Overseas Investment of Chinese Enterprises

A Casebook on Corporate Social Responsibility

Overseas Investment of Chinese Enterprises

A Casebook on Corporate Social Responsibility

Liu Baocheng/Chandni Patel

Globethics.net China Ethics No. 9

Globethics.net China Ethics

Publications Director: Prof. Dr Obiora Ike, Executive Director of Globethics.net in Geneva and Professor of Ethics at the Godfrey Okoye University Enugu/Nigeria.
Series Editors: Prof. Dr Liu Baocheng, Founder and Director of Center for International Business Ethics (CIBE) at University of International Business and Economics in Beijing/China. Director of Globethics.net Regional Programme China.
Prof. Dr Dr h.c. Christoph Stückelberger, President and Founder of Globethics.net. Executive Director of Geneva Agape Foundation GAF Professor of Ethics in Moscow/Russia, Enugu/Nigeria, Beijing/China.

Globethics.net China Ethics Series 9
Liu Baocheng/ Chandni Patel, *Overseas Investment of Chinese Enterprises: A Casebook on Corporate Social Responsibility*
Geneva: Globethics.net, 2020
ISBN 978-2-88931-355-6 (online version)
ISBN 978-2-88931-356-3 (print version)
© 2020 Globethics.net

Managing Editor: Ignace Haaz

Globethics.net International Secretariat
150 route de Ferney
1211 Geneva 2, Switzerland
Website: *www.globethics.net/publications*
Email: *publications@globethics.net*

All web links in this text have been verified as of November 2020.

TABLE OF CONTENTS

PREFACE

The global Covid-19 pandemic was an earthquake and shock for the global economy and its supply chains. A large part of humanity was staying at home in lockdown and large parts of business on all continents was closed for months in the first half of 2020. International supply chains have been developing exponentially during the last three decades of globalization. Its vulnerability became now visible. The pandemic experience and political tensions may modify some supply chains, but nevertheless, international exchange of good services will remain important in order to reduce poverty and increase sustainable economic growth.

Chinese Outbound Direct Investment (ODI) is a fairly a recent phenomenon, which has been accelerating over the past two decades. Under the national campaign of "stepping overseas", Chinese government has devised a slew of policies to incentivize domestic firms to stretch their business operations beyond Chinas national border. Given its position as a manufacture hub in the global supply chain, and spurred by its massive foreign exchange reserves, ODI is instrumental to serve the strategic objectives: to secure steady supply of raw materials on one hand, and to expand channels to global market places on the other hand. While state-owned firms take a lion's share in Chinese ODI programs, private firms quickly follow suit.

Initial ODI efforts concentrated on merger and acquisition of existing foreign entities with strong market potential but which are hit by the financial crisis. In more recent years, Chinese ODI has been converging along two tracks – targeting access to technology and brands in the developed world, and natural and labor resources in the lesser developed regions.

Despite its long imperial history, China has no past experience of colonization. Iron curtail in the post-World War II era capsulated China from engaging with the world economy when multinational companies surged to dominate global economy. Lack of experience and knowledge, Chinese ODI has undergone a painful learning curve through trial and error. Major challenges encountered by Chinese overseas operation lie in misalignment of strategic objectives and cross-cultural communication amongst multi-stakeholders, which brings corporate social responsibility under scrutiny.

This book offers unique case studies on Corporate Social Responsibility (CSR) in overseas investments of Chinese Enterprises. They deeply analyze successes, failures and lessons to learn in CSR in order to improve ethical, values-driven business to serve societies.

Beijing/Geneva, 1 June 2020
China Ethics Series Editors
Prof. Dr. Liu Baocheng, Beijing/China
Prof. Dr Christoph Stückelberger, Geneva/Switzerland

INTRODUCTION

Background: Reform and Opening

China's spectacular economic growth and structural transformation is attributable to its domestic reform and open-door policy to the outside world, a grand change initiated 40 decades ago. Shifting from the mandate economy stereotyped after the Soviet Union onto a steadfast track of dynamic market economy while avoiding major political upheavals, Deng Xiaoping, with his vision, wisdom and courage, is accredited as the mastermind behind such a historical manoeuvre. In retrospect, his entire notion is liberalization coupled with measured privatization through containing state intervention into economic decisions by individuals and institutions.

Domestic reform was rolled out in four tracts: rural reform, urban reform, tax reform and price reform. 1) In the rural area, collective land in the hands of communes was divided into small plots and redistributed to individual households. 2) In the urban area, factories vertically controlled by the State Planning Commission were gradually transformed into business enterprises that were responsible for their own profit and loss, while allowing individuals to set up their business proprietorship. 3) Business entities were required to surrender tax instead of profit to the government, and local governments were allowed to retain a percentage of tax collected from businesses instead of relying entirely on the budget of the central government. 4) A large portion of pricing mechanism was left to the supply and demand of market forces. With materialistic motivation in place, productivity in all sectors and at all levels resurged.

Open-door policy was instituted by diverting the country's partnership from the socialist bloc within which trading activities were conducted on escrow basis in the absence of currency exchanges. The first phase was aimed at attracting contract manufacture opportunities into the Special Economic Zones (SEZs) charted in southeast coastal regions adjacent to Hong Kong and Taiwan. Businesses from these places served as catalysts to expose mainland China to global investment when the world was experiencing a dramatic wave of production reallocation at the tag end of the 20th century. With windfall success, the experience drawn in those 5 pilot SEZs was duplicated and scaled up along the entire coastal regions by adding on 14 Economic and Technological Development Zones (ETDZs), shifting from simple processing trade to more value-added operations. At a dazzling speed, China was integrated into the global value chain presenting itself as the world largest assembly line. Cashing in on its abundant cheap workforce, large landmass and lower environmental standard, China, with a variety of incentive schemes, was able to allure continuous flow of foreign direct investment in the manufacture sector when neighbouring regions, typically the four Asian Tigers – South Korea, Taiwan, Hong Kong and Singapore – were declining in their comparative advantage. By the end of 2015, China for the first time in history toppled the United State and became the top recipient of foreign direct investment (FDI). According to John Dunning's Investment Development Path (IDP), foreign multinational enterprises might help indigenous firms to upgrade their capabilities, and thus aid the economy in its development. Foreign investors did not only bring their technology and management expertise, but also sales channels to the world marketplace. With aggressive policies deployed to spur its export drive, China is able to amass the mammoth foreign exchange reserve (FER). Most of the foreign exchange eventually ended up in the government coffer because exporters were required to surrender their foreign currencies earned in exchange for local currency.

> *Although foreign invested enterprises (FIEs) are no more than 3%*
> *in number, they provide 1/10 urban employment, contribute 1/5 tax*
> *revenue, 1/4 industrial output, and nearly 1/2 import and export.* [1]

-- Chen Deming, Former Minister of Commerce

From being an exporter in primary goods, the country began to import raw materials – all sorts of commodities such as energy, mineral, timber, grain, as well as spare parts, and export manufactured goods with added value. Trade pattern reversed with rest of the world largely resulting from the import substitution program, where Chinese companies were incentivized by government procurement programs and direct subsidies to digest foreign technologies and manufacture process. As scale and scope economy accelerated, Made in China was enabled to outbid competitors both local and from third countries in the global market. For the same reason, Chinese firms faced increasing anti-dumping and counter-veiling duties levied those importing countries. This turns out to be major driver for outbound investment in order to circumvent such sort of tariff barriers.

Through interaction with intermediaries like export agents and local distributors, Chinese managers gradually gained direct access to the end market. Deeper knowledge and local connection with end buyers boosted the confidence to localize their production while avoiding customs tariff, transaction cost and freight charges. Time to market was also placed under better control. More importantly, direct feedback from the market helps the company to make continuous improvement over their products and services.

By the end of 2017, China for 9 consecutive years remained the world largest exporter. Among the total trade value at $4.28 trillion,

---

[1] 40 years for China to Integrate into and Deeply Impact on Global Value Chain, International Trade Issues, February 28, 2018, http://www.globalview.cn/html/economic/info_23049.html

export stood at \$2.39 trillion with an annual increase of 10.8%, and import at \$1.92 trillion with an annual increase of 18.7%, leaving the country with a surplus of \$0.47 trillion.[2] The contrast is stunning when the total trade value of \$20.64 billion in 1978 when China adopted the open-door policy and \$509.65 billion in 2001 when China joined the World Trade Organization are brought in to comparison.[3]

Strategic Drivers Behind ODI

To secure steady influx of raw materials, from energy to iron ore, is a critical part to maintain Chinese domestic growth and export momentum. By 2017, China surpassed the United States on the importation of petroleum hallmarked by 400 million metric tons. Even with that, China's storage capacity can only sustain the country's consumption in no more than 40 days, which is far below the energy security line set by the International Energy Agency (IEA). The same year witnessed another surge of iron ore import by 5% amounting to 1.07 billion metric tons despite the worldwide rejection to steel products and the country's resolve for massive reduction in its excess steelmaking capacity. In addition to long-term supply agreements, the most comfortable approach to exercise control over location-bound resources is merger and acquisition. These are handled almost without exception by state-owned conglomerates backed by state-owned banks.

Rising demand for quality life among Chinese people with more disposable income is another propeller behind Chinese investment overseas. Food safety concern after the Sanlu milk scandal (mixing mela-

---

[2] MOFCOM, January 15, 2018. http://www.mofcom.gov.cn/article/ae/ag/201801/20180102698781.shtml. Trade value is calculated at an exchange rate of \$1=RMB6.5.

[3] MOFCOM, March 10, 2004, http://zhs.mofcom.gov.cn/article/Nocategory/200405/20040500218163.shtml

mine) which broke out in 2008 aggravated Chinese people's distrust in home-made food. During the past decade, nearly 90% of baby milk formula is imported from overseas. In response, Chinese diary companies had to acquire in a slew farms and milk plants in the Netherland, Australia and New Zealand to serve their high-end consumers at home. Many Chinese firms are no longer content with importing and distribution foreign branded products in the home market. They typically target 2nd tier brands either for equity participation or acquisition in entirety in hope to enhance brand value for their entire product portfolio.

John Dunning outlined three specific advantages sought after by overseas activities in his eclectic paradigm: ownership, internalization and location. He also distinguished between four kinds of objectives on mutually non-exclusive basis: market seeking, natural resource seeking, strategic asset seeking, efficiency seeking and strategic asset seeking. While his analysis is utterly true to the extent of micro decision by individual firms, China's outbound investment at its macro level has also been invoked increasingly by the excessive amount of FER in the hands of the central government. By the end of 2017, total amount of FER reached $3.14 trillion, counted down from the peak of $3.8 trillion, as a result from chronic trade surplus. This is larger even than that of the G7 countries combined. The inflationary pressure and depreciation of domestic currency would be phenomenal should a large chunk of FER is brought back to domestic market. For the sake of security, its biggest portion is used to purchase treasure bonds from developed countries regardless of the negligible interest returns. Despite of the fact that the long-waited liberalization of capital account is still hanging in the air, the government has gradually loosened its grip on FER, granting limited access to sizeable Chinese firms for outbound direct investment (ODI) over projects in line with the national strategy.

China's domestic policies have experienced much change over the last few decades, integrating ODI within larger economic goals. As introduced by the Third Plenum of the 11th Central Committee of the Communist Party of China (CPC) in 1978, the country witnessed far reaching changes for achieving socialist modernisation; with an aim towards instituting open economic policy in favour of reciprocal cooperation with other countries.[4] Said goals for establishing a more open economy were reinforced but a year later in 1979, whereby Chinese enterprises were given authorisation to establish overseas corporations in accordance with the State Council's newly issued "Fifteen Economic Reform Measures."[5] Further efforts to solidify Chinese ODI were even invested in 1983 with the Ministry of Foreign Trade and Economic Cooperation (now Ministry of Commerce, MOFCOM), placed as the lead body in charge of overseeing procedure and authorisation; coupled with later developments in 1990 on behalf of the State Administration of Foreign Exchange (SAFE), for regulations on standardising foreign exchange management within ODI.[6] These moves established the first framework for the outbound investment of Chinese companies, facilitating greater clarity and predictability in how enterprises ought to navigate international investments. Indeed, the pace of these reforms continued to quicken throughout the remainder of the 20th century, with the CPC's

---

[4] China Daily Information Company, Brief History of the Communist Party of China, *A New Era of Socialist Modernization Construction (October 1976 – April 1991)*: <<http://cpcchina.chinadaily.com.cn/2010-09/07/content_13901594 _7.htm>> [accessed: 21st November 2017]; News of the Communist Party of China, People's Daily, Liang Jun and Yao Chun, *Communist Party of China in Brief,* (March 2013).

[5] Lu, G., *Reform of the administrative approval system to boost the sound development of OFDI*, Review of Economic Research (2002) Vol. 66: 18–26.

[6] Center for International Forestry Research (CIFOR), Huang Wenbin and Andrea Wilkes, *Analysis of China's Overseas Investment Policies,* Working Paper 79 (2011).

14th Congress Party voicing a need for "active expansion of overseas investment and cross-border operations of Chinese enterprises."[7]

However, despite such pro-outward policies, the State Planning Commission in 1991 heeded caution on the basis of observations that Chinese enterprises engaging in unfamiliar international markets, with unfamiliar laws and inadequate experience, may risk suffering business and economic loss.[8] As such ODI was limited to smaller scale investments and solely to those specifically in line with national macro-economic goals.[9]

Notwithstanding the aforementioned efforts to open the Chinese economy, this pinnacle development (Going Out strategy) came in the wake of the 1997 Asian financial crisis, attributing further importance to the direct role of ODI to economic stability; not just in and amongst its role for promoting inbound investment. Alongside newer regulatory mechanisms[10], lower restrictions to foreign exchange[11] and entry into

---

[7] 14th National Congress of the Communist Party of China, Jiang Zemin Speech, To Accelerate Reform and Open-door in order to Achieve Bigger Victory of Socialist Cause with Chinese Characteristics, (12th October 1992), accessible via: <<http://www.china.com.cn/guoqing/2012-09/12/content_26748045.htm>> [accessed: 21st November 2017].

[8] State Planning Commission, Opinions on Tightening Supervision over ODI Projects, (5th March 1991), accessible via: <<http://www.chinalawedu.com/falvfagui/fg22016/56330.shtml>> [accessed: 21st November 2017]:
"However some projects, owing to an unfamiliarity of foreign markets and foreign laws, coupled with inadequate experience, lack clarity in intended objectives and have even resulted in business loss").

[9] Shen Yang Industrial University, S.F. Chen, *China OFDI Policy System Research*, (2009).

[10] *Temporary Method for Complaints by Chinese Overseas Companies*, (2006); MOFCOM establishment of the "China Companies Overseas Business Complaints Service Centre" to provide free complaints service.

investment-related treaties, notably China's accession to the World Trade Organisation[12]; the following years also emphasised economic policy development aligned with greater investor responsibility within ODI.

ODI as a national strategy was officially initiated in 1997, when the 15th Chinese Communist Party (CCP)'s Congress Report announced "to encourage outbound investment when comparative advantage permits, so as to better utilize two markets and two resources at home and abroad." The popular concept of "stepping overseas" or "going abroad" which denotes outbound investment was coined in the 10th Five-Year Plan for National Economic and Social Development in 2001, the year when China joined the World Trade Organization (WTO) with the purpose of "expanding the field, path and mode of international economic and technological cooperation". It was reiterated in 2002 by the 16th CCP Congress report, in the year when its GDP per capita reached $1 135 with $286.4 billion foreign exchange reserve at hands. Thus far, China's open-door strategy evolved on four pillars – external trade, FDI, project construction and ODI. In 2004, the Ministry and Commerce and the Ministry of Foreign Affairs jointly issued "Country based Industrial Guideline for ODI" to prioritize countries and industries according to bilateral relationship and respective economic structure.

Growing economic might is naturally followed by geographic expansion. China's rise is perceived by big powers as a shockwave to the current geopolitical equilibrium. During the APEC summit in November 2010, President Barak Obama assumed the driver seat to push forward further integration with the Southeast Asian countries aiming at a trade

---

[11] SAFE, *Notice on the Issues Regarding Removing Deposit for Repatriated Profit Gained from Overseas Investment* (2002); SAFE, *Notice on the Issues Regarding Simplifying the Review of the Source of Foreign Exchange,* (2003).

[12] World Trade Organisation (WTO) <<https://www.wto.org/english/thewto_e/countries_e/china_e.htm>> [accessed: 21st November 2017].

pact between 12 countries known as the Trans-Pacific Partnership (TPP). This deal arguably was intended to reduce dependence on China by the member countries and entrench U.S. leadership in the Pacific Rim, although the Trump administration decided to withdraw in January 2017. China was propelled to accelerate its own geopolitical ambition by actively engaging the Regional Comprehensive Economic Partnership (RCEP) encompassing 16 countries. While only 3 out of 18 chapters have been approved so far due to widely divided interest among the RCEP participants, China since 2013 unilaterally launched its own grand strategy known as the One Belt and One Road Initiative (OBOR) comprising of countries along the ancient Silk Road from Chinese east coast all the way to western Europe, and countries along the maritime route southbound to Oceania, southeast Asia and all African countries surrounding the Indian Ocean.

In order to entrench the bulkhead against the contagion of global financial crisis that broke out in 2008, China funnelled RMB4 trillion stimulus package into its economy, primarily targeting the manufacture sector, planting the seed for excessive production capacity. Overburdened by its excessive industrial capacity, particularly when domestic demand has withered for stockpiles of steel, cement and glass largely due to heightened strain on real estate development, the enticement for infrastructure development over the OBOR countries is irresistible. In addition, China's capability, efficiency and cost advantage in building power plants, transportation and communication networks stand almost unrivalled in the world. The two domestic policy banks – China Development Bank (CDB) and Export-Import Bank of China (CEXIM), with humongous financial capacity, are firm supporters of large Chinese companies offering seller's credit and low-interest loans. The establishment of the Asian Infrastructure Investment Bank (AIIB), a multilateral development bank funded by 70 countries as of 2017, headquartered in Beijing, which was put in operation since the beginning of 2016, further helps to boost China's confidence to invest heavily along the OBOR countries.

The OBOR Initiative is neither comparable to Marshall Plan nor a rule-based free trade area, but rather a conceptual framework drawing closer relationship based on political will among participating countries. According to the White Paper on China and WTO published by Chinese State Council in June 2018, more than 80 countries and institutions have signed up with China on the OBOR Initiative. In the absence of specific set of rules, implementation of OBOR is identified by collaborative projects. Between 2013 and 2017, trade value reached $5 trillion among OBOR members. Within these countries, Chinese investment exceeded $70 billion and 75 economic and trade zones have been established, creating $1.6 billion tax revenue and 220 000 jobs for the host countries. $60 billion is committed by China to aid the social welfare projects in those developing countries and international institutions associated with OBOR.

The policy developments undertaken by China are a perfect starting point in assessing the motivations, directions and considerations underpinning the country's recent surge in outbound investment. Until 2004, ODI was rather sporadic, and was approved on case-by-case basis. In October 2004, MOFCOM issued the first official sketchy regulation in this field: The Provisions on the Examination and Approval of Investment to Run Enterprises Abroad. In March 2009, Regulation on ODI was promulgated requiring national level approval of project involving $100 million investment. January 2014, National Development and Reform Commission (NDRC) opened the floodgate to allow ODI up to $1 billion by its Approval and Recording of Overseas Investment Project. To check the excessive capital flight, partly triggered by the interest hike in the United States, August 2017 witnessed a sudden halt when NDRC, MOFCOM, People's Bank of China (PBOC) and Ministry of Foreign Affairs (MOFA) jointly issued a document "Guideline on Further Orienting and Regulating ODI" to particularly restrict ODI in real estate, hotels, cinemas, entertainment, sports clubs. Over the past 14 years, Chinese policy toward ODI is generally placed on a steady track of liberalization punctuated at different occasions by certain restrictions and orientations. There are three watchdogs over ODI. The NDRC is responsible for the approval of specific overseas project, MOFCOM accesses the qualification of outbound investors, and the State Administration for Foreign Exchange (SAFE) looks after the amount, conversion and remittance of foreign exchange needed for ODI. From beginning of the 21st century, Chinese ODI had been growing exponentially (Exhibit 1). Nonetheless, as a result of stringent curb over what was termed as "irrational investment", the year end of 2017 saw a steep decline in Chinese ODI by a margin of 29.4%.[13]

Exhibit 1 Volume of Chinese ODI, 2002-2016 (unit: US$ 100 million)

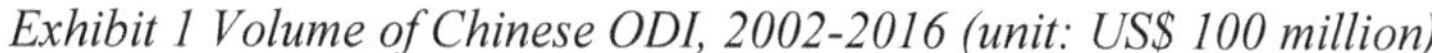

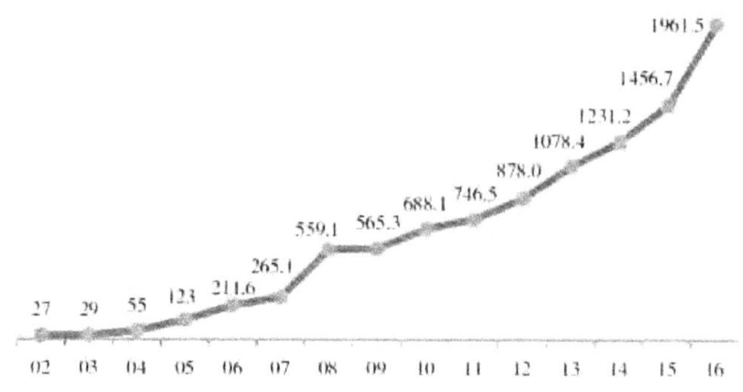

图 1　中国对外直接投资流量．2002—2016（单位：亿美元）

Source: Source: Chinese Investment Consulting Net, 2017-12-19,
http://www.ocn.com.cn/chanye/201712/raatf19090013.shtml

Construction of infrastructure projects overseas is statistically calculated as part of ODI. By the end of 2017, gross revenue accomplished

---

[13] MOFCOM, January 16, 2018, http://www.mofcom.gov.cn/article/ae/ag/201801/20180102699398.shtml

reached $168.59 billion, 5.8% annual increase. The value of new projects contracted hit on $265.28 billion, registering 8.7% increase over the previous year. These projects – from highways, railways to seaports, airports, from residential housing to power plants - are gigantic. For example, 782 contracted projects were valued above $50 million in 2017, thus were able to absorb more building materials and equipment excessively available in China in addition to its abundant and cheap labour resources. Export in goods accompanying these projects was $15.59 billion, a 15.7% increase which is far higher than the average normal trade growth rate. Expatriate labour force accounted for 522 000 people among the total of 979 000 working overseas on various construction projects.

In 2017, ODI from China was $120.08 billion on accumulative basis and omnipresent in 174 countries by 6 236 enterprises. Major sectors covered are leasing and business service (29.1%), distribution (20.8%), manufacture and data transmission (15.9%) and IT services (8.6%). ODI of Chinese enterprises has become a topic of much discussion amongst various stakeholders around the world. Such dialogue is not only attributable to its dramatic surge in volume and spread in economic sectors, but also more significantly to its behaviour and impact on the host countries. In 2015, Chinese ODI in the amount of $145.67 billion, for the first time in history preponderated over its FDI, and turned China as the 2nd world largest source of direct investment outflow.

Regulatory Orientation: Responsible ODI

Indeed, from a practical perspective, successful ODI necessitates that market entry decisions consider the environmental backdrop of both home and host countries. Such knowledge can aid enterprises in their decision-making process when selecting which host country they wish to target for their endeavours. At the very least, contextual understanding of domestic policies, foreign policies and any pre-existing bilateral relations, will help companies to better position themselves for entry overseas.

Alongside China's 40 year opening process, there has long existed an emphasis on the need for companies to recognise their role in ensuring responsible investment based on apt considerations and prudent preparation. In particular arises the need for Chinese enterprises to ensure that they are familiar with the investment background of a target host country prior to market entry. This focus later permeated policies such as the "stepping abroad" strategy, consolidated in the 10th Five Year Plan during the 4th Meeting of the 9th National People's Congress in 2001.[14]

"We must seize the opportunity to speed up development, implement strategy for revitalising the country through science and education [and] implement sustainable development strategies... in our efforts to promote economic development."[15]

--16th National Congress of the CPC

Subsequently in the early 2000s, MOFCOM invested efforts into information sharing, releasing its first series guidance for potential investors to aid in the assessment of overseas investment markets.[16] In doing so it aimed to rectify the unfamiliarity and knowledge deficit that the State Planning Commission had commented on some years before. Fur-

---

[14] Note: the strategy was first suggested during the Fifth Plenary Session of the 15th Congress of the CPC in 2000.

[15] 16th National Congress of the Communist Party of China, *Party Constitution*, (14th November 2002), accessible via: <<http://cpc.people.com.cn/GB/64162/ 64168/64569/65444/4429114.html>> [accessed: 21st November 2017].

[16] First report to be published: MOFCOM, *2002 Country Trade and Investment Environment Report*, (released on 20th May 2003) <<http://www.mofcom. gov.cn/article/ae/ai/200305/20030500092182.shtml>> [accessed: 22nd November 2017].

thermore, in cementing the role of sustainability within investment decisions, 2006 brought with it the integrated concept of "green finance"; establishing that a company's environmental background would be included within the Company Credit Database used for reviewing credit applications.[17] In this way a holistic approach was endorsed towards responsible investment, spanning the entire length of investment projects; not just during the course of actual operations, but from the initial market entry stages concerned with raising capital and selecting a market.

This same focus on social responsibility has been reiterated within current ODI-driven domestic policies and initiatives, including China's OBOR Initiative as first mentioned by President Xi Jinping in September 2013. Officially detailed by the National Development and Reform Commission (NDRC), the Ministry of Foreign Affairs, and MOFCOM in 2015; the initiative aims to rejuvenate the Ancient Silk Road in establishing *"peace and cooperation, openness and inclusiveness, mutual learning and mutual benefit"* in the shared aim of economic prosperity. In doing so, it has been key in drawing attention to *"green"* development and *responsible* investment in order to achieve mutual political trust, economic integration and cultural inclusiveness.

"We support localized operation and management of Chinese companies to boost the local economy, increase local employment, improve

---

[17] People's Bank of China and State Environmental Protection Administration, Notice on Sharing Enterprise Environmental Protection Information, Publication No. 450 (19th December 2006). Accessible via: <<http://www.zhb.gov.cn/gkml/hbb/gwy/200910/t20091030_180727.htm>> [accessed: 22nd November 2017]. See also: Opinions of the General Office of China Banking Regulatory Commission on Strengthening Social Responsibilities of Banking Financial Institutions, Publication No. 252, (5th December 2007). Accessible via: <<http://www.cbrc.gov.cn/govView_91D73B8D49484BF4B1D87D29F9577C2D.html>> [accessed: 22nd November 2017].

local livelihoods, and take social responsibilities in protecting local biodiversity and eco-environment."

--Belt and Road, Action Plan (28th March 2015)[18]

As initiated in the same year by the State Council, the same holds true for the Made in China 2025 policy which outlines a 10-year plan to upgrade China's manufacturing capacity in the hopes of transforming the country into a manufacturing powerhouse.[19] With the policy's main guiding principles fixated on: *innovation, quality first, green development, structural optimization and talent orientation*, the initiative focuses on increasing the quality, efficiency, capacity and sustainability of Chinese manufacturing to secure its foothold in higher global production chains.

Within this role, it was emphasised by the State council that there exists a need to:

"Guide enterprises in their assimilation to local cultures, enhancing their awareness of social responsibility and operational risk management, improving their localisation capacity."[20]

Thus, alongside the policy's superior emphasis on "green" development, embodying a core caveat of responsible investment, lies an additional focus on the need to familiarise oneself with a host country's environment; particularly with regards to the risks that may arise given differing regulatory conditions and substantive cultural differences. In

---

[18] National Development and Reform Commission of China (NDRC), Vision and Actions on Jointly Building Silk Road Economic Belt and 21st-Century Maritime Silk Road, FIRST EDITION, (28th March 2015). Accessible via: <<http://en.ndrc.gov.cn/newsrelease/201503/t20150330_669367.html>> [accessed: 22nd November 2017].

[19] State Council, Notice of the State Council on Printing and Distributing "Made in China 2025", Publication. No 28, (8th May 2015) Accessible via: <<http://www.gov.cn/zhengce/content/2015-05/19/content_9784.html>> [accessed: 22nd November 2017].

[20] Supra note 15, State Council Notice.

turn, such considerations ought to be aligned with the greater need for promoting localisation and social responsibility, as a driving force behind the success of investment decisions.

It is thus clear that underpinning China's economic reform and pro-outward investment policies, is the need for Chinese enterprises, when taking advantage of the hospitable domestic environment, to engage in responsible investment in line with macro-economic goals. In achieving such aims, securing familiarity with host countries prior to market entry is key; whereby it is necessary for Chinese companies to account for wider socio-political considerations, alongside the business, legal and economic environment of its overseas target market.

With this in mind, a potential cornerstone of ODI lies in the existence of any bilateral investment treaties (BITs) held between the home and host country. Such agreements aid in an enterprise's understanding in the scope of legal discourse, as well as the extent to which both countries vouch to protect its investment interests. BITs cover a range of different investment related matters, including: fair and equitable treatment; protection from expropriation; dispute resolution; national treatment etc. As such, they aim to better clarify investment-related regulations, providing a more stable environment against which potential business ventures may be pursued. By virtue of their added protectionism, or at the very least their greater degree of certainty in how disputes ought to be handled, companies are provided with a safeguard in the event that things go wrong.

In and amongst such relationships the existence of Bilateral Tax Agreements (BTA) are also notable, handling additional matters such as issues of dual taxation, tax evasion and stimulating greater trade efficiency. The notable benefit of BTAs thereby lies in providing greater financial clarity to potential investors, whilst outlining the scope of their tax obligations. In fact, as early as 1983 China entered into its first dual taxation avoidance agreement with Japan, recognising the need to protect investment interests of overseas enterprises[21]; since then it has entered into such agreements with over 100 countries. The same applies for BITs, with China having entered into such treaties with 129 countries (including 65 Belt and Road nations)[22]; with more than 60 of these agreements having already been signed between 1988 and 1998 alone.[23] Indeed, attempts have even been made to launch BIT negotiations with the European Union and United States. Today, with the exception of Germany, China is recognised as having signed more BITs than any other country in the world.[24]

The significance of such extensive bilateral relations within ODI is notable in light of the investment losses suffered by Chinese companies operating in Libya. Within 2011, 50 Chinese contracted projects in the North African country with an accumulated valuation of up to USD 18.8 billion, were forced to abandon ship owing to the volatile domestic situation stirred by social unrest. As a result, Chinese investments suffered direct economic losses of up to RMB15 billion.[25] Despite the fact that these formal business undertakings were founded upon contractual relationships, the existence of contractual duties were still insufficient to provide enterprises with certainty, nor predictability, as to the level of

---

[21] Agreement Between the Government of the People's Republic of China and the Government of Japan for the Avoidance of Double Taxation and the Prevention of Fiscal Evasion with Respect to Taxes on Income, Signed in Beijing, [6th September 1983]; Supra note 3, CIFOR Working Paper.

[22] UNCTAD, Investment Policy Hub <<http://investmentpolicyhub. unctad.org/ IIA/CountryBits/42>> [accessed: 30th November 2017].

[23] Congyan Cai, *Outward Foreign Direct Investment Protection and the Effectiveness of Chinese BIT Practice*, Journal of World Investment and Trade Vol. 7 (2006).

[24] Supra note 18, UNCTAD, Investment Policy Hub.

[25] Zhang Juan and Wei William X., *Managing Political Risks of Chinese Contracted Projects in Libya,* Project Management Journal, Vol.43 (4), (2012).

compensation they were entitled to in such an event.[26] In the absence of any BITs in force at the time,[27] ambiguity ensued as to the method of dispute resolution available; with the Chinese government eventually stepping in, calling for Libyan authorities to adequately handle the matter and ensure that enterprises be fairly compensated.[28] Without BIT agreements rendering that dispute resolution take place in an international arena, determination of business losses and adequate compensation was thus left to the discretion of local courts based on local laws and legal interpretation.

Given the uncertainty this caused surrounding the recourse and remedy available to Chinese enterprises, calls were made at the time for improvements to bilateral relations between China and Libya[29]; along with reiterating the need to regularly evaluate host countries and their business environments prior to investing.[30] The example demonstrates the need for investing companies to factor the existence of BITs within risk management; whereby the absence of such relations ought to merit that additional safeguards be put in place. In fact Chinese enterprises have since been critiqued for overlooking the political risk in Libya before engaging in its market. As such, whilst is noted that some enterprises had prepared for the already unstable socio-political environment

---

[26] China Daily, Li Jiaboa, *Firms Awaiting Libya Loss Compensation* (April 2012); Global Times, Song Shengxia, *China Seeks Compensation in Libya,* (March 2012).

[27] Note: China and Libya had signed a BIT in 2010, however it is still yet to come into force - Supra note 18, UNCTAD, Investment Policy Hub.

[28] China Daily, *China asks Libya to Compensate for Companies' Losses,* (March 2012).

[29] Supra note 22, China Daily (Li Jiabao) quoting E. Ali Saleh Huwedi (counsellor of the Libyan Embassy in China).

[30] Global Times, *China Counting Financial Losses in Libya,* (March 2011); quoting Lin Guijun (Professor at University of International Business and Economics, Beijing, China).

by investing in safeguards such as political risk insurance; others had failed to do so.[31]

"[M]ost Chinese companies that have business in Libya have been subjected to great losses because most of them underestimated the risks in Libya and neglected to buy disaster insurance for their projects".[32]

--Wang Xiyan (China National Machinery
Industry Corp, Strategy Research
Department, Manager)

The Guideline on Further Orienting and Regulating ODI 2017[33] delineated the objectives of Chinese government for its outbound investment: 1) to permeate the philosophy of innovation, harmonization, greenness, opening and sharing; 2) to diversify global markets based on supply side reform; 3) to prioritize on OBOR; 4) to foster rationalization of Chinese ODI; 5) to prevent and address ODI risks; 6) to promote sustainable development of ODI; 7) to realize mutual interest and common development with the host countries. Based on these objectives, 3 categories of ODI are identified for differentiated treatment:

The encouraged list includes: 1) infrastructure development along the OBOR and neighborhood countries; 2) projects that are able to promote the export of production capacity and technical standards; 3) cooperation on high-tech development and advanced manufacture; 4) energy and mineral exploration and development; 5) agricultural development; 6) distribution and logistics services. The restrictive list includes: 1) investment in countries with which China has no diplomatic ties or torn by wars, or sensitive countries China is committed to restrictions based international treaties; 2) real estate, hotels, cinemas, enticement and sport clubs; 3) variable interest entities (VIEs) or investment platforms

---

[31] Supra note 21, Zhang Juan and Wei William X.

[32] Supra note 22, China Daily (Li Jiabao).

[33] http://www.gov.cn/zhengce/content/2017-08/18/content_5218665.htm

that are detached from real project; 4) projects that involve substandard equipment; 5) projects that are uncompliant with environmental and safety standards in the host countries. The forbidden list includes: 1) core technologies or products in the military industry; 2) gambling and pornographic industries; 3) projects that violate China's commitment to international treaties; 4) projects that endanger national interest and national security.

It is therefore pertinent that enterprises begin making market entry decisions by looking at the official guidance published by institutions such as MOFCOM. This will aid in the selection process for an overseas market by providing companies with a familiarity and understanding of the investment climate in their target region, whilst unveiling any former problems that may have previously been incurred which could alter the dynamic of the investment at hand. At the same time, it is paramount that socio-political factors do not go unnoticed. It is therefore apt that enterprises invest time and effort into better understanding local cultures and social risks within host countries, in appreciation of the role and influence that local society may have as stakeholders to large scale ODI projects.

It is worth noting that overwhelming debate and existing literature surrounding Chinese ODI is aggregated on why and how companies should step overseas, but little is devoted to how to address challenges in the host market. This book attempts to showcase a host of typical issues encountered by Chinese companies in this particular regard, to be followed by analysis and recommendations.

Reaction by Host Countries toward Chinese ODI

Indeed, socio-political risks may not only come in the form of purely domestic matters; but may further arise in light of how receptive a host country is for foreign investment. Such considerations must be taken into account when choosing a target host in order to forewarn investors of the types of social and market challenges they could face in overseas territories. This in turn will enable companies to better determine an appropriate market for their investment, and prepare for sustainable operation.

In this regard, the perception of Chinese investment in host countries has tended to receive a mixed reception. This is no doubt partially owing to its expansive nature in covering both developing and developed countries [Exhibit 2], along with an entire array of different industry sectors.

Exhibit 2 Geographical Distribution of China's OFDI Stock, 2004 and 2013

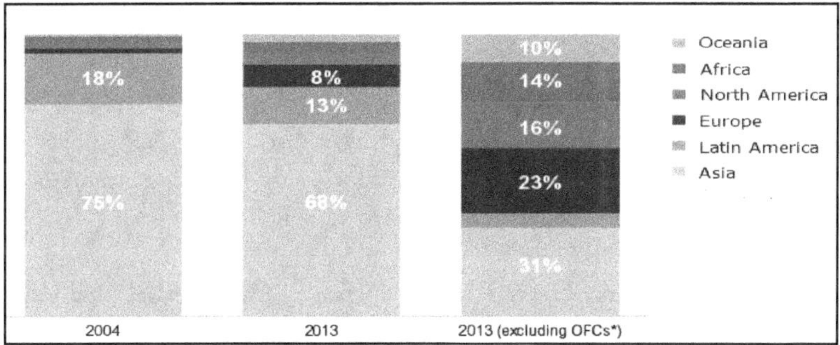

Source: World Resources Institute, Lihuan Zhou and Denise Leung, China's Overseas Investments, Explained in 10 Graphics, (January 2015), http://www.wri.org/blog/2015/01/china%E2%80%99s-overseas-investments-explained-10-graphics

Nevertheless, with research conducted for measuring and categorising such perceptions, companies are better able to position themselves in host markets and foresee the challenges they are likely to face as Chinese corporations operating in a foreign territory. Indeed such research identifies, broadly speaking, a division between how developed countries receive and view Chinese ODI, as compared with the attitude of developing countries.

Developed Countries

Chinese ODI within developed nations are largely carried out through merger and acquisition (M&A) targeting existing businesses saddled with established brands and/or technologies, but are plagued by the looming financial crisis. Such modus operandi tends to face market entry issues related to governmental receptiveness. Within the USA,[34] EU,[35] Canada[36] and Australia[37] for example, Chinese investment projects have received scrutiny over whether the substance of their ventures are in line with overreaching national interests and national securi-

---

[34] See: Politico, Megan Cassella, *Trump Blocks Chinese Purchase of U.S. Company for National Security Reasons,* (September 2017); Peterson Institute for International Economics, Theodore H. Moran, *Chinese Investment and CFIUS: Time for an Updated (and Revised) Perspective,* Policy Brief No. PB15-17 (September 2015).

[35] Financial Times, Guy Chazan, *Germany Expands Power to Block Takeovers,* (July 2017); The Diplomat, Magda Tsakalidou, *Has Winter Come for Chinese Investments in the EU?* (October 2017); Financial Times, Charles Clover and Jim Pickard, *UK to Tighten Foreign Investment Reviews,* (July 2017).

[36] The Globe and Mail, Jeff Gray, *Ottawa's "National Security" Review a Warning to Foreign Investors,* (July 2015); Canadian Council of Chief Executives, Theodore H. Moran, *Chinese Foreign Direct Investment in Canada: Threat or Opportunity?,* (March 2012). However, consider: The Canadian Press, *Norsat International Investors Approve Takeover Bid from Chinese Firm,* (June 2017).

[37] The Telegraph, Jonathan Pearlman, *Australia Blocks Electricity Deal with China for "National Security" Reasons,* (August 2016); ABC News, Tom Iggulden, *Government Warned Chinese Investment Could Threaten Australia's National Security Interests,* (April 2016); ABC News, Chris Berg, *Rejecting a Chinese Bid for Land is in "The National Interest"? Show me how,* (May 2016); Australian Centre on China in the World, The Australia-China Story Archive, *Chinese Investment in Australia,* (2015).

ty.[38] As a result this has given rise to higher market entry standards, comprehensive screening processes, and greater limitations to ODI, along with a general caution amongst local society in welcoming Chinese investment.

Worth noting is that the definition of "national security" or "national interests" may differ from the stance generally adopted by China; causing greater difficulties for Chinese enterprises in predicting the likelihood of market entry success. For instance, it is noted that Australian tests for determining whether an investment is in accords with national security interests, rely on a case-by-case discretionary basis, contrasting with that of the more standardised negative list system used in China.[39] Indeed, even countries like the USA opt for a more open and flexible screening process,[40] differing from Chinese processes which favour certainty in providing codified lists for "encouraged," "restricted" and "prohibited" industry sectors.

Whilst this may render the process of market entry difficult to predict, companies can improve their chances of success by ensuring transparency in the motivations and business information surrounding their proposed investments. This is in recognition of the fact that a large motivating factor underpinning a host country's national security concerns, is owing to the large market share still enjoyed by Chinese state-owned

---

[38] Karl P. Sauvant and Michael D. Nolan, *China's Outward Foreign Direct Investment and International Investment Law,* Journal of International Economic Law, Vol 1. (42), (2015) p. 11.

[39] Vivienne Bath, *Foreign Investment, the National Interest and National Security – Foreign Direct Investment in Australia and China,* Sydney Law Review, Vol 34:5 (2012)

[40] University of Pennsylvania Journal of International Law, Christopher M. Tipler, *Defining 'National Security': Resolving Ambiguity in the CFIUS Regulations,* Vol. 35:4, (2014); Berkley Business Law Journal, Xingxing Li, *National Security Review in Foreign Investments: A Comparative and Critical Assessment on China and U.S. Law Practices,* Vol. 13, No. 1, Article 5, (2015).

enterprises (SOEs); along with the close relationship between Chinese investment and larger macro-economic strategies.[41] This in turn has led developed nations to query the impartiality of proposed Chinese ODI within their territory. Accordingly, proposed investments face greater obstacles with regards to market entry, particularly within sensitive industries such as agriculture, infrastructure development, telecommunications etc. The net result has been to trigger tighter measures placing limitations on market access, generally requiring a greater degree of transparency and disclosure to prove political neutrality.

For instance within Australia, 2008 brought additional criteria for assessments made when evaluating whether a foreign investment ought to be allowed into the country.[42] The updated criteria was primarily directed towards foreign SOE investments and included:

"Whether an investor's operations are independent from the relevant foreign government, [and] whether the investor observes common standards of business behavior."[43]

Indeed the same holds true for the Canadian government, who released guidelines in December 2007 establishing that:

"For the purposes of evaluating proposed investments by foreign SOEs, Section 20 of the ICA [Investment Canada Act] and supporting

---

[41] Peter Drysdale, *A New Look at Chinese FDI in Australia,* China and World Economy Journal, Vol 19:4 (2011): *"The scale and speed of the surge of Chinese investment into Australia, largely from state-owned enterprises (SOEs), has raised the question of whether investments by SOEs require special scrutiny."*

[42] Peter Drysdale, Shiro Armstrong and Neil Thomas, *Chinese ODI and the Need to Reform Australia's Foreign Investment Regime,* Eaber Working Paper Series, Paper No. 117, (March 2015) p.7.: *"In 2008, in what was widely perceived as a reactive response to the beginnings of large-scale Chinese ODI, Australia introduced added FIRB [Foreign Investment Review Board] assessments and conditions for SOEs."*

[43] Supra note 33, Karl P. Sauvant and Michael D. Nolan.

Guidelines require that the investor satisfies the Minister of the investment's commercial orientation; freedom from political influence; adherence to Canadian laws, standards and practices that promote sound corporate governance and transparency..."[44]

Such measures evidence a particular need for Chinese SOEs to ensure that when targeting developed nations as host countries, they focus their attentions on emphasising the commercial motivations for entering the market, and clarify the extent of their affiliation to the Communist Party of China. Doing so shall hopefully aid in dispelling the security concerns of host governments, whose general wariness towards Chinese ODI is largely resultant of safeguarding against political risks. That being said, it is noted that the sudden influx and substantial volume of Chinese ODI has given rise to economic risks which may further limit market entry.

However, it is not just Chinese SOEs who need to prove their commercial independence and political neutrality in order to secure governmental approval in developed host countries. Within the U.S., a comprehensive review of national security issues has long been entrenched as part of the procedural mechanisms used in determining whether or not foreign investments in the form of mergers, acquisitions or takeovers ought to be authorised. In this case, all companies both state-owned and private, may be subject to review from the Committee on Foreign Investments in the United States (CFIUS). It is noted that review of privately owned Chinese enterprises is down to the voluntary discretion of the American company involved in the transaction; however, those transactions perceived to be under a foreign government's control (en-

---

[44] Government of Canada, Investment Canada Act, *Statement Regarding Investment by Foreign State-Owned Enterprises,* (last modified 2012), accessible via: <<http://www.ic.gc.ca/eic/site/ica-lic.nsf/eng/lk81147.html>> [accessed: 1st December 2017].

compassing SOE related transactions), are mandatorily subjected to review.[45]

The CFIUS committee, comprised of the heads of department for: the department of treasury; the department of justice; the department of defense; department of homeland security etc., is then tasked with the duty of investigating into the proposed ODI on a case by case basis. Their analysis is primarily concerned with identifying and addressing any risks posed to national security.[46]

Indeed, on the basis of the CFIUS extensive review process, both state-owned and private Chinese enterprises have already faced market restrictions. A slew of attempted acquisition cases have been denied, notably: China National Offshore Oil Corporation (CNOOC) vs. Unocal (2005)[47]; Huawei vs. 3Leaf (2011)[48], and Sany Heavy Industry Group vs. four Oregon Wind-power Projects (2012)[49], and more recently Ant Financial vs. MoneyGram (2018). All such cases represented attempts of Chinese ODI in sensitive sectors perceived by CFIUS (oil exploration and pipeline, telecommunications, adjacency to military base, financial security and privacy). They were marred by concerns over the political neutrality of the enterprises involved; demonstrating that the burden to

---

[45] United States, Foreign Investment and National Security Act of 2007, 121 Stat. 246, Public Law 110-49 (26th July 2007), ss8 (B).

[46] US Department of Treasury Official Website: <<https://www.treasury. gov/resource-center/international/Pages/Committee-on-Foreign-Investment-in-US.aspx>> [accessed: 1st December 2017].

[47] North Carolina Law Review, Michael Petrusic, *Oil and National Security: CNOOC's Failed Bid to Purchase Unocal,* Vol. 84 No. 4 Article 9, (May 2006); See since: Financial Times, Leslie Hook, *CNOOC Heeds Lessons of Failed Unocal Bid,* (July 2012).

[48] Cheung Kong Graduate School of Business, *Huawei and 3Leaf: What went wrong? Chinese telecoms set sights on strategic foreign assets,* (March 2011); Reuters, *Huawei Backs away from 3Leaf Acquisition,* (February 2011).

[49] Reuters, Rachelle Younglai, *Obama Blocks Chinese Wind Farms in Oregon Over Security,* (September 2012).

prove independence from the government not only lies with Chinese SOEs but also with purely private enterprises too.[50]

In fact, it is noted that since President Trump's first state visit to China in November 2017, a bill entitled: "Foreign Investment Risk Review Modernisation Act"[51] was put forward for reforming CFIUS. The bill is intended to strengthen the review process of other investment types, particularly within the technological sector. According to the authors, motivations underpinning it were openly attributed to closing:

"gaps in the existing CFIUS review process, [whereby] potential adversaries, such as China, have been effectively degrading our country's military technological edge by acquiring, and otherwise investing in, U.S. companies."[52]

Such concerns are voiced primarily in light of current fears regarding the protection of U.S. based technology; whereby alongside national security concerns, hesitancy to accept Chinese investment has also arisen in developed nations owing to a greater focus for the protection of

---

[50] Note, commenting on the need to bar private enterprises, such as Huawei, from entry into the USA: Mike Rogers and C.A. Dutch Ruppersberger, House Permanent Select Committee on Intelligence, 112th Congress, *Investigative Report on the U.S. National Security Issues Posed by Chinese Telecommunications Companies Huawei and ZTE*, (2012): *"Huawei and ZTE cannot be trusted to be free of foreign state influence and thus pose a security threat to the United States and to our [telecommunications] systems."*

[51] Senate of the United States Bill, 115th Congress, 1st Session, (2017) Accessible via: <<https://www.feinstein.senate.gov/public/_cache/files/8/d/8ddd5830-5e2b-4e7c-9c6f-2c206c953868/5A37EAB23418E531304A42ABA8CF0B2F. cfius.pdf>> [accessed: 1st December 2017].

[52] John Cornyn, *Cornyn, Feinstein, Burr Introduce Bill to Strengthen the CFIUS Review Process, Safeguard National Security,* Press Release (8th November 2017). Accessible via: <<https://votesmart.org/public-statement/1204881/cornyn -feinstein-burr-introduce-bill-to-strengthen-the-cfius-review-process-safeguard-national-security#.WiEWKu2GPIV>> [accessed: 1st December 2017].

intellectual property rights in sensitive tech-based fields.[53] Indeed, such fears may be part and parcel of the reasons why Chinese companies such as Huawei have faced added scrutiny when it comes to proposed investments.[54]

Indeed, even leading EU countries such as Germany, France and Italy have started debate as to whether there ought to exist a unified process for screening FDI projects targeted towards EU countries. CFIUS attempts to call for a more integrated approach across the Atlantic in light of similar concerns regarding sensitive high-tech industries, as well as issues of unfair competition owing to speculation that certain Chinese ODI projects may be closely affiliated, and even sponsored by, the Chinese government as part of larger macro-economic strategy.[55] The €670 million deal of Fujian Grand Chip Investment Fund via its Germany based subsidiary Grand Chip Investment GmbH (GCI) to take over Aixtron, a semiconductor manufacturer in Germany (2016), was revoked by the Federal Ministry for Economic Affairs and Energy (Bundesministerium für Wirtschaft und Energie). Such rejection is considered a rare case within European Union for fear that it might uproot

---

[53] European Parliamentary Research Service, Briefing, *Chinese Investment in the EU,* (May 2014): *"When investing in China, European businesses have experienced problems in protecting their key technologies due to copying. This could also be the case where a European business is acquired by a Chinese investor."* Supra note 45, Investigative Report: *"The protection of intellectual property and compliance with United States export control laws are a core concern for U.S. interests."*

[54] Reuters, Phil Stewart, *U.S. Weighs Restricting Chinese Investment in Artificial Intelligence",* (June 2017): *"United States appears poised to heighten scrutiny of Chinese investment in Silicon Valley to better shield sensitive technologies seen as vital to U.S. national security."*

[55] European Parliamentary Research Service, Members Research Service, Gisela Grieger, *Foreign Direct Investment Screening: A debate in light of China-EU FDI flows,* Briefing (May 2017).

Germany's leading position in the technology for MOCVD reactors, and that it might be used for military purpose in China.[56]

Such considerations cumulatively demonstrate that a core obstacle for Chinese companies attempting to gain market entry into developed nations, is how to convince foreign governments of the political neutrality of their proposed investments. In order to help rectify this, companies ought to ensure: greater transparency; disclosure of essential information for proving commercial independence, and recognition of intellectual property rights in safeguarding high-tech industries. One method for achieving these aims would be to subscribe to internationally recognised standards for responsible business conduct, predominantly with regards to corporate governance structures which ensure accountability and transparency at all levels of business.[57]

Developing Countries

China has a long tradition cultivating close ties with developing countries. It has an upper hand dealing with their heads of government as well as political elites with special emphasis on generating personal rapport. As a basic diplomatic principle of non-intervention, Chinese government refrains from attaching political conditions over either aid programs or commercial projects. Nor is there stringent surveillance and auditing in place over budget in the hands of the host government or partners. On the other hand, developing countries come with greater localisation risks, whereby gaining the approval of local community is the bigger challenge; unlike developed countries where political risks, in

---

[56] Caixin Net, Approval Followed by Rejection, 2016-10-25, http://m.companies.caixin.com/zknews/2016-10-25/101000565.html?utm_source=Zaker&utm_medium=ZakerAPP&utm_campaign=Hezuo

[57] Note, this need had been voiced as far back as 2008 by the Organisation for Economic Co-operation and Development: *OECD Investment Policy Reviews: China 2008,* OECD Publishing (2008).

securing government approval, is key. Therefore, the challenge confronting Chinese investors lies much less with host government receptiveness, but largely with the receptiveness of local society at large.

The roaring campaign over the flagship OBOR Initiative has encountered criticisms from the western world where Germany, UK, U.S. and Australia show hesitation to endorse raising concerns of transparency and conformity to global governance standard. More recently, an article titled "China's Belt and Road difficulties are proliferating across the world" by Financial Times (July 11, 2018) portrayed Sino-centrism citing cases of China-funded projects that are either suspended or mismanaged resulting in public opposition, corruption scandals and environmental damages. Discontent at home is centered on the unpredictable return on investment for big projects in those debt-ridden countries, worrying that the splurge may end up in the Myth of Danaides – condemned to fill a bottomless vessel with water.

Indeed, the idea that governments of developing country are more receptive to Chinese ODI is logical; given the role of strategies like OBOR, in aiding core development such as infrastructure building, energy and resource generation, and knowledge transfer. As such, Chinese ODI provides the private financing, skills and resources needed to aid in the economic development of those countries who lack sufficient public resources to independently achieve such progress. In essence it is seen that there is a greater governmental dependency on Chinese ODI to meet domestic policy objectives in developing countries.

However, this dependency has led to concerns by civil society that the fruits of Chinese ODI may not be reaped in equal measure[58]; notably

---

[58] Dorothy-Grace Guerrero and Firoze Manji, *In China's New Role in Africa and the South: A Search for New Perspectives,* containing: Dot Keet, *The role and impact of Chinese economic operations in Africa,* (Oxford: Fahamu) 2008: *"the objective and fundamental problem is that these relations are based upon highly uneven levels of development and a very different capacity to benefit from*

that it may have little to no impact, or alternatively a negative impact, on local communities. With fears that China's involvement may be partially motivated by a resource-push, and inadequacies in a host country's domestic governance for the protection of local society, employees and the environment; there arises a risk of ODI projects being perceived as exploiting developing nations. Such fears are exacerbated in industry sectors closely related to mining and natural resource extraction, contrasting with developed countries where utmost caution is currently paid to the technological sector.

What's more in those countries where corruption is rife, the lack of transparency around Chinese enterprises (as previously noted in the context of developed countries), is once again a problem; this time for gaining local society approval. In countries that are currently undergoing political transformation or uncertainty, lack of transparency coupled with society's general distrust of government motivations, creates tensions for Chinese ODI. This is especially considering that a large proportion of ODI projects currently take the form of government-based contracts.

For instance, within South East Asian countries such as Myanmar and Cambodia, where recent years have given rise to political unrest, a failure to address the concerns of local society head-on has given rise to a growing anti-Chinese sentiment.[59] Perceived as only interested in the host government's agenda as well as their own commercial pursuits, Chinese companies are more and more likely to face social prejudice in these markets; making it harder for companies to enter these countries in future.

---

such interactions and cooperation [...] there cannot be genuine win-win development scenarios in such a situation."
[59] Vanessa Lamb and Ngo Dao, *Perceptions and Practices of Chinese Investment: China's Hydropower Investments in Mainland Southeast Asia,* BICAS Working Paper Series, Conference Paper No. 21, (May 2015).

"At a popular level, anti-Chinese resentment abounds... [Many] said they felt the Chinese had trampled over local interests, propped up the unpopular military regime and pillaged the country's natural resources."[60]

--China Dialogue

(Commenting on the situation in Myanmar)

Indeed distrust is worsened in cases where Chinese enterprises operating abroad have been seen to import labour from back home, limiting the positive benefits of their investment upon local society.[61] To address such labour concerns, it was noted in 2010 that the Ecuadorean government passed its new Hydrocarbons Law requiring that local citizens make up 95% of unskilled workers, and 90% of skilled workers in foreign ventures.[62] Then again, even where job creation has been stimulated, problems may still arise with regards to poor working conditions, non-compliance of domestic laws and regulations, and unequal treatment of local workers.[63]

---

[60] China Dialogue, Beth Walker, *Anti-Chinese Sentiment on Rise in Myanmar,* (May 2014).

[61] Chris Alden and Davies Martyn, *A Profile of the Operations of Chinese Multinationals in Africa,* South African Journal of International Affairs, Vol. 13:1 (2006), p.93; Eric Farnsworth, *The New Mercantilism: China's Emerging Role in the Americas,* Journal of Contemporary World Affairs, Vol. 110, Issue 733 (2011).

[62] Global Economic Governance Initiative, Rebecca Ray, Kevin Gallagher, Andres Lopez and Cynthia Sanborn, *China in Latin America: Lessons for South-South Cooperation and Sustainable Development,* (2015). Note: the tensions caused within Latin America owing to Chinese companies importing local Chinese labourers from back home: R. Evan Ellis, *China on the Ground in Latin America: Challenges for the Chinese and Impacts on the Region,* (Springer) 2014. p.156-158.

[63] The China Quarterly, Ching Kwan Lee, *Raw Encounters: Chinese Managers, African Workers and the Politics of Causalization in Africa's Chinese Enclaves,* Vol. 199, (2009) 647-666.

At the same time Chinese ODI has been criticised widely in the international domain and media circles as having negative impacts upon local communities and the environment, with respect to: exacerbating the resource curse; disregarding local community rights, and a general lack of environmental and social impact assessments within investment decisions.

It is noted that social and environmental challenges and fear of exploitation, is not limited solely to Chinese ODI. Rather, it has been witnessed with regards to companies emerging from developed countries too.[64] In addition, the responses to Chinese investment within developing countries tends to be rather mixed [Exhibit 3], signifying that perceptions may be more closely related with wider political and economic factors, including: the flow of Chinese imports into the host country; the existence of any trade imbalance; political affiliations, domestic policies and institutions etc.[65]

Exhibit 3 Perceptions of China in Africa

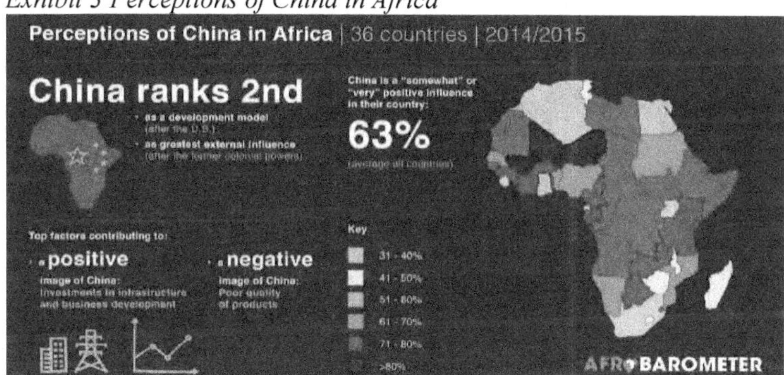

---

[64] International Institute for Sustainable Development (IISD), Yuan Wang and Simon Zadek, *Sustainability Impacts of Chinese Outward Direct Investment: A review of the literature,* IISD Report, (January 2016).

[65] Supra note 58: IISD Report; Afrobarometer, Working Paper Series, Aleksander Gadzala and Marek Hanusch, *African Perspectives on China-Africa: Gauging Popular Perceptions and their Economic and Political Determinants,* (January 2010).

Source: Afrobarometer, AD122: China's Growing Presence in Africa wins Largely Positive Popular Reviews, (2016).

Africans' Perceptions of Chinese Business in Africa, a survey conducted by Ethics Institute of South Africa, University of Stellenbosch, revealed ambivalent views on the presence of Chinese companies in Africa. While some portray China as a benevolent investor and friend of Africa, others accuse China of being a 'new colonial power', extracting resources for their own benefit with little return for Africa. [Exhibit 4]

Exhibit 4 Reputation of Chinese Business in Africa: Combined results for South Africa, Nigeria and Kenya

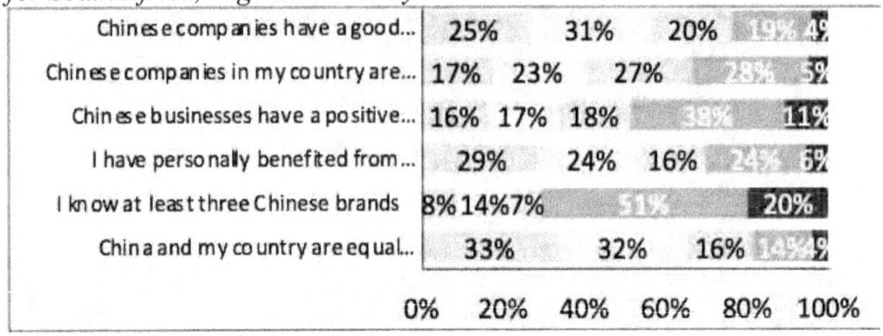

Chinese companies have a good...	25%	31%	20%	19%	4%
Chinese companies in my country are...	17%	23%	27%	28%	5%
Chinese businesses have a positive...	16%	17%	18%	39%	11%
I have personally benefited from...	29%	24%	16%	24%	6%
I know at least three Chinese brands	8% 14% 7%		51%		20%
China and my country are equal...	33%	32%	16%	14%	5%

0%   20%   40%   60%   80%   100%

Source: Ethics Institute of South Africa, 2014

Therefore, Chinese enterprises targeting developing countries ought to recognise the need to build closer relationships with civil society; first and foremost, by improving the level of direct communication and public disclosure surrounding their intentions, plans and operations. This is in recognition of China's aforementioned domestic economic policies, emphasising the need for localisation and social integration of projects. With this in mind, it is important during the initial market entry stages that companies recognise the existence of any prejudices about their activities that they will need to dispel, and ensure that their investments remain sensitive to wider socio-environmental concerns.

In addition, when selecting developing countries as a target market, Chinese companies ought to assess the social stability within those regions to help them identify potential sources of conflict that may arise. Controversies surrounding previous investment projects may also help indicate the general public and media consensus on investments, specifically in regards to certain industry sectors within the said region. Understanding this dialogue will help companies better position their entry, whilst aiding in public relations management. After all, key to market entry for developing regions is for Chinese enterprises to recognise that government receptiveness is not enough for long term success; efforts need to be invested into securing the trust of local communities, particularly where there exists the risk of political rebellion or insurgency.

Conclusion

Having addressed the policy background which has given rise to such large volumes of Chinese ODI, it is clear that the role of social responsibility within such investment cannot be overlooked. As a key trend underlying China's economic policies, and as a determining factor within the very initial market entry stages of investment (in securing governmental and market receptiveness within host countries), this is but the tip of the iceberg in terms of why social responsibility is key to investment success.

As the following case studies shall demonstrate, at every stage of investment, enterprises ought to consider the needs and interests of its wider stakeholders. Learning from past example, it shall be seen what can go wrong where such interests go unnoticed.

Questions for Thought

1. Are the National Security concerns surrounding Chinese ODI in developed countries warranted?

2. Is there strategic alignment between the goals of home country and the host country?

3. Which is more pressing – receptiveness of a host country's government or local society? Does this change depending on the industry sector being invested in?

4. To what extent may Chinese macro-economic policies affect private investments overseas, and how?

5. How might recent policy developments within the U.S. affect the overall rate of Chinese investment globally?

6. Concerning a specific ODI project, who are the key stakeholders and what are their core interest involved?

Appendix

China Economic Background &Policies

Exhibit 5 China Opening Up Reform_GDP Growth (% increase on year earlier) 1980-2014

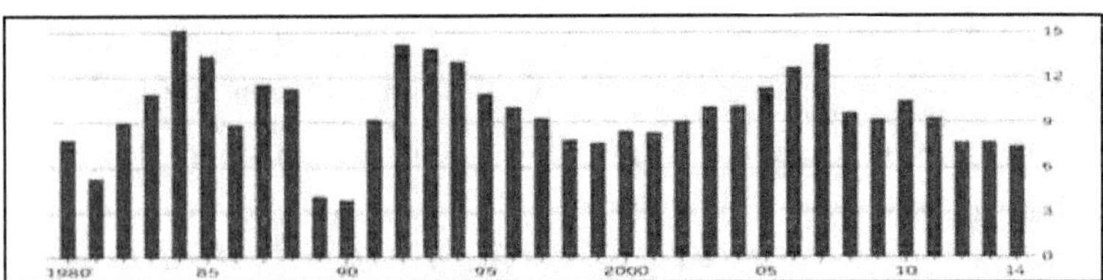

Source: Haver Analytics, National Bureau of Statistics
Via: The Economist, China's Slowdown From a Very Big Base, (2015).

Exhibit 6 China GDP Growth Slowing Down (% increase on year earlier) 2014 -2016

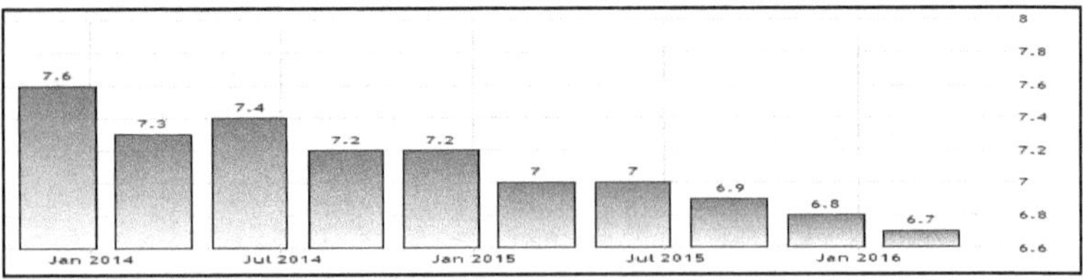

Source: National Bureau of Statistics, China

Via: World Economic Forum, Andrew Wright, This is how China's Economy has Changed in the Last 10 Years, (2016)

Exhibit 7 Belt and Road Plan

Exhibit 8 Made in China 2025 Initiative

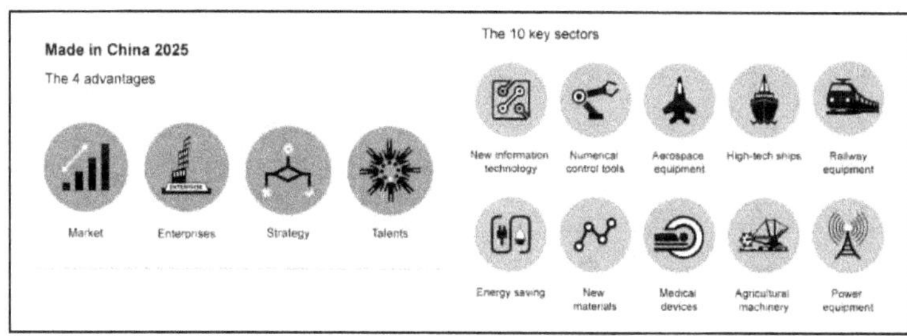

Chinese ODI: Host Country Receptiveness
Exhibit 9 Chinese ODI Host Country Spread 2015
Source: Statistical Bulletin on China's Outward Foreign Direct Investment 2015

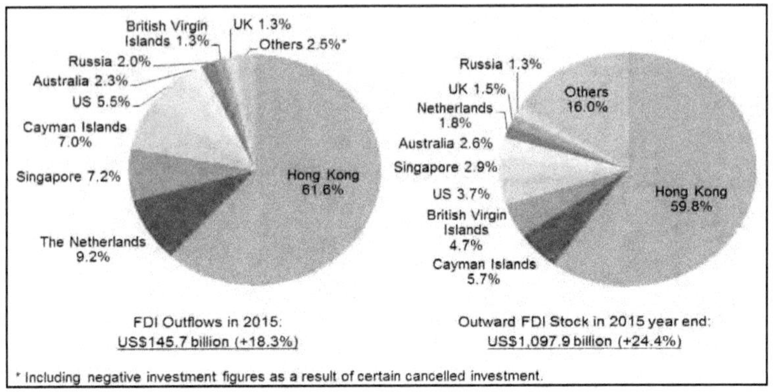

Via: Hong Kong Trade Development Council, China Takes Global Number Two Outward FDI Slot: Hong Kong Re-mains the Preferred Service Platform, (2016).

Exhibit 10 International Perceptions of China Generally

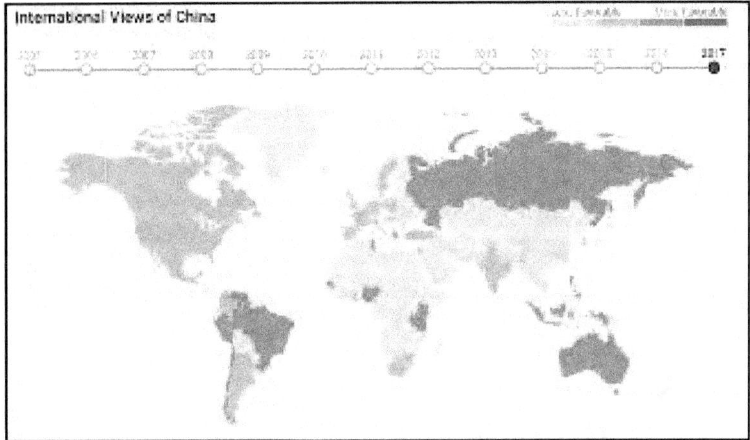

Source: Pew Research Center, Natural Earth Via: Center for Strategic and International Studies, China Power Project

Exhibit 11 Distribution of Chinese Related BITs (Currently in force - 2017)

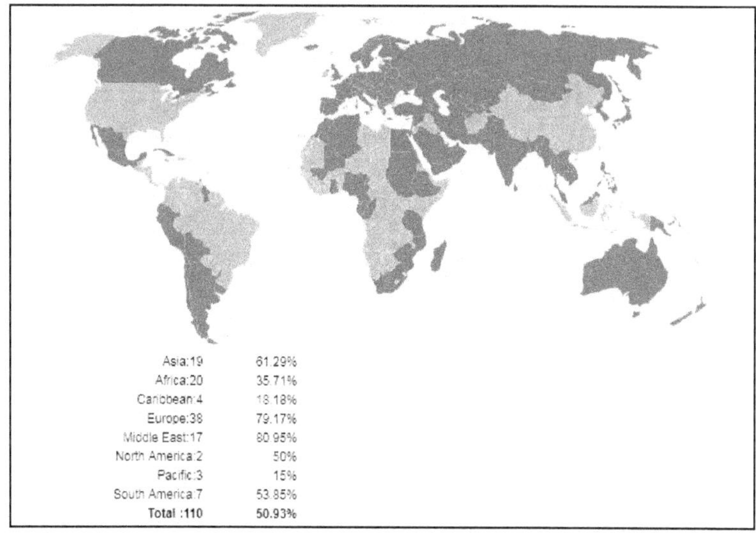

Source: United Nations Conference on Trade and Development (UNCTAD), Investment Policy Hub. Graph created by the Author.

Exhibit 12 Extent of CFIUS Review on Chinese Transactions

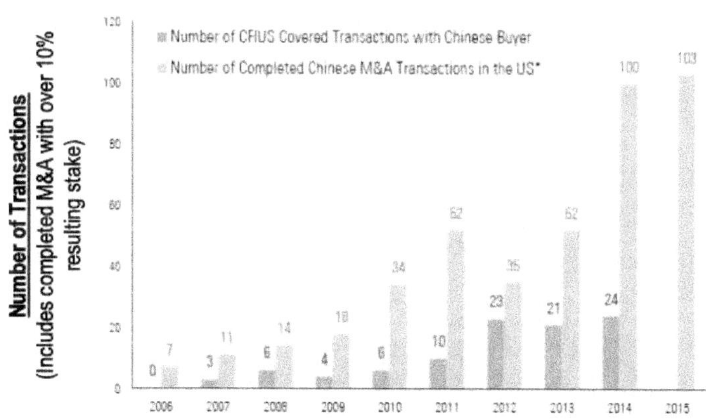

Source: Rhodium Group and the US Department of Treasury
Via Rhodium Group, Thilo Hanemann and Daniel Rosen, Don't Misread Old Tealeaves: Chinese Investment and CFIUS, (2016).

The graph indicates that the level of scrutiny paid by CFIUS over Chinese-related transactions has grown as a response to the rapid increase in Chinese ODI. Significantly the rise in CFIUS reviews is disproportionately less than the growth of Chinese ODI in the U.S.

1

INFRASTRUCTURE BUILDING

Watch out for the "White Elephant": The 'Rushing in' Phenomenon

1.1 Background: Belt and Road

The landscape for Chinese ODI has been greatly shaped by its national policies designed to aid in China's economic transition and rising global presence by strengthening economic ties through trade and investment with major partners. Of particular note is the ambitious OBOR Initiative; aiming at a revival of the Ancient Silk Road concept, by facilitating movement of all productive factors along maritime and land-based trading routes. As the world 4th most populous country, largest economy in Southeast Asia with huge natural reserves, founding member of Association of Southeast Asian Nations (ASEAN), Indonesia occupies a strategic position in China's OBOR program.

According to the report by Asian Development Bank (ADB), "the cost of building the infrastructure that developing countries in Asia will need in order to maintain the economic growth that lifts people out of poverty is estimated at $8 trillion between now [2013] and 2020."[66] Aside from geopolitical considerations by Chinese government, this

---

[66] Who Will Pay for Asia's $8 Trillion Infrastructure Gap? 30 September 2013. https://www.adb.org/news/infographics/who-will-pay-asias-8-trillion-infrastructure-gap

sheer market potential is irresistible in the eye of Chinese investors counting on their manifold strong advantages: geographic proximity, historical ties with Indo-Chinese tycoons, abundant supply of building materials, expertise in infrastructure development, and green light to the financial powerhouse in the backyard.

As depicted in Exhibit 1.1, Chinese ODI was already concentrated in Asia for obvious reasons by the time when the OBOR Initiative was launched in 2013. Focus has been greatly sharpened extensively on the development of infrastructure as a prerequisite to the proposed trade routes. In doing so, a majority of infrastructure projects initiated in a wide variety of countries ranging from Africa, South East Asia and even Latin America[67], may not only be intertwined with the OBOR initiative, but may have also enjoyed China's support in its drive for global expansion.

Exhibit 1.1 Continental Distribution of China's OFDI Stock, 2013

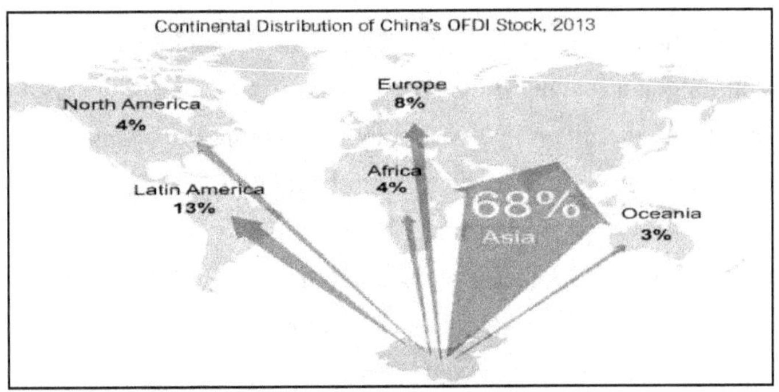

Source: World Resources Institute, Lihuan Zhou and Denise Leung, China's Overseas Investments, Explained in 10 Graphics, (January 2015), http://www.wri.org/blog/2015/01/china%E2%80%99s-overseas-investments-explained-10-graphics

---

[67] China Daily, Jorge-Tuto Quiroga, *Time for a 'Belt and Sea Lane' for Latin America,* (May 2017); CGTN, Zhang Ruijin, *Latin America, Another End of the Belt and Road?,* (November 2016).

Indeed within China, large cash reserves have been dedicated to financing overseas projects on the concept of 'win-win'; whereby host countries are provided with especially low interest loans for infrastructure development, on the condition that the projects are contracted to Chinese companies.[68] The idea here is that countries lacking in industrial capacity still rely on export of commodities key to their wealth accumulation, whilst providing Chinese companies with a wider market to do business. Along these lines, such an engagement is of mutual practical benefit, particularly when it is considered that for certain countries lacking expertise in infrastructure building, outsourcing these projects to countries with know-how, such as China, may be the only viable option for their development.[69]

After all it has been noted that Chinese companies are rather experienced in the field of infrastructure building, having had much practice in their own home territory.[70] However, failure to appreciate the level of influence contextual factors can have on the operations and success of projects, has led to a number of problems with respect to Chinese infrastructure-led ODI. Issues have mainly arisen with respect to: localisation of projects, undue delays, inaccurate financial projections, and environ-

---

[68] European Council on Foreign Relations, Commentary: Agatha Kratz, *Paying the China Price: The Costs of Chinese Investment,* (July 2015).

[69] King's College London, Lau China Institute Working Paper Series, Agatha Kratz and Dragan Pavlićević, *China's High-Speed Rail Diplomacy: Riding a Gravy Train?,* (January 2016).

[70] Foreign Affairs, Jeffrey D. Sachs, *Government, Geography and Growth: The True Drivers of Economic Development,* (October 2012): *"China has proved itself highly effective at building large and complex infrastructure (such as ports, railways, fiber-optic cables, and highways) that complements industrial capital".*

mental concerns; prompting changes in domestic policy to encourage a closer interaction between Chinese companies and local enterprises.[71]

These problems may be attributed to the initial stages and decision making processes involved in the investment process; with the result being large scale projects that are ultimately abandoned or suspended for long periods of time.[72] Subsequently, the investment which once showed much promise for economic growth on both sides of the fence, is left nothing but a white elephant; a pursuit which at best causes next to no change, and at worst results in economic loss.

With this in mind, the issues highlighted by the following cases focus on the initial decision making processes when determining whether to invest in a project or not. After all, it has been emphasised that central to the OBOR Initiative lies the concept of strategic long term investments and partnerships, whereby 'long term' necessitates effective planning and preparation prior to the going out process. This ensures during market entry, that a proposed project has been carefully selected and structured to safeguard continuous growth and development:

"Only if the financial base is solid, growth prospects sustainable, and multi-year collaboration in place will an investment support the government's strategy." [73]

--Liu Jiahua (former Deputy Director General of China's State Administration for Foreign Exchange/Chief

---

[71] Ministry of Foreign Affairs of the People's Republic of China, *China's Policy Paper on Latin America and the Caribbean,* (November 2016) <<http://www.fmprc.gov.cn/mfa_eng/wjdt_665385/2649_665393/t1418254.shtml>> [accessed: 10th June 2017].

[72] Financial Times, James Kynge, Michael Peel and Ben Bland, *China's Railway Diplomacy Hits the Buffers,* (July 2017); Fortune, Minxin Pei, *Why China Keeps Throwing Trillions in Investment Down the Drain,* (December 2014).

[73] World Economic Forum, Liu Jiahua, *China's New Model of Investment, Explored,* (May 2017).

Managing Director of China-LAC Industrial Cooperation Investment Fund (Claifund)

As of August 2017, in line with the Chinese government's recent policies for outbound investment, which adopt the same classification framework as is used for inbound investment ("encouraged", "restricted" and "prohibited" categories); there now exists an even greater need for ODI in:

"Exploration and development of energy resources such as oil gas and minerals [to ensure they operate] on the basis of careful evaluation of economic benefits".[74]

--General Office of the State Council

The changes emphasise that diligent financial assessments are a crucial factor within market entry decisions; particularly for those industry sectors in more sensitive fields or operation in countries with less predictable political and legal environment.

1.2 Rushing-in

However, despite this focus on long termism, it has been noted that a number of projects fall short of their intended aims. A common and problematic outcome for infrastructure investments relates to unnecessary delays and high costs that materialise during delivery of projects.

Whilst delays and extra expenses are an intrinsic risk in any investment, particularly large scale ones in riskier fields such as infrastructure and the extractive industries; the current track record of Chinese investments implies that there may be a more substantive underlying issue present. Indeed a study published by Oxford University in 2016, noted

---

[74] Notice of the General Office of the State Council on Forwarding the Guiding Opinions of NDRC, MOFCOM, PBOC and MFA on Further Guiding and Regulating the Direction of Outbound Investments, (August 4th 2017).

that of 95 large scale Chinese rail and road projects analysed between 1984 and 2008, 75% had all been over budget[75]; a factor which ultimately led the study to predict that:

"Unless China shifts to a lower level of higher-quality infrastructure investments, the country is headed for an infrastructure-led national financial and economic crisis, which - due to China's prominent role in the world economy - is likely to also become a crisis internationally."[76]

--Oxford Review

In this regard, one of the main obstacles preventing Chinese companies from securing higher-quality investments lies in their motivations and attitudes when pursuing investment opportunities. It is noted that with policies such as China's Going Global and the OBOR initiative, there exists a lot of temptation for companies to invest here and there. Indeed, the incredible speed of China's development and the surge in capital that had entered the country following its Open Door policy, have meant that a number of companies now enjoy staggering amounts of capital that only a short period of time ago could only have been dreamed of. What's more, the near future continues to hold a number of possibilities as China experiences one of the fastest emerging middle income markets, in which consumers and companies are aggressively wetting their appetite for navigating the open waters.

This combination of factors: pro-outward investment policies, huge surplus in capital, and a growing market appetite; provides Chinese companies with the position, resources and drive needed to invest into large scale projects overseas. However, this has also resulted in problems of rushing in, whereby investment opportunities are selected prem-

---

[75]Atif Ansar, Bent Flyvbjerg, Alexander Budzier, Daniel Lunn, *"Does infrastructure investment lead to economic growth or economic fragility? Evidence from China"* Oxford Review of Economic Policy, Vol 32, No. 3, (2016), pp. 360-390.

[76] Supra note 9, Oxford Review, at p.385.

aturely without adequate checks and proper assessments conducted beforehand to ensure that they are not only viable, but within the company's best interests[77].

A case in point is that of the 2015 Bandung High Speed Rail project in Indonesia, managed by Kereta Cepat Indonesia China (KCIC). KCIC was a joint venture established between China Railway International Co. Ltd. (CRI) and PT Pilar Sinergi BUMN Indonesia (a consortium of Indonesian SOEs). Relative ownership was split in the proportion of 40% - 60% respectively. The project, to construct high-speed rail connecting Jakarta to Bandung [Exhibit 1.2], was first announced by the Indonesian government in July 2015, and was awarded to the Chinese company by late September of the same year. Indonesia's decision to award the project to CRI over a competitive Japanese bid, was primarily rooted in the Chinese company's offer to build the railway without requiring a government loan guarantee as a prerequisite. In essence, CRI had agreed to shoulder the entire financial risk inherent in the infrastructure development.[78]

---

[77] China Dialogue, Zhang Chun, *Why doesn't anyone like Chinese companies overseas?* (September 2014): *"don't jump on bandwagons. That's a major reason for investment failures in recent years...Companies need to be realistic and only expand overseas when they actually need to, rather than just following others."*

[78] Institute of South Asian Studies, Yusof Ishak Institute, Issue 2016 No. 16, Wilmar Salin and Siwage Dharma Negara, *Why is the High-Speed Rail so Important to Indonesia,* (April 2016), PERSPECTIVES; Tempo, *Sayonara to the Shinkansen,* (18 October 2015) - National Development Planning Minister, Sofyan Djalil, sent to Japan to inform Prime Minister Shinzo Abe that Indonesia could not accept Japan's proposal; Indonesia Investments, *Construction of Indonesia's Jakarta-Bandung Railway Should Start Soon,* (March 2016).

Exhibit 1.2 Jakarta-Bandung High Speed Railway Plan

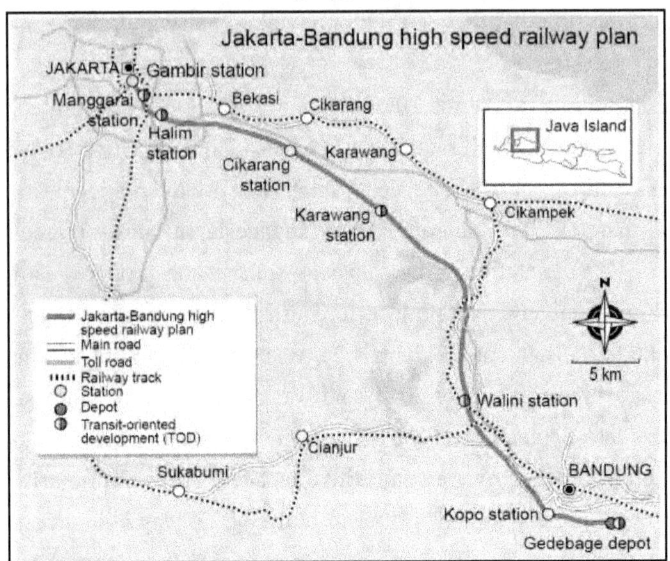

Source: Kompas Research Center. Via Railway Pro Communication Platform, "Loan Signed for Indonesia High Speed Railway Project, (2017).

Shortly after, the project appeared to be smoothly underway with its opening ceremony having been officiated by President Joko Widodo in mid-January 2016. However, just six days later, it faced its first obstacle when it was suspended over incomplete paperwork, which had been submitted to obtain necessary approvals for the project's construction. It was found that vital details were still missing, including: technical drawings of the rail design, field data, and other specifications. As a result, the consortium only possessed licences to build the first 5km of the railway,[79] and has ever since been struggling to secure the land permits needed to build the railway as intended. The primary issue at the present time of writing, lies in securing access to 49 hectares of land which are

---

[79] South China Morning Post, Kristine Kwok, *China's High-speed railway project in Indonesia suspended over incomplete paperwork* (January 2016).

currently utilised by the country's Ministry of Defence: the Indonesian Air Force.

Such delays have resulted in an inflated purchase price, caused as a result of design adjustments necessary for obtaining licenses. At the same time, the delays have further prevented the project from securing a loan agreement from its largest financier: the China Development Bank.[80] To make matters worse, the situation has been exacerbated by the fact that the plan, developed by CRI, aimed to have the 140km project completed regardless its useable condition by 2019. Providing only a mere 3 year timeline, little room was left for such setbacks.

What is of particular note here, is why such setbacks were unforeseen in the first place. As a direct result of Indonesia's geographical terrain, high levels of bureaucracy and land acquisition rights, the country had long gained a reputation for being particularly cumbersome as an investment target for infrastructure development[81]; giving reason to anticipate additional challenges and burdens.

It so happened that the year 2015 marked entry into force of the Indonesian government's new law: the Law No. 2/2012 on Land Acquisition for Development in Public Interest. The law had been passed in order to resolve some of the more pressing and urgent matters which had caused difficulties in earlier high profile projects. In particular, it aimed to improve Indonesia's investment landscape in order to entice foreign investors, and encourage future infrastructure projects central to devel-

---

[80] Jakarta Post, Dylan Amirio, *Indonesia might see high-speed rail costs swell amid changes,* (April 2017).

[81] Indonesia Investments, *Infrastructure Development in Indonesia,* (2017) <<https://www.indonesia-investments.com/business/risks/infrastructure/item381>> [accessed on 15th June 2017].

opment.[82] As such, CRI's bid for the Bandung High Speed Rail can be argued to have been rather well timed.

Nonetheless, whilst the investment opportunity may have been well timed, CRI's decision to offer a bid which required no government loan guarantee and proposed a fairly tight time schedule, was far less strategic. Despite reasons for renewed optimism about the venture in light of these regulatory changes, it was still necessary to remain cautious given uncertainties surrounding the legislation's real impact upon investments. This was especially pertinent in view of Indonesia's internal fragilities relating to: weak governance; absence of the rule of law; and, loose enforcement of regulations.[83] Such factors ought to have provided CRI with enough caution that the same delays and practical challenges faced by earlier infrastructure projects, were still fairly likely to resurface, notwithstanding the regulatory changes.

Surely enough, despite the new law's aims to make it increasingly easier and quicker for infrastructure development projects to acquire necessary land, the problem is still far from having been solved. Rather, it is these very issues associated with land acquisition rights that have plagued the Bandung rail project into a tailspin. The outcome emphasises that even where regulatory environments have been strengthened in host countries, some form of government loan guarantee is a necessary buffer to truly protect long term rights and investments; particularly in

---

[82] East Asia Forum, Nicholas Morris and Irene Tsjin, *How to Resolve Indonesia's Infrastructure Crisis,* (June 2015): *"Indonesia's past performance in delivering infrastructure projects does not inspire confidence that the infrastructure gap will be filled. Poor coordination between different levels of government, long delays in permit issuance and major difficulties with land acquisition have led to major delays for even those projects where funding was available. And this has discouraged private investors from participating in public–private partnerships."*

[83] Asia Development Bank, Research Policy Brief No. 17 Governance, Peter McCawley, *Governance in Indonesia: Some Comments,* (2005).

developing countries where regulatory enforcement is weaker. That explains why the more sophisticated Japanese competitor who had been courting the Indonesians as an early bird chose to risk losing the business by insistence on such a bottom-line.

Indeed, CRI's decision to absorb all financial risk despite Indonesia's poor track record with previous infrastructure ODI projects, appears to have been motivated by the short term aim in securing its bid over Japanese competition, which is also extolled as an emotional triumph deeply embedded in the Chinese nationalistic sentiment against Japan. This indulgence was further supported by the company's somewhat ambitious projections for the railway to be completed in a mere matter of 3 years.[84]

With this in mind, it is emphasised that strategic long term partnerships need to be carefully cultivated on the basis of a diligent cost-benefit analysis; whereby mutually beneficial "win-win" investments take into consideration the needs of both parties to a transaction. Accordingly, the starting position of any investment decision ought to consider the economic interests and wider strategies of the company itself, prior to engaging in bidding wars. Without such a crucial self-evaluation, it becomes particularly easy for companies to make more and more challenging promises in their effort to secure bids, ultimately made at the expense of the company's own interests.

In fact, studies have found that the primary reasons for economic loss in majority of infrastructure projects can be rooted back to: poor justifications for selecting the project in the first place; misalignment of the project and company needs; insufficient planning, and crucially, unrealistic projections that underestimated the project's costs whilst

---

[84] Financial Times, Robin Harding (Tokyo), Avantika Chilkoti (Indonesia) and Tom Mitchell (Beijing), *Japan Cries Foul after Indonesia Awards rail contract to China"* (October 2015).

overestimating its benefits.[85] It appears that all such misgivings had been present in CRI's case, highlighting the importance of pertinent cost-benefit analysis in paving the way for sound investment decisions.

When targeting an underdeveloped country endowed with rich natural resources, a rudimentary reflection should be addressed: why it remains underdeveloped after decades of independence? By the same token, why a project that apparently holds huge promise failed for years to find a proper partner other than myself? This is not naval gazing; after taking a pause followed by a simple reflection, certain hidden bugs may turn out to be self-evident at a glance.

1.3 Problems of Feasibility

Yet, assessment of macro level fundamentals is no substitute for thorough examination on all risk factors in a dynamic fashion. In and amongst the need for more integrated cost-benefit analysis, lies a further need for feasibility reports. After all, long term strategic decision-making not only requires an assessment of the value in proposed projects, determining whether investments are in the true interests of the investing company; but also whether they are practical, taking into account all the contextual factors surrounding the proposal. Without such considerations, the expectations and mechanisms employed to determine project performance later on, inevitably become skewed. As the Chinese proverb goes: *a gigantic dyke may collapse with an overlooked ant hole.*

Indeed, the impact of feasibility reports is crucial to establishing realistic financial projections and timescales for the commencement of large scale overseas projects. Such projections establish the baseline upon which the entire project's management decisions and ultimate success rate will be determined, and are therefore pivotal at the very

---

[85] Mckinsey & Company, Nicklas Garemo, Stefan Matzinger and Robert Palter, *Megaprojects: The Good, The Bad, and the Better,* (July 2015).

beginning stages when conducting due diligence on proposed investment opportunities. However, the aforementioned rushing in phenomenon, coupled with overly optimistic attitudes towards investment opportunities, have undermined the overall accuracy of feasibility reports in certain cases. Therefore, it is utterly important to unlearn the assumptions at the very onset.

Take for example the project to build a 471.5km long railway between Tinaco in the Cojedes State of Venezuela, and Anaco in the country's Anzaotegiu State. The project announced in 2009, was part of a National initiative to construct 8,500 miles of railway in Venezuela by 2030; and culminated in a joint venture worth USD 7.5 billion. The joint venture was established between a consortium of Chinese companies headed by China Railway Engineering Corporation (CREC) with 40% ownership, and Venezuela's national railway company: Instituto Ferrocarriles del Estado (IFE), holding the remaining 60%. The project marked Latin America's largest non-oil related investment contract, and was intended for completion by 2012.[86]

However, come 2012 the project was still a long way from completion and indeed, later in 2013, it was ultimately suspended when the Venezuelan government became unable to pay the contract underpinning the venture. Since then the project's construction sites have been all but abandoned, with raw materials ransacked and stolen, leaving little to show for the investment project as a whole. Consequently, five years overdue, the project has only added to the list of Chinese overseas high-speed rail initiatives that are yet to come to fruition; with it being voiced that of all the Chinese-led projects currently under discussion and con-

---

[86] Venezuela Analysis, Spencer Earl, *Venezuela Inaugurates New Line for Extensive Rail System Project*, (March 2009).

struction around the world, there have been very few that can actually be deemed successful.[87]

Exhibit 1.3 Around the World Sovereign Credit Default Swaps (CDS) 2016

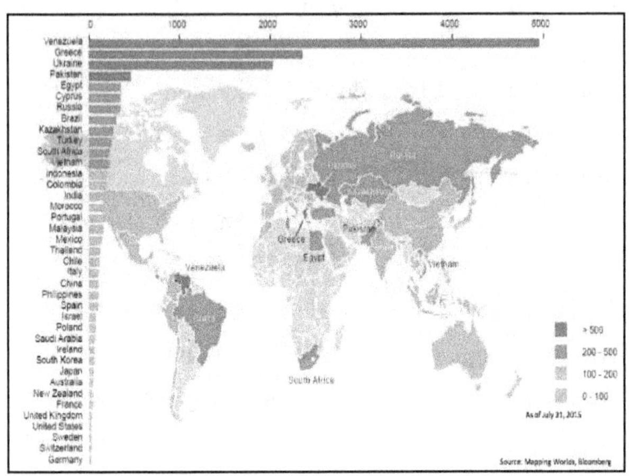

Source: Mapping Worlds, Bloomberg, Via Business Insider, Ben Moshinsky, RANKED: The World's National Debts, From Safest to Most Risky, (2015)

In evaluating the case, it is to be remembered that the ultimate factor which rendered the project a failed attempt was down to larger macroeconomic considerations. Venezuela's weakening economy necessitated that cut backs were needed, as the country became more and more unable to meet outstanding debts owed to foreign enterprises. After all, the

---

[87] South China Morning Post, Kristin Huang, *Why China's bid to sell high-speed rail technology overseas is losing steam,* (April 2017): *"There is no case of China exporting high-speed rail that can be described as very successful."* [quoting Dou Xin, CRRC Qingdao Sifang spokeswoman]; Financial Times, *China Rethinks Developing World Largesse as Deals Sour,* (October 2016): *"Even though about 20 Chinese high-speed rail projects are officially under discussion around the world, only one in Turkey is operational outside China"* [quoting Agatha Kratz].

particularly high costs associated with high speed rail technology gives rise to higher risk of defaulting, especially in the context of countries such as Venezuela, which had been suffering from low cash reserves, food shortages and inflation.

However, whilst such factors may well be outside the realm of strict business, it is worth considering that once again, tell-tale signs did exist to warn the Chinese company that the investment bore such heavy risks. Indeed, Venezuela's credit history highlighted that the country had often entered into dealings which were ultimately cast off mid-way, having defaulted on creditors and extended overseas loan repayments a handful of times in just the last 30 years[88] [see Exhibit 1.3 for Venezuela's sovereign credit default rating]. In light of such statistics, it appears that the decision and expectations surrounding CREC's investment in the Tinaco-Anaco high speed rail, may have been somewhat misjudged.

Feasibility reports alongside risk management considerations ought to have taken credit factors into account when determining whether such an endeavor was a viable option or not. After all, credit checks are an integral part of any investment decision. However it has since been suggested that the issue at hand lies not with oversight, but with technique. Attention has been drawn to the manner in which Chinese assessment strategies, unlike Western ones, focus on the potential for development and future returns more heavily than on past considerations: *"They look backwards, [China] looks forwards."* [89]

However, this forward-looking perspective nullifies cost-benefit considerations at the expense of project feasibility per se. From this lens of risk interpretation, it is acknowledged that the proposed project would have appeared positive; given the future potential of Venezuela as a

---

[88] Financial Times, *What China can learn from its Venezuela Blow,* (October 2016).

[89] Supra note 22: Financial Times.

country rich in commodities such as oil, coupled with its larger potential in and amongst government aims to build 8,500 miles of domestic railway by 2030. Yet, when such considerations are taken into account alongside feasibility assessments, past considerations such as credit ratings must inevitably take a front seat; as factors vital to determining the security of the investment when attempting to answer pragmatic questions such as: is this investment viable?

Exhibit 1.4 Great Hole of China

Source: The Economist, Special Report, Banks Breaking Bad, (2016)

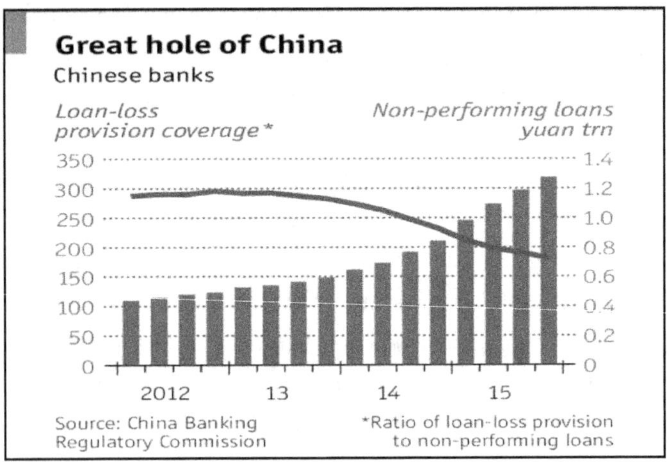

After all, feasibility studies not only have implications on the Chinese companies that are managing overseas projects, but also on host countries, and importantly the banks and financiers that provide the necessary capital for ODI. A company's track record and own credit rating so to speak, is therefore also in need of safeguarding; something which can best be achieved where adequate checks have been made to maximize every possibility of success. Indeed, this is especially prudent given the current trend and rising volume of non-performing loans within the Chinese banking sector [Exhibit 1.4]. China's banks extended a record 12.65 trillion yuan ($1.88 trillion) in loans in 2016 as the government encouraged credit-fueled stimulus to meet its economic growth target. The credit explosion stoked worries about financial risks from a rapid build-up in debt, which authorities in 2017 pledged to contain.[90]

"In the end, if they are not delivering on the returns, then the banks that are lending will eventually say we need to be careful and we cannot keep doing this...it has to be commercially viable."[91]

--Rajiv Biswas

Asia-Pacific Chief Economist, IHS Markit (Singapore)

Regardless of how renowned a company may be, its overall track record in overseas investments, will ultimately determine the cost and timeline for the company to raise capital in future; a fact best evidenced by the infamous Wanda Group under the real estate magnate Mr. Wang Jianlin. Despite Dalian Wanda representing China's largest commercial enterprise with exceedingly high net worth, reports have circulated of warnings sent to Chinese financial institutions against financing the company's future overseas acquisitions. Such warnings come in spite of the company's well-known brand, and in light of its recent history with 'unusual' foreign investment choices[92]; reinforcing the long term need for all companies, regardless of size, to strategically and pragmatically orchestrate ODI opportunities. Wanda purchased in 2014 the landmark Spanish Building in Madrid city center for €265 million for rebuilding and renovation, with the intention to transform it into a commercial plaza composed of a deluxe hotel, shopping center and apartment build-

---

[90] Weizhen Tan, The trade war is complicating China's efforts to fix its economy, July 19, 2018, https://www.cnbc.com/2018/07/18/us-china-trade-wars-impact-on-chinas-economy.html

[91] Knowledge@Wharton, Special Report: *China, New Ambitions, New Directions*, (June 2017), *Where will China's 'One Belt, One Road' Initiative Lead?*, p3. Quoting Rajiv Biswas, Asia-Pacific Chief economist at IHS Markit (Singapore).

[92] BBC News, *Dalian Wanda $9.3bn deal in 'crazy' restructuring*, (July 2017).

ing. Notwithstanding the 4-500 job opportunities created and handsome tax revenue generated in the process of reconstruction and subsequent operation for this building idling there for half a century, the project encountered roaring opposition from interest groups and newly elected government which forfeited its predecessor promise.[93] After a standstill for 3 years, Wanda was compelled to resell the property to Baraka Global Invest Co., occurring a net loss of nearly RMB200 million.[94]

Political entanglement both at home and abroad can make matters worse, however lucrative the project might be by economic calculation; not only for the project at stake, but it can be perilous for the entire company. Wanda met its Waterloo when it was identified among five Chinese private companies to be targeted by Chinese regulators amid a crackdown on overseas acquisitions. Chinese regulators had instructed the country's largest lenders to cut funding for six of the company's overseas acquisitions. It was widely rumoured that Wanda was accused of maculating the OBOR program by outbidding the state-owned China Railway Engineering Corp (CREC) for the acquisition deal of Bandar Malaysia and privately meeting the Malaysian Prime Minister Najib Razak in May 2017. The Bandar Malaysia project, owned by state fund 1Malaysia Development Berhad (1MDB), had originally been awarded to CREC and its Malaysian partner, Iskandar Waterfront Holdings (IWH), in December 2015. The joint venture's alleged failure to meet key conditions under the transaction, among other things, prompted the Malaysian government to unilaterally cancel the contract in May. The

---

[93] Richest Chinese Criticized the Resistance Posed over his Investment on the Spanish Building, May 23, 2016, https://www.bbc.com/zhongwen/simp/business/2016/05/160523_wanda_spain_investment

[94] Epoch Times, Wang Jianlin Sold the Spanish Building in Madrid at a Loss of RMB200 million, June 7, 2017, http://www.epochtimes.com/gb/17/6/7/n9235261.htm

rail project, valued at US$5.2 billion, is part of Beijing's Belt and Road infrastructure development push.[95]

In addition, as highlighted by the Tinaco-Anaco High Speed rail case, feasibility reports are not only essential for strengthening credit checks when determining financial feasibility; but also for calculating time schedules and deadlines. Indeed, the Tinaco-Acaco High Speed rail case is not the only one of its kind to have far exceeded the proposed timeline for completion, with many Chinese-led overseas projects in all industry sectors facing the same problems.[96] This in turn has led to setbacks such as: unexpected cost overruns, tensions and reputational damage to the 'China' brand.

Whilst it is conceded that China's capacity for achieving remarkable levels of speed and efficiency in infrastructure building is next to no other,[97] it needs to be remembered that executing such tasks in overseas territories brings with it operational, legal and technical challenges that may not be present back home. In appreciation of this fact, it is worth adopting techniques such as *reference-class forecasting*; looking at

---

[95] South China Morning Post, China's Dalian Wanda scraps bid for Bandar Malaysia project after regulatory scrutiny at home, 25 July, 2017, https://www.scmp.com/business/companies/article/2104005/wanda-scraps-bid-develop-bandar-malaysia-rail-project

[96] Liu, J, Flanagan, R and Li, Z (2003) *Why does China need risk management in its construction industry?* In: Greenwood, D J (Ed.), 19th Annual ARCOM Conference, 3-5 September 2003, University of Brighton. Association of Researchers in Construction Management, Vol. 1, 453-62.

[97] The Economist, *The Lure of Speed: China has Built the World's Largest Bullet-Train Network*, (January 2017): *"Less than a decade ago China had yet to connect any of its cities by bullet train. Today, it has 20,000km (12,500 miles) of high-speed rail lines, more than the rest of the world combined."* See also: World Bank, Gerard Ollivier, Jitendra Sondhi and Nanyan Zhou, *High Speed Railways in China: A Look at Construction Costs*, China Transport Topics No. 9, (July 2014); Global Construction Review, Rod Sweet, *Why Can China Build High-Speed Rail so Cheaply?*, (July 2014);

former cases that have already been completed in similar terrains, to get a better idea of the types of challenges that might be faced, and of the requisite timelines that ought to be realistically attributed for the project's commitments.[98] In essence, looking backwards may not be such a bad thing.

1.4 Internal Controls

In fact, looking inwards may be a more pressing matter in the context of those financial institutions who have been funding such large scale infrastructure ODI. Indeed, the contextual backdrop of China as previously explored, in which the regulatory environment, influx of capital and market drive have inspired particular enthusiasm; has not only prompted a rise in opportunities for businesses but for financiers.

Statistics show that since the Belt and Road initiative was first announced in 2013, related investments in terms of infrastructure projects and M&As have already totalled USD 494 billion.[99] Accordingly, alongside the USD 124 billion pledged by the Chinese government in state-owned investment funds (Silk Road Fund) and policy banks (China Development Bank and Export-Import Bank of China)[100]; there remain phenomenal opportunities for commercial banks of the likes of: ICBC, Bank of China, and China Construction Bank to invest[101] [Exhibit 1.5].

---

[98] Supra note 19, Mckinsey & Company.

[99] Jiemian News Source Official Website: <<http://www.jiemian.com/article/1318829.html>> [accessed: 3rd July 2017], Statistics accurate up until May 2017.

[100] Reuters, Brenda Goh and Yawen Chen, *China Pledges $124 billion for New Silk Road as Champion of Globalization,* (May 2017).

[101] Caixin, Peng Qinqin and Denise Jia, *China State Banks Provide over $400 Bln of Credits to Belt and Road Projects,* (May 2017); Reuters, Shu Zhang and Matthew Miller, *Western Banks Eclipsed by China's Along the new Silk Road"*

In turn, given that the funding sourced by these banks originates from public deposits, the need for stringent risk management mechanisms within their investment policies and processes, is vital to safeguarding the overall wealth of the Chinese public.

Exhibit 1.5 Widening Belt

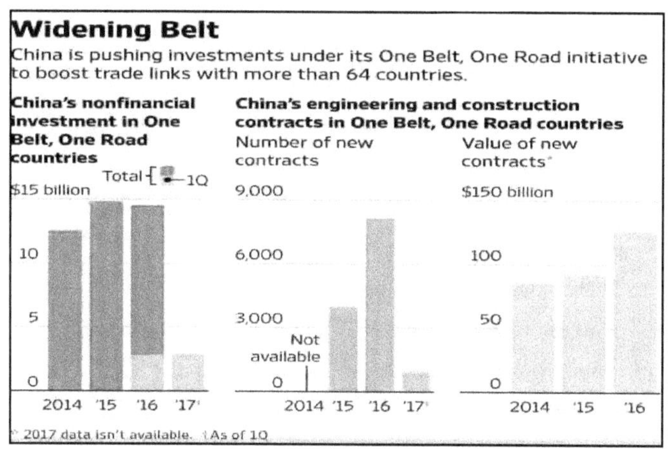

Source: Data from Ministry of Commerce China
Via The Wall Street Journal, Mark Magnier and Chun Han Wong,
China's Silk Road Initiative Sows European Discomfort, (2017).

However, it isn't just these large scale policy-driven investments that are on the rise within China; opportunities overseas have already grabbed the attention of many individuals and small businesses, a fervency much like the European adventures during the Great Discovery. This is in part reflects the chorus of anxiety among investors over the lackluster stock market and frozen housing market at home. Since the turn of this century, massive emigration from China has brought about large magnitude of ODI by individual households, particularly in the

---

(May 2017); Caixin, Wang Yuqian, *Fact Box: Financial Aspects of Belt and Road,* (May 2017).

real estate sector in those developed countries. In addition to wealth security and education for children, concerns over living quality such as food safety, environmental degradation and skyrocketing housing prices, have set off a new wave of emigration from China. United States, Canada, Australia, New Zealand, Singapore and United Kingdom are the most favorable destinations for Chinese middle class seeking permanent residence or naturalization. According to the Report on Chinese Emigration (2015), in 2013 alone, 133 000 Chinese were granted green cards in the 3 countries – United States, Canada and Australia. The report describes it as the third wave of emigration because most of the emigrants settled by investment, as contrasted with the first wave by relatives and second wave by professional expertise.

With this influx of investment opportunities arises a public safety concern, as members of the public who lack either the experience, the access to information, or both, need to be safeguarded against dishonest attempts in procuring their money.[102] This in turn necessitates that the internal controls adopted by commercial banks and financial institutions are comprehensive enough to prevent fraud and money laundry. It is noted here, that once again these risks emerge as a direct result of the phenomenon of rushing in, whereby safety measures and essential checks are overlooked, in and amongst the overarching frenzy to invest.

"China's financial markets were opened in the 1990s and the pace at which they have developed has brought many risks...People are eager to achieve high returns, but they do not have adequate knowledge of the financial risks." [103]

--Zhao Xijun (Renmin University, Deputy Dean School of Finance)

---

[102] Consider the prevalence of Ponzi Schemes in China today: Reuters, Matthew Miller and Shu Zhang, *China's $7.6 billon Ponzi scam highlights growing online risks,* (February 2016); South China Morning Post, Frank Tang, *Why Ponzi Schemes are thriving in China despite crackdowns,* (July 2017).

[103] Supra note 32, South China Morning Post (Frank Tang).

A case in point, brought to light in 2017, was that of Minsheng Bank; China's biggest privately owned joint-stock bank possessing over 500 branches across China, and which is listed in both Hong Kong and Shanghai. The case concerned a Beijing branch (Minsheng Hangtian-qiao) which had raised RMB 3 billion (approx. USD 440 million) from the Chinese public through investments made into a wealth management product. However, in early April when an inquiry was made into the product, it was discovered by chance that the investment upon which the RMB 3 billion capital had been raised, was in fact a sham.[104]

Since then, the head of the branch Zhang Ying has been detained, and an internal investigation conducted into the institution's affairs. Indeed, private investors informed local and international media that the investment opportunity had been pitched to them as risk free, with a high return of 8-27%:

"I invested because they told me it's a product that would guarantee my capital...My fund manager stressed again and again that there is no risk."[105]

Not only do such testimonials reinforce the nature of the fraudulent activity, but they exacerbate the heavy reputational loss and legal back-lash caused to the corporation as a whole; tarnishing future prospects for the bank to secure public capital in investment projects.

The case has become renowned in highlighting the problems inher-ent with the internal control mechanisms in Chinese financial institu-tions, whereby a weak governance structure fails to provide the appro-priate checks and balances to identify and mitigate fraud related risks.

---

[104] Caixin, Wu Hongyuran, Wu Yujian and Wang Yuqian, *Minsheng Bank Official Probed for Alleged Fraud,* (April 2017); South China Morning Post, Zheng Yangpeng, *China's Minsheng Bank sees investor trust vanish – along with 3bn yuan,* (April 2017).

[105] The New York Times, Sui-Lee Wee and Own Guo, *Chinese Investment Scandal Highlights 'Shadow Banking' Risks,* (April 2017).

"There are gaps in the internal control mechanisms and internal control management of individual base level entities."[106]

--China Minsheng Bank Official Statement

The repercussions of such weak internal controls pose a direct threat to public safety, and it has thus been announced by the chairman of the China Banking Regulatory Commission, Guo Shuqing, that there exists a need to standardize the sales operations of wealth management products. Stricter controls such as monitoring and video surveillance of the process have thus been suggested.[107] In addition March-April 2017 brought with the introduction of 8 new rules for commercial banks and financial institutions; aimed at improving internal regulation and risk management, in order to safeguard public wealth. After all, Minsheng Bank is not alone in having experienced such scandals, with other notable banks such as ICBC falling foul of the same problems.[108]

The case illustrates that in and amongst all the rising opportunities for ODI, there also exists a need back home to strengthen the transparency and internal controls of those institutions that are hoping to become part of funding overseas projects. Preparatory checks and risk assessments into potential investment decisions is not only a subject matter that concerns those Chinese companies managing ODI, but also those Chinese institutions that aim to raise the capital to finance them.

---

[106] China Banking News, *Minsheng Bank Scandal Highlights Wealth Management Product Risks,* (May 2017), quoting: China Minsheng Official Statement (27th April). <<http://www.chinabankingnews.com/2017/05/02/minsheng-bank-scandal-highlights-risk-wealth-management-products/>>

[107] Supra note 36, China Banking News; Financial Times, Tom Mitchell, *China Orders Videotaping of Retail Investment Sales,* (August 2017).

[108] South China Morning Post, Don Weinland, *World's Biggest Bank gets caught up in China Investment Scandal,* (May 2016).

1.5 Change in Attiude

The culmination of the above factors finds, when approaching ODI there is a dual need for:

a). Strengthened cost-benefit analysis alongside feasibility reports in Chinese companies,

b). Strengthened internal controls in Chinese financial institutions. Such groundwork will greatly improve the decision making process involved in selecting higher quality investment opportunities, building trust and reliability around the 'China' brand.

These factors all require greater emphasis on strengthening management decisions and structures, to ensure that projects are not only developed in a strategic manner, but that first and foremost, they are actually selected in a strategic manner. Indeed, it is worth remembering that strategy involves knowing when to say 'no' to a particular opportunity; especially where it is either misaligned with the interests of the company or is unlikely to realistically yield the return it promises. With such a change in attitude, problems relating to the rushing in phenomenon may be mitigated.

However, inspiring this change in attitude also requires the further challenge of emphasising the need for ODI to be fuelled by rule-based transactions as opposed to traditional relationship-based ones. After all, rule based transactions, by proxy of their added transparency and certainty, provide companies with necessary information for strategic decision making; i.e.: cost-benefit analysis, feasibility reports, internal controls, checks and balances etc. Accordingly they provide a more solid framework upon which to make appropriate risk assessments.

Analysts suggest that such a shift in approach has already been prompted by the Chinese government in line with the country's SOE reforms. Through the increasing inclusion of private stakeholders into SOE structures, it is seen that Chinese enterprises are able to *"up-*

grade[s] their decision-making capacity for evaluating overseas invest-ments, especially in regards to risk control."[109]

In other words, the increasing homogeny between State-owned and private sector corporations, may ensure that decision making processes are fueled more strongly on the basis of prudent commercial considerations; in line with international investment rules and recognised business strategies. This in turn will help to integrate Chinese policies, such as the Going Global Strategy and the Belt and Road initiative, within a more stable and certain market environment. Investments may be made in a transparent and predictable manner, aiding both market entry rationality and host country receptiveness.

1.6 Knowledge Sharing

Transparency and predictability may also be improved in light of information exchange. Information exchange, or knowledge sharing, ensures that both sides of an investment are better positioned to control any uncertainties that may exist within the proposed ODI. As such it may aid a company in safeguarding that their feasibility reports and cost-benefit analyses are based on prudent evaluations.

It is noted here that knowledge sharing within the realm of social responsibility often focuses on the need for companies to disseminate technology and resources when investing overseas. However, knowledge sharing is as much about what a company can learn, as about what it has to teach.

---

[109] The Jamestown Foundation, China Brief Vol. 15 Iss.2, Zhibo Qiu, *The Impact of SOE Reform on Chinese Overseas Investment,* (2015). Also consider the traditional organisational structure of Chinese SOEs and its impact on short termism/strategic decision making, Supra note 8, China Dialogue: *"Officials in charge of SOEs are subject to evaluations, and are only in their posts for five years. That means they are unlikely to undertake large-scale prospecting projects which take longer than five years to come to fruition."*

A perfect example of this two-way approach, is best embodied in the success story surrounding the 470km Madaraka Express High Speed Rail project. Opened in May 2017, the high speed rail connects the two cities of Nairobi and Mombasa in Kenya. The project was formerly established in 2011 when Kenya signed a memorandum of understanding (MOU) for China Road and Bridge Corporation (CRBC) to build the train. Therein it was established that 90% of the project's USD 3.8 billion costs would be financed by the Export-Import Bank of China. The repayment plan provided for a 10 year grace period, after which repayments would be spread out over the following 30-40 years.[110] The project proposal anticipated construction of the train to take approximately 50 months, with a scheduled completion date for December 2017.[111]

In recognition of the technical challenges posed by the Kenyan terrain, particularly with regards to Kenya's great wildlife, the company reached out to local experts to aid in their understanding of potential risks. This ensured that feasibility projections and design plans were adequately informed. Accordingly, preliminary efforts were invested into liaising with local rangers and zoologists,[112] making use of local expertise and know-how. Such expert opinion ensured that as many foreseeable challenges as possible, had been appropriately considered in the planning and design stages. As such the train incorporated raised platforms into its design, whilst simultaneously taking into account the animals migration patterns in determining its overall route. Through the combined efforts of CRBC and Kenyan locals, impacts of the infrastruc-

---

[110] BBC News, *Kenya Opens Nairobi-Mombasa Madaraka Express Railway,* (May 2017).

[111] Railwaytechnology.com   <<http://www.railway-technology.com/projects/mombasa-nairobi-standard-gauge-railway-project/>> [accessed on 19th June 2016].

[112] Shanghaiist, Alex Linder, *Kenya Launches $3.2billion China-built Railway with Promises of Economic Prosperity for All,* (May 2017).

ture development on the animals' natural habitat, were thereby mitigated.[113]

"In the construction of the Nairobi-Mombasa railway, we devoted ourselves to environmental and wildlife protection."[114]

--Wen Gang (Vice President, China
Communication Construction)

Whilst locals were able to provide the company with greater insight into contextual matters, the company focused efforts into hiring a local workforce and providing over 3,000 local railway technicians and 44,000 others with training. In doing so, it recognised the practical challenges that might later arise should locals be unable to properly maintain the infrastructure on their own. In essence, the upfront investment for CRBC to mitigate the risks will most likely later on come to well outweigh the potential costs.

Diligent risk assessments thus allowed the company to pragmatically structure the overall investment, including an agreement for CRBC's continued management over the train for the first 10 years commencing operations. This provided leeway for both sides to implement additional mechanisms for securing the project's long term success; ensuring in the meantime, that the train could continue to thrive under the mutual care and supervision of the Chinese company and local Kenyans alike.[115]

Such careful planning and preparation, taking account of technical feasibility risks, financial risks, risks associated to localisation, and so and so forth; enabled the project to be completed 18 months ahead of time. The case thus evidences the positive impact that strategic decision

---

[113] CNN, Briana Duggan and Idris Muktar, *Nairobi to Mombasa high-speed railway opens,* (May 2017).

[114] XinhuaNet, Xiang Bo, *Chinese Companies Fulfill Social Responsibilities Globally: Report,* (July 2017).

[115] China Daily, Pan Zhongming and Lucie Morangi, *Kenya expands infrastructure with new Chinese-built train,* (May 2017).

making and prudent preliminary assessments can have on the success of a venture. The train already in operation as of today, has shortened the travel time from more than 12 hours to 4.5 hours between the two cities. Indeed, whilst there have been some contentions concerning the overall costs of the project, with it highlighted that the Madaraka Express cost twice as much per kilometer than the Chinese built Djibouti-Ethiopia train; it's overall reception remains strong with many hopeful that it has not only benefited the Chinese companies involved, but may also increase the Kenyan GDP by 1.5%.[116] At present the project is even intending to extend further through Western Kenya and on to 6 other East African countries [Exhibit 1.6].

Exhibit 1.6 New East Africa Railway

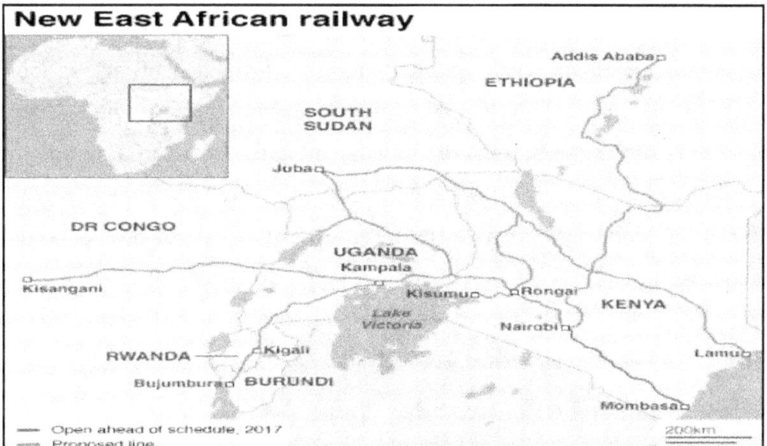

New East African railway

Source: Kenyan Railways, Ethiopian Railway Commission, Transit Transport Coordination Authority

Via BBC News, China to Build New East African Railway Line, (2014)

---

[116] Aljazeera, *Kenya Inaugurates new Chinese-funded railway,* (May 2017): quoting Kenyan Transport Minister James Macharia.

1.7 Conclusion

China is a big emerging economy yet under swift transformation with swinging pendulum in its policy gradient. On top of that, since a majority of infrastructure related ODI shall settle in developing countries with higher political volatility, a close watch of the political climate and regulatory changes on both sides is the very basic homework before embarking on the journey of outbound investment. Direct investment intrinsically differs from trade in that it looks for long-term engagement rather than transactional gains. Of course, the long termism central to Chinese investment policies especially on the Belt and Road, does not mean that companies risk overshooting the runway simply to earn more credits from either side of the government; political agenda may not always fall in line with business pursuit.

A good beginning makes a good ending. As a matter of fact, serious decision making begins by unlearning hearsays and assumptions that may have aroused initial interest. Then, suitability of investment opportunities is by and large determined by the company's mission, financial capability, and more crucially in-house expertise. Fallout of apparently good business deals is often attributed to the syndrome of "eyes bigger than stomach", which wastes resources and tarnishes creditability. Reliance on a good local partner is always advisable than leaning on a subsidiary or representative office staffed by expatriates. Here, suitability must be defined from the perspective of all major stakeholders involved for based on strategic interest alignment. Therefore, it is important for honest cost-benefit analysis, accurate feasibility reports and strengthened checks and balances to be put in place prior to signing the investment contracts.

Such preliminary preparations will not necessarily eliminate all risks inherent in large scale overseas projects, but may at least ensure that when projects do begin, they do so on the right foot and move forward on the right track. After all, more haste does not only mean less speed, but also more cost.

1.8 Questions for Thought

1. Large scale infrastructure investments tend to run over budget and over time (not just with regards to Chinese ODI). With this in mind, is it better to overestimate time and cost projections to try and absorb these uncertainties, or is it better to try and establish realistic, but tight deadlines in the hope (but not guarantee) of meeting them?

2. In the Madaraka Express case, CRBC negotiated that it would have management control over the train for the first 10 years of its operation. Why do you think this was the case?

3. What factors need to be considered when making a cost-benefit analysis? How might these factors be prioritised at the time of negotiating/bidding for a contract?

4. What is the lesson learned by Wanda Group?

5. What are the measured steps necessary to identify a suitable investment project?

1.9 Appendix

China Infrastructure Building

Exhibit 1.7 Demand for Infrastructure Investment Globally (2015)

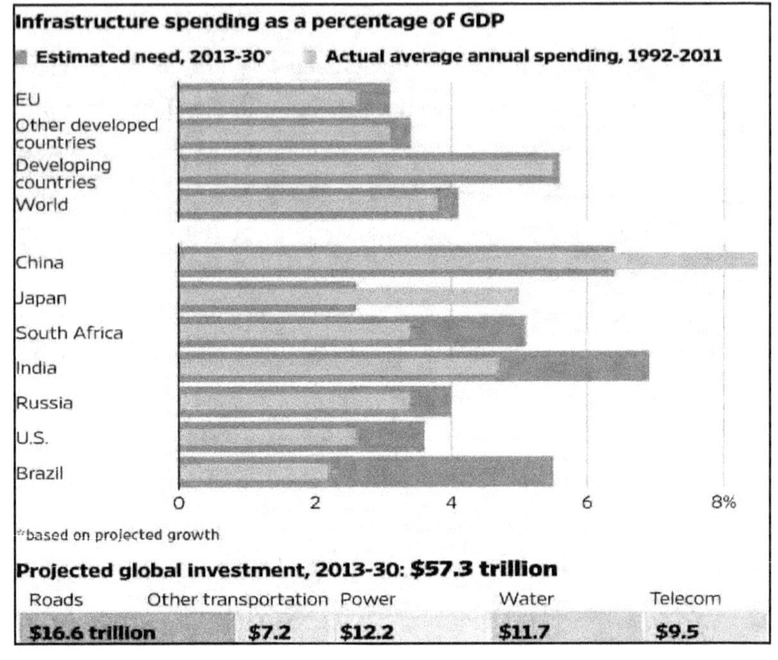

Source: Mckinsey Global Institute

Via The Wall Street Journal, Ian Talley, U.S. Looks to Work with China-Led Infrastructure Fund, (2015).

Exhibit 1.8 Chinese Expertise on Infrastructure Building_Domestic High Speed Rail Network

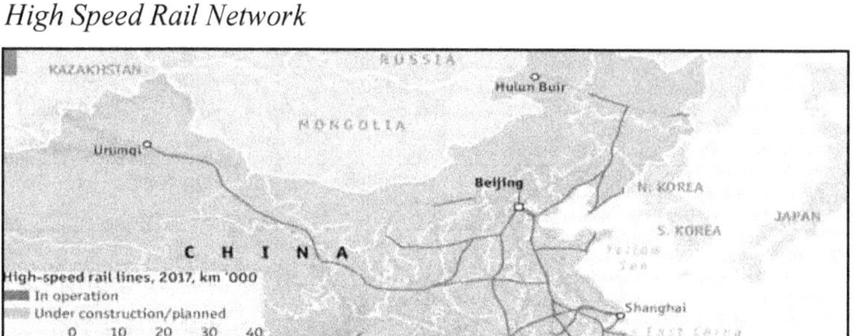

Source: China NDRC, National Railway Administration, International Union of Railways Via: The Economist, China's high-speed trains are back on track, (2017)

Table 1.1 China To-Date Overseas Railway Projects

CHINA OVERSEAS RAILWAY PROJECTS *(as of February 2017)*					
Host Country	Project Name	Valuation	Participation	Status	Date of Contract Signing
Tanzania	Tazara Railway	/	Entire Project	Operational	1970
Nigeria	Modern Train (Abuja-Kaduna)	850 million USD	Design and Construction	Operational	2009
	Modern Train (Lagos – Ibadan)	1.487 billion USD	Entire Project	Ongoing	Aug. 2012
	Modern Train (Kaduna-Kano)	1.685 billion USD	Entire Project	Commencing Soon	Sep. 2016
	Coastal Railway (Lagos – Calabar)	11.1 billion USD	Entire Project	Commencing Soon	July 2016

Turkey	High Speed Rail: Second Phase (Ankara – Istanbul)	1.27 billion USD	Entire Project	Operational	July 2006
Libya	Coastal Railway	2.2 billion LYD	Construction	Interrupted	Feb. 2008
	South-North Railway	1 billion LYD	Construction	Interrupted	Feb. 2008
Algeria	175km Double-Tracked Electrified Railway Line	16.505 billion RMB	Entire Project	Ongoing	June 2009
	55km Double-Tracked Electrified Railway Line	4.117 billion RMB	Entire Project	Ongoing	June 2009
Saudi Arabia	South-North Railway (CTW 400 Project)	728 million USD	Entire Project	Operational	Sep. 2009
Sierra Leone	African Minerals Limited (AML) Iron Ore Railway New Line Construction	/	Entire Project	Operational	2010
Ethiopia	Ethiopia and Djibouti Railway	1.98 billion USD	Entire Project	Operational	Dec. 2011
Chad	Chad Railway	5.631 billion USD	Entire Project	Ongoing	Jan. 2012
Zambia	Zambia East Line Railway	2.264 billion USD	Entire Project	Commencing Soon	Nov. 2016

1. China Railway International Group					
Host Country	**Project Name**	**Valuation**	**Participation**	**Status**	**Date of Contract Signing**
Bolivia	Montero - Bulo Bulo	/	Design	Ongoing	Sep. 2013

	Railway Project		Design		
Indonesia	South Sumatra Coal Transportation Project	/	Design	Ongoing	March 2010
	Central Kalimantan Coal Transportation Project	/	Design	Commencing Soon	April 2014
Cambodia	Preah Vihear Mine Railway Project, Mano Port Project	/	Design	Ongoing	/
Angola	Luanda Railway Reconstruction Project: Phase 1 and 2	/	Design	Operational	/
Laos	Sino-Laos Railway	/	Design	Ongoing	Sep. 2016
Djibouti	Djibouti Doha Ray – Nagad Railway Project	/	Design	Ongoing	/
Iran	Tehran – Qom – Isfahan High Speed Rail	/	Design	Commencing Soon	Nov. 2016
Sudan	Khartoum – Sudan Port Railway Project	/	Design	Suspended	March 2007
	Reconstruction Project of a 100km railway, equipment funded by assisted project (20	/	Equipment Purchasing	Completed	May 2014

	million USD)				
Senegal	Dakar – Bamako Railway Restoration Project	8.136 billion RMB	Design and Construction	Commencing Soon	Dec. 2015
Hungary	Hungary – Serbia Railway Project	2.89 billion USD	Sub-contract	Ongoing	Nov. 2015

2. China Communication Construction Group Ltd.

Host Country	Project Name	Valuation	Participation	Status	Date of Contract Signing
Malaysia	South Railway	2.67 billion MYR	Sub-contract	Commencing Soon	October 2016
	Southern Coastal Railway	46 billion MYR	Entire Project	Commencing Soon	Nov. 2016
Kenya	Mombasa–Nairobi Standard Gauge Rail	3.804 billion USD	Entire Project	Operational soon	May 2014
	Nairobi – Malabar Railroad Project: Section 1	1.483 billion USD	Entire Project	Ongoing	Sep .2015
	Nairobi – Malabar Railroad Project: Section 2 and 3	/	Entire Project	Commencing Soon	March 2016

Source: China Rail Transit, Overview of Chinese Enterprises Building Overseas Railway Projects, Issue 76 (April 2017). Translations by the Center for International Business Ethics.

2017 Changes: China Banking Regulations

Exhibit 1.9 2017 Pledge for Additional Funding of Belt and Road_Distribution of Funds

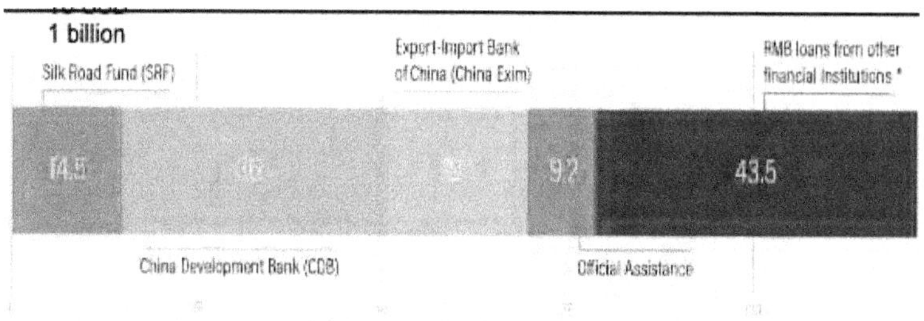

Source: World Resources Institute, ShouQing Zhu, 4 Ways China's Belt and Road Initiative Could Support Sustainable Infrastructure, (2017).

As depicted, an estimated 35.6% of additional funding (USD 43.5 billion) is to be sourced from other financial institutions" including commercial banks. This in turn demonstrates the pub-lic safety need for greater risk management and strengthened internal controls within the Chinese banking/financial sector.

Exhibit 1.10 China Bank Regulatory Commission (CBRC) 2017

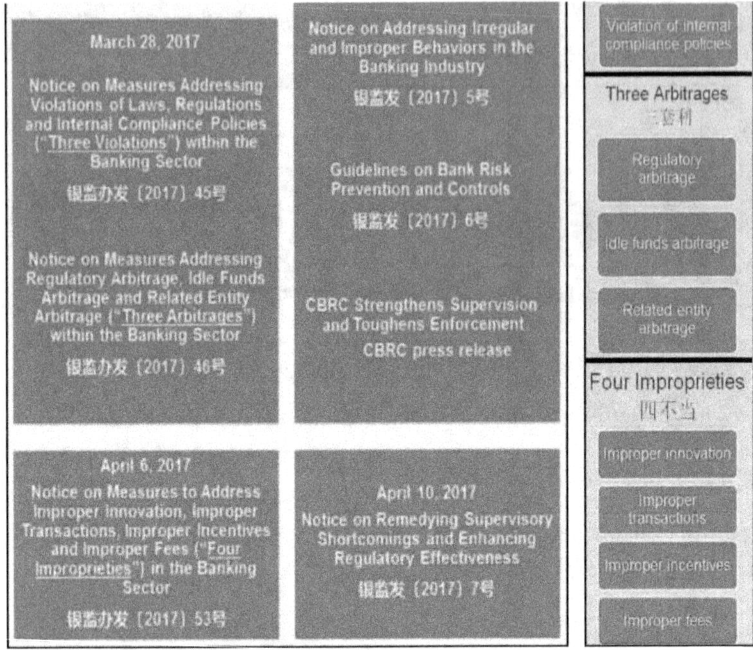

Source: China Law Insight, Chen Yun, Andrew Fei and Wang Rong (King & Wood Mallesons), CBRC's New Supervisory Storm is Here – Implications for Foreign Banks in China, (2017).

The CBRC released 8 new Rules in 2017 for improving: risk management within the financial system, regulatory and supervisory framework for banks/financial institutions, and better integration with national development policies. Officially heralded as the major underlying weaknesses within the Chinese banking and financial sector, are the "Three Violations, Three Arbitrages and Four improprieties," deemed responsible for irregularities therein. [117]

---

[117] See: KPMG, 2017 Q2 China's Banking Sector: Performance of Listed Banks and Hot Topics, (October 2017) for a more detailed background on the current banking and financial sector in China, and analysis on the impact of the 2017 strengthened regulations.

2

MERGERS AND AQUISITIONS

Policy Changes: Calls for Strategic Investment

2.1 Background Context

Compared with the size of national economy, the absolute level is still very low. For example, in 2015, Chinese companies spent around 0.9 percent of GDP on outbound acquisitions; EU companies spent 2 percent, and US companies spent 1.3 percent. However, its mere double digit speed of growth in recent decade is rather eye catchy. In 2012, Chinese ODI was $87.8 billion. The following year broke the hallmark of $100 billion. 2016 saw a stride of $170.1 billion.

It is not just ODI in the form of infrastructure development and the extractive industries that have surged in recent years for Chinese enterprises. The number of Chinese companies entering into merger and acquisition (M&A) deals overseas has also been growing at a staggering rate [Exhibit 2.1] with noticeably expanded industrial scope and regional territory. In 2016, total value of overseas M&As reached $221 billion, six times of that of domestic acquisitions by foreign firms.[118] This has occurred both with respect to the sheer amount of Chinese outbound M&A transactions, and the magnanimity of value involved in many landmark deals. The total amount of China outbound acquisitions had

---

[118] Phoenix Finance, 2017-07-24, http://finance.ifeng.com/a/20170724/15546590_0.shtml

grown dramatically, from \$49 billion in 2010 to \$227 billion in 2016. Chinese companies have almost unlimited firepower for overseas acquisitions, and that makes them willing to pay unrealistically high prices for high-profile megadeals.[119]

Exhibit 2.1 Overseas Shopping Spree

Source: Source: Bloomberg, Vinicy Chan, Wall Street M&A PayDay at Risk as China Curbs "Irrational" Deals, (2016).

For instance, ChemChina's acquisition of Pirelli for EUR €9,000 million, marked the largest singular European takeover in 2015; amounting to 60% of the net value of all European based M&As concluded that year. The company then went on in the following year, to conclude the largest cross border takeover of any Chinese company; acquiring the Swiss-owned Syngenta for USD \$47 billion.[120] For this entire deal, \$33

---

[119] David Cogman, Paul Gao, and Nick Leung, Making sense of Chinese outbound M&A, July 2017. https://www.mckinsey.com/business-functions/strategy-and-corporate-finance/our-insights/making-sense-of-chinese-outbound-m-and-a

[120] Deloitte, Press Release, *Continuous Growth of Chinese M&As in Europe Despite Economic Slowdown in China* (February 2016).

billion was financed by debt, a typical behaviour for Chinese acquirers with a propensity for high leverage.

Reports from 2016 point out the magnitude of this growing surge in M&A interest, with the total net worth of Chinese M&A deals from 2015 having been quickly surpassed in just the first six months of 2016 alone.[121] This continuing trend eventually resulted in China overtaking the US for the first time, as the country with the highest volume of outbound takeovers; evidencing the significance of Chinese companies' new role in influencing global markets.[122]

Such a phenomenon is likely to have been underpinned by a number of factors, including steady decline of the Chinese renminbi, and shift of China's economy from export-driven manufacturing to technology based high-end research and development, accompanied with a focus on consumer-based industries.[123] For some, the move was even deemed inevitable from a business and economic standpoint for any Chinese company wishing to excel either by growing into or securing their position as a Fortune Global 500 company.[124] As a matter of fact, the last two decades saw a dramatic surge in the number of Chinese companies on Fortune Global rank. [Exhibit 2.2] They achieved their position either through monopoly granted by the state, reorganization at the order of the

---

[121] Fortune, Scott Cendrowski, *Chinese Companies Have Already Set an Outbound M&A Record This Year,* (June 2016).

[122] South China Morning Post, Xie Yue, *Record year for China's outbound M&A as it overtakes US for the first time* (December 2016).

[123] J.P. Morgan, *Asian Corporates Aggressively Using M&A to Pursue Growth,* (November 2015).

[124] Telegraph, Ashley Armstrong, *China's M&A boom is forcing the heavyweights to open up,* (2nd April 2016) Quoting Wang Jianlin, founder of Dalian Wanda: *"Relying solely on organic growth will only get you so far. You won't find one Fortune 500 company who made it to where they are today without acquiring other businesses."*

state (tantamount to a matryoshka scheme) or aggressive takeover backed by state banks.

Exhibit 2.2 Number of Chinese Companies on Fortune 500, 1995 – 2017

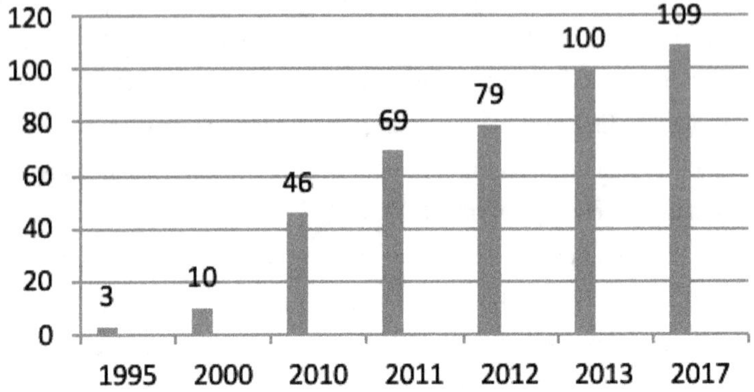

Herein, amongst the handful of incentives encouraging Chinese companies to abandon purely organic growth models for expansion, the role of public policy in recent years and its role in cultivating business takeovers is highly visible. The "Go Global" campaign as of 2001, the aforementioned "Belt and Road" policy and "Made in China 2025" initiative, have all brought with them a regulatory environment that is well suited to companies' pursuit of outbound M&A opportunities. Yet, notwithstanding such public policies, 2017 brought with it changes to this once open regulatory framework. With tightened control over capital restrictions and outbound takeovers, it has been noted that despite 2016 elevating China above the US with respect to outbound M&As, the Chinese government has since felt a need to step in and curtail what is considered "irrational transactions".

Reasons for tightening control may be plentiful, with a specific objective on stabilizing the country's economy and curbing capital flight.[125] Nevertheless, it is of note that the new regulations aim to deter

---

[125] Reuters, *China forex regulator tightens controls to stem capital outflows – sources*, (November 2016).

only those decisions which are deemed "irrational"[126] or "fake"[127] investments. As such, it is the role of China's SAFE to scrutinize proposed M&As more vigilantly. Interestingly enough, SAFE occupies this role despite its own vested interest in ODI as a 65% shareholder of the Silk Road Fund. What this once again reinforces, is that the essence of the aforementioned public policies do not simply lie in promoting ODI, but crucially, in ensuring the integrity of such investments as rational long term operation in line with the national development strategy.

2.2 Past Failouts

Indeed, the new regulations come as no surprise in light of the high percentage of Chinese outbound M&A failings. Statistics note that whilst countries such as the US and UK tend to have success rates of 80-90% in proposed takeovers, the statistics in China are much lower, with only around 44% of transactions actually successful.[128]

A number of reasons have since been attributed to these low success rates, and whilst in-depth information concerning failed takeovers is not so easy to come by, trends in behaviour can help to pinpoint inherent problems that have prevented long term success. Thereof Chinese companies are reminded of three core notions key to securing a prosperous M&A opportunity: transparency, due diligence and synergy. The three principles are necessary for corporations to ensure that:

1). they are transparent and genuine in nature, so as to increase their chances of finding suitable partners and building trust;

---

[126] Supra note 6, Reuters; The Wall Street Journal, Lingling Wei, *China Issuing 'Strict Controls' on Overseas Investments*, (November 2016).

[127] Financial Times, Gabriel Wildau, Don Weinland, Tom Mitchell, *China to clamp down on outbound M&A in war on capital flight,* (November 2016)

[128] China Daily Mail, Craig Hill, *The China Challenge: Why Mergers and Acquisitions Often Fail,* (May 2012).

2). that they are strategic, by which it is ensured that proper due diligence is exercised with respect to planning and structuring takeovers; and

3). that the motivations underpinning M&As are driven by the concept of synergy in aiding growth and adding value[129], as opposed to simply attempting to add companies together in the hope of generating new revenue streams.

Another underlining reason is that Chinese acquirers tend to be less patient in the negotiation process, focusing on a broad picture. As soon as nod is obtained from the government, they are eager to close a deal by offering prices that are hard to resist by the acquiree. For instance, in 2012, Chinese company CNOOC offered \$15.1 billion, or \$27.50, for all the outstanding shares of Canadian oil company Nexen. That was 61% more than where the latter's stock had been valued at before the deal.[130]

2.2.1 Transparency and Trust

Taking the former notion into account, it is to be borne in mind that M&As are primarily concerned with the amalgamation of companies in the hope of establishing an altogether more competitive business. Accordingly, it is particularly important from the outset for the company acting as the acquirer, to understand as fully as possible: the financial position, reputation, market share, competitive edges, growth prospect, relationship with key stakeholders, and business operations of the target company it hopes to enter into M&A dealings with. Only then may it possess the information key to determining whether a merger/takeover is not only a viable option, but a good one.

---

[129] Financial Times, Don Weinland, *Chinese M&A boom faces regulatory checks,* (December 2016).

[130] Stephen Gandel, Companies are paying up for deals, Fortune, August 1, 2012, http://fortune.com/2012/07/31/companies-are-paying-up-for-deals/

In this regard, Chinese companies have faced problems on both sides of the fence: as both the target of foreign companies, and as the acquirer of them. As a target for acquisition, it has been noted that the general lack of transparency into the inner workings of Chinese corporations, has prevented them from attracting potential foreign investors who are looking to strengthen themselves inorganically.

As a direct result of limited publicly available information surrounding Chinese enterprises, all the preparatory work necessarily falls on the Chinese companies' shoulders, bearing the entire burden of having to look for acquisition targets themselves. As an acquirer, the Chinese company is arguably placed in the less favourable situation [Exhibit 2.3]. In turn the process of finding suitable corporations for M&A deals becomes a one-way street: like looking through a blacked-out window, the Chinese company may be looking for potential targets, but very few are looking for them.

Exhibit 2.3 Better Bought Than Buyer

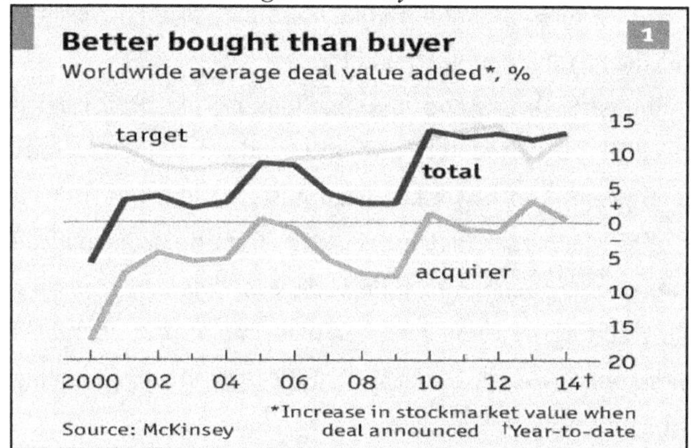

Source: McKinsey Via The Economist, Mergers and Acquisitions: The New Rules of Attraction, (2014).

On the other side of the fence, this lack of transparency is further likely to inspire a respective lack of trust in Chinese corporations as the acquirer; when they attempt to reach out and approach foreign prospective companies. This is not only by virtue of the importance that enterprises (particularly Western ones) tend to place in transparency, but further in light of past cases such as the Caterpillar scandal acting as a blip on the record of Chinese outbound M&As. Indeed, the case offers a better understanding of why transparency and openness are key to not only protecting the overall reputation of an M&A, but to further protecting the singular reputation of both companies involved in the transaction.

The Caterpillar scandal involved the acquisition of Hong Kong listed company ERA Mining Machinery Ltd. (ERA Mining) by the Fortune 500 Company Caterpillar Inc. for US $677 million. Given that ERA Mining owned the subsidiary company Zhengzhou Siwei Mechanical & Electrical Equipment Manufacturing Co Ltd. (Siwei), which bragged a particularly large market share developing hydraulic roof supports in China's coal mining industry; the merger was motivated by Caterpillar's focus on entering the Chinese coal market. Owing to Caterpillar's status as a leading manufacturer of mining equipment and locomotives, the proposition was thereby a seemingly good fit.

Despite preliminary checks and investigations having been carried out, the deal went through smoothly only to unveil a few months later that the financial position of Siwei had been misrepresented as a result of poor accounting standards. In January 2013, Caterpillar announced that they had uncovered *"deliberate multi-year, coordinated accounting misconduct"*[131], resulting in a non-cash goodwill impairment charge of US $580 million, and losses in business contracts for Siwei, devaluing the overall acquisition.

Whilst it has since been contended by Siwei's former CEO, Wang Fu, that the accounting mishaps ought to have been evident had Caterpillar ensured they had a "comprehensive understanding" of Siwei's

---

[131] Forbes, Simon Montlake, *Alleged Fraud at Caterpillar's Chinese Acquisition Puts Spotlight on U.S. Principals,* (January 2013).

financial affairs[132], it is important to note that such an exchange of information is the dual responsibility of both companies. As such, the expectation did not solely lie with Caterpillar to secure such an understanding, but with both Caterpillar and Siwei to have ensured that all vital financial information had been relayed, properly understood and taken into account during the takeover.

However, the lack of openness and proper communication in identifying such problems earlier on, naturally meant that upon discovery of such improper accounting methods, distrust ensued. Siwei maintained that the accounting mishaps had not been intentional but rather were resultant of inexperience in accounting practices, and Caterpillar maintained its allegation of fraud. The outcome resulted in the firing of a number of Siwei's senior management team, including a director of its parent company ERA Mining. Unsurprisingly these internal tensions prevented smooth integration following the takeover.

In addition, a dispute settlement of US $135 million ensued, paid by ERA to Caterpillar in light of the circumstances. Significantly, the scandal resulted in a loss of reputation for both parties individually, let alone for the acquisition as a whole. Given the high profile of the case, it has since resulted in a backlash that may have left future foreign investors wary of entering into cross border M&As with Chinese companies more generally.[133]

The case reiterates the importance of transparency and proper information exchange between both companies to an M&A; not only in making themselves aware of each other's circumstances, but in situations like Siwei's, in even helping a company to better understand its own internal affairs through the expertise of an outside perspective.

---

[132] Reuters, Clare Baldwin, John Ruwitch, *Special Report: How Caterpillar got Bulldozed in China,* (January 2014).

[133] Supra note 12, Reuters.

In fact, the case further acts as a warning for Chinese companies to appropriately scrutinize foreign acquisitions, ensuring that any unknown or unforeseen setbacks in the target companies for M&A are uncovered. To avoid such costly setbacks coupled with unwelcome surprises, securing effective disclosure of vital information on both sides is critical to building an open and transparent relationship. As such, companies ought to make adequate preparations prior to takeover for market entry decisions, risk assessments, and transaction structures. In short, do not shy away from asking the important questions.

Indeed, companies have a tendency to rely on purely written correspondence for the exchange of information; whereby the existence of a paper trail ensures higher levels of accuracy and accountability. However, it is worth noting that important information can also be harboured through field visits and face-to-face dialogue exchange, providing companies with a better understanding of the underlying value system and culture of the organisation that it hopes to enter into an M&A with.

Pragmatically speaking (as previously explored), transparency may even be a make it or break it for a large number of Chinese outbound M&As, who face obstacles when attempting to secure host government authorization. A prime example of this lies with Huawei; one of the world's largest telecommunications manufacturers, one of China's leading international brands, and a company that has previously boasted a number of awards for its leadership, innovation and influence. Yet despite this sparkling reputation, the company was still unable to secure a number of proposed outbound M&As within the U.S., with the American Government stepping in to block such endeavours.

In 2011 for example, the company announced its plans to acquire the US based company 3Leaf, but was later unable to proceed with the deal after CFIUS expressed concerns over national security. This marked the third time that Huawei's proposals for outbound investment had been barred in the U.S. for security reasons; with the other two attempts namely: its 2008 attempt to acquire 3Com, and its 2010 attempt to become the primary supplier of Sprint Nextel Corp.

In this regard, it has since been suggested that the solution to such problems lies in transparency:

"Making corporate governance more open and visible will go a long way towards making [Huawei] more trustworthy in the eyes of foreign governments."[134]

--Teng Bingsheng
(Cheung Kong Graduate School of Business, Professor of Strategy)

"I think [Chinese companies] start from a point of disadvantage because Americans have some stereotypes about China that have to be disputed...companies can do it by surprising American audiences with openness, transparency and fairly broad-based communications approach."[135]

--Bill Black
(Fleishman-Hillard, Senior Partner)

In fact, in response to its failed attempt at acquiring 3leaf, the company recognized for itself the need for stronger transparency in securing outbound M&As. In 2011, Huawei established its first local board of directors in Australia, including non-executive members. This was achieved in acknowledgement that the company "had done a very poor job of communicating...and must take full responsibility for that."[136]

---

[134] *Cheung Kong Graduate School of Business, Huawei and 3Leaf: What went wrong? Chinese telecoms set sights on strategic foreign assets, (March 2011).*

[135] Financial Times, Reuben Miller, Joy C. Shaw, *Chinese outbound M&A: an examination of best practices*, (November 2011).

[136] Reuters, James Grubel, *China's Huawei vows to become more transparent*, (October 2012). Quote from John Lord, Chairman of Huawei Technologies Australia Pty Ltd.

Within the same year, it further continued to strengthen transparency and disclosure standards in the hope of securing greater trust from local governments, revealing for the first time the identities of its board of directors.[137] Since then the company has continued to grow more and more open and transparent in its communication internationally, having learnt from its past failings that: "*It is certainly a positive influence and help with our global business when we are open towards the government, media, customers and the general public.*"[138]

However it's not just transparency that is key. The acquirer, instead of getting obsessed with linear profit calculation, must take into full consideration of the expectations of major stakeholders. Concurrently benefits to these stakeholders must be effectively communicated in a constructive fashion. For instance, prospects for tax revenue to be generated to the host government, job opportunities available to the community, receptiveness to trade union, effective measures for pollution control, are all important factors to gain popular support for the takeover, and more meaningfully for the ensuing operation of the project in question, because this shall help unplug some of the potential backlashes as the project moves forward. For this purpose, it is advisable to involve selected representatives from stakeholders at critical junctures before announcement of conclusion in such deals.

It has been stressed that some of the major reasons for unsuccessful M&As are down to: poor due diligence; bad integration; incompatible cultural values and making acquisitions for the wrong reasons.[139] By and large all these factors can be traced back to the initial decisions

---

[137] The New York Times, Kevin J. O'Brien, *New Openness from Chinese Telecom Giant*, (March 2013).

[138] Supra note 17, New York Times, quoting Mr Ryan Ding (Executive Director of Carrier Network BG).

[139] Supra note 17, New York Times, quoting Mr Ryan Ding (Executive Director of Carrier Network BG).

surrounding how a company determines which foreign enterprise to target during takeovers. Within this process it is essential that the importance of due diligence and synergy be kept in mind, with an eye to ensuring effective long term integration of both corporations.

2.2.2 Due Dilligence and Decision-making

In a nutshell, the purpose of due diligence exercise is to avoid harm through careful verification and thorough evaluation of all the facts related to a prospective project. From the acquirer's perspective, it is necessary to scrutinize the financial standing, operational activities, procedures and standards of the target company. This is in appreciation of the primary role of due diligence: to determine the risks associated with proposed takeovers, and determine the most appropriate cause of action in structuring a transaction. Typically, a professional team composed of accountants, lawyers and lenders, headed by a corporate strategist, are charged with such responsibility.

One particular case emphasizing this point, is that of China National Offshore Oil Company (CNOOC) and its mistimed acquisition of Nexen in the meltdown of global oil market. The acquisition concluded in 2013, faced serious problems as a result of CNOOCs failure to properly educate itself on Nexen's financial situation, coupled with its lack of understanding with regards to the company's environmental context and daily operations. This meant that not only did CNOOC overestimate the value of Nexen when acquiring shares in the company, but it equally underestimated the risks and obstacles associated with oil extraction in the Canadian territory.[140]

In essence, the company had failed to undergo necessary preliminary investigations in a diligent manner, resulting in overpayment during the

---

[140] Reuters, Charlie Zhu, Bill Powell, *Special Report: The Education of China's oil company,* (October 2013).

course of later negotiations. Subsequently, the entire M&A was set off on the wrong foot, with skewed expectations as to the profitability of the new venture.[141] Given that strategic business decisions need to be underpinned with realistic goals and projections in the hope of achieving success; the project became undermined, with it becoming increasingly harder to strategize the takeover when the outgoings spent for the acquisition were disproportionately deluged. Indeed, this is a crucial factor worth considering within the context of Chinese enterprises, where it has been noted that a large percentage of Chinese outbound M&As has either been overpaying for target companies or paying particularly large premiums. In some cases, premiums have reached as much as 33% over the market price of shares that are acquired.[142]

Consequently, CNOOC's overly optimistic financial projections coupled with its lack of understanding surrounding the contextual factors of doing business in Canada, left the company facing greater financial obstacles than originally anticipated. This included the operational challenges of working with a different geology when attempting to access landlocked oil sands,[143] and the higher labor costs involved in recruiting employees from a developed country with higher wage expectations.[144] Regardless the company's commitment to the highest standards of safety and regulatory compliance, its newly installed pipeline in 2014 at Nexen's Long Lake oil sands facility in northern Alberta spilled more than 31,000 barrels of emulsion – a mixture of bitumen, water and sand – into the surrounding muskeg in what remains the largest such

---

[141] Lehman Brown International Accountants, Official Website, "Mergers and Acquisitions: Drivers, Issues and Countermeasures" <http://www.lehman brown.com/insights-newsletter/mergers-acquisitions-drivers-issues-countermeasures/> [accessed on 5th June 2017].

[142] Supra note 19, *Cheung Kong Graduate School of Business.*

[143] The Economist, Industry Briefing, *Key Player – CNOOC Ltd.,* (April 2014).

[144] Financial Post, Jeff Lewis, Claudia Cattaneo, *Life After CNOOC's Nexen Deal: Is China's Honeymoon with Canada's Oil Patch Over?* (Dec. 2013).

spill in Alberta history.[145] With no real strategy for overcoming these unanticipated setbacks, financial loss ensued.

However, whilst CNOOC's misjudgements arose largely within a financial context with regards to acquisition price, it is to be borne in mind that due diligence aims to mitigate risks which do not solely exist within the context of finances. A number of risks may equally arise in respect to substantive matters associated with an acquisition. Indeed, a case in point is that of Zijin Mining Group and its purchase of Monterrico Metals in 2007.

The acquisition enabled Zijin (a Hong Kong registered company) to take over the highly controversial but lucrative Río Blanco Copper mine in Peru, and to do so at a price that was at least 3 times lower than desired. Despite Monterrico Metals' largest shareholder insistent that the fair value of the company lay within the region of US $500 million to US $1 billion,[146] it was ultimately acquired at the bargain price of approximately US $180 million.

On the basis of a purely quantitative assessment, the venture was therefore exceptionally attractive. Commencement of the copper mine would cost approximately US $1.44 billion, and given the capacity of the mine to generate vast amounts of copper and molybdenum, it was anticipated that the project would yield a four year payback.[147] In addition, the original plans that Monterrico Metals had put in place aimed to establish an even larger mining district in the region, providing greater scope for future business. However, whilst the Río Blanco Copper mine

---

[145] Jameson Berkow, 'A parade of broken promises': How CNOOC stumbled with its Nexen takeover, bnnbloomberg, Sep. 15, 2017. https://www.bnnbloomberg.ca/a-parade-of-broken-promises-how-cnooc-stumbled-with-its-nexen-takeover-1.857533

[146] The Economist, *The Economist Warns of Dangers Ahead for Zijin in Peru*, (June 2007).

[147] Reuters, *UPDATE 2 – Monterrico Metals agrees $186 mln bid from Zijin*, (February 2007).

may have appeared, on the surface, to be a rather attractive investment opportunity by virtue of its vast quantity of reserves; the reality painted a very different picture.

The mine, which had been taken over by Monterrico Metals in 2003, had a long history of turmoil as a result of heavy opposition faced by locals. The local community feared for: the ecological impact that the mine would have on their land, its impact on their livelihood, and the risk it would pose to the international organic farming certificate that the local Piura communities had managed to obtain. Tensions ran so high that by 2004, a series of protest marches resulted in multiple injuries and a few fatalities, whilst in 2005, 28 protestors were even detained and allegedly tortured by police and mine security.

Legal challenges had even surmounted against the mine, with Peruvian law stating that such a project could not commence without the approval of local persons. Given the lack of local consent, the mine was thus rendered as having been in constant violation of the regulatory framework put in place to protect the needs of local communities. In light of these factors, it was found by Zijin's own Supervisory Committee that the company had overstated the value of certain assets by overlooking:

"problems [arising] from the social and environmental protection in local society, higher political, economic and cultural risk for overseas investments." [148]

Indeed, taking such factors into account, the reasons for the cheap acquisition price of the mining project quickly transposed. Sure enough by 2009, not only was the entire project ultimately suspended by the Peruvian government (a mere 2 years after Zijin had taken it over), but

---

[148] Friends of the Earth Updates Blog, Kelly Trout, *Groups Call on Hong Kong Exchange to Ensure Zijin Mining Comes Clean about Overseas Investment Risks*, (March 2011).

Zijin also faced heavy legal costs defending Monterrico staff during court cases for the 2005 alleged torture accusations.

What is of particular note here, is that despite Zijin's attempts to distance itself from the controversial history suffered by Monterrico Metals, having attempted to invest in social projects and rebuild ties with the local community; such attempts were of little to no avail. Indeed, the animosity and stigma surrounding the mine had clearly built to such a serious level, that there was little the company could do to gain full community support. In short, the company had bitten off more than it could chew.

Resultantly, notwithstanding its short lived involvement in what had been a long tumultuous relationship with locals, Zijin still faced the brunt of reputational damage. In 2011 the company faced reprimand from NGOs for its failure to properly disclose the risks associated with its investment decisions. A petition letter signed by Friends of the Earth, CooperAccion, Fundación Ecuménica para el Desarrollo y la Paz (Fedepaz) and CATAPA, was sent to the Hong Kong Stock Exchange (where Zijin's stocks were publicly listed), requesting that the company be made to disclose all material risks associated with the Río Blanco Copper mine, so that investors may be placed in a better position to make informed decisions.

The case of Monterrico Metals is only to be dwarfed by another "international scam" that hit on the world headlines – the development of Nicaragua Canal by a Hong Kong listed Chinese firm. Wang Jing, the Chinese billionaire who came forward to bankroll the project through his Hong Kong-based HK Nicaragua Canal Development Group (HKND). He vowed to turn this poverty-striken country into one of the richest countries in the region with his ambitous project. Nicaragua was rated by World Bank as the second poorest in Latin America and the Caribbean with total GDP at US \$10.98 billion. The 276-kilometre canal would cut through the country to link the Pacific and Atlantic oceans

[Exhibit 2.4]. In June 2013, Nicaragua's National Assembly approved a bill to grant a 50-year concession to finance and manage the project to HKND Group. The concession could have been extended for another 50 years once the waterway was operational.[149] A free trade zone with commercial facilities as well as tourist hotels, a Pan-American highway and an international airport at Rivas were planned to be built when canal construction was advanced. Traffic is expected to more than double that of the Panama Canal with the capacity to accommodate far larger tonnage vessels. The project costs were estimated at $50 billion, nearly 5 times of GDP of the entire country, not to mentioned it was later on raised to UD $100 billion.

Exhibit   2.4   The   Blueprint   of   Nicaragua   Canal   Source:

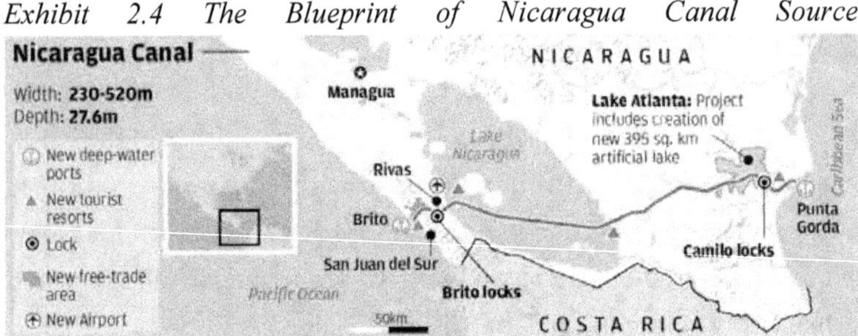

https://www.scmp.com/news/world/americas/article/2134250/nicaragua s-us50b-rival-panama-canal-going-ahead-slowly-funding

The project was initially designed to be completed by 2020, but now has turned out to be a pipe dream. The fallout is primarily due to insufficient financing capability as a result of big loss in wealth encountered by Mr. Wang. But on the other hand, the resistance from environmentalist groups from this entire region would present persistent blows on the ground of disruption to natural habitat, damage to the Lake Nicaragua as the largest source of freshwater, and possible oil spillages once the canal

---

[149] De Cordoba, Jose (2013-06-13). "Nicaragua Revives Its Canal Dream". The Wall Street Journal Online. Retrieved 2014-03-09.

is put into operation. It was also rumoured that the Chinese government favoured more the existing Panama Canal due to the fact that Panama cut off diplomatic ties with Taiwan and moved closer to Mainland China with 19 treaties.

These two cases notably highlights Zijin's failure to appropriately determine all risks associated with the proposed venture; both financial and non-financial [Exhibit 2.5].

Exhibit 2.5

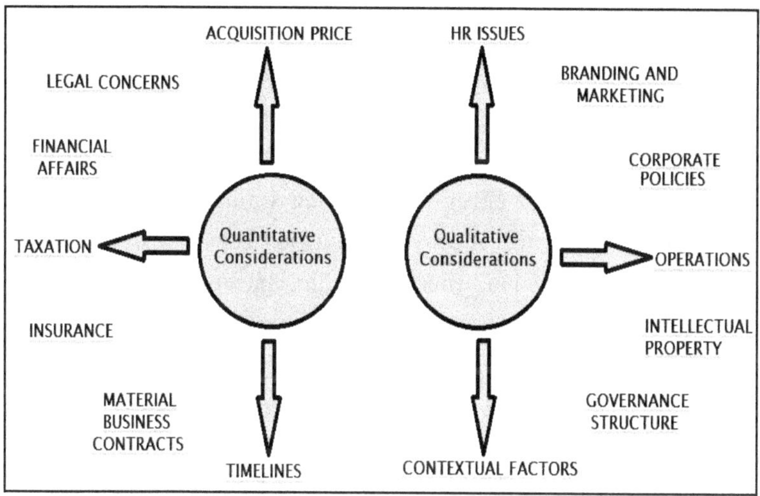

Source: Created by the Authors

Indeed, the aforementioned two cases of CNOOC and Zijin both stress that choosing a suitable acquisition, requires realistic quantitative projections as to a target company's profitability/resources, and further due diligence checks as to qualitative considerations such as: contextual factors; business operations; consumer base; management issues; branding and marketing, etc. The need to effectively assess both, is key.

Thus Chinese companies ought to allocate more resources towards developing their understanding of acquisition companies prior to finalizing an M&A; as opposed to the current trend of securing acquisitions through over-evaluations. Whilst this may initially appear to put companies at risk of losing out on bids for particularly attractive target companies, investing resources into substantive matters such as: developing strategic business plans, refining models for restructure, and ensuring that risk assessments have been conducted diligently; will provide them with a better reputation long term, strengthening their foothold within the international M&A arena.

2.2.3 Synergy and Success

The final relevant consideration in choosing a suitable M&A lies with the concept of synergy. 'Synergy' is a term often associated with M&As, as the underlying concept of takeovers. It operates in recognition of the fact that in either situation: acquisitions or mergers, there persists a need to ensure effective assimilation between the companies involved in the transaction. After all, the fundamental aim of M&As lies in the concept of value-adding, and thus rests in the ability to retain the core elements that made each respective company so successful in the first place, whilst doing so in a manner that integrates them into an even bigger and better corporation.

However, within the context of China, past cases reflect that this notion of 'value adding' has tended to result in companies literally attempting to add together two highly profitable corporations. This is achieved from a purely mathematical standpoint, without much afterthought as to effective integration or compatibility of company values, governance structures and corporate cultures.[150] This somewhat reductionist approach has resulted in later problems where the exact opposite is

---

[150] Global Times, Liu Tian, *High Failure Rates Plague China's M&A Sector,* (March 2015).

achieved: value destruction, or failure to carry through the M&A.[151] The resulting observation notes that the true meaning of synergy goes much deeper than simply adding companies together under one general umbrella.

One initial area worth examining here, is the target acquisitions of recent high-profile M&As concluded by Chinese enterprises. Before even assessing compatibility with the acquisition company's internal affairs such as: values, structure and cultures; there is a need to consider the very industry sector that the acquisition company operates in. Indeed, synergy is best achieved when the two companies involved in the M&A operate in similar industries, so that their experiences, brands and expertise may be assimilated. Where the M&A is intended to diversify the acquiring company's portfolio, the need for well-planned and controlled diversification is essential. However, recent practices have demonstrated the opposite trend within the context of China's larger conglomerates, leading to 2017 policy measures for tightened scrutiny over proposed takeovers.

The M&A portfolios of China's most acquisitive companies including the aforementioned Wanda Group and HNA Group (Hainan Airlines), have not only evidenced substantial volumes of outbound M&As funded on excessive borrowing, but incorporate increasingly diversified acquisitions which stray from the company's own primary operations. For instance, HNA's core business activities fall within the travel industry, as an airline provider. However, notwithstanding this fact, the company's recent M&As have seen investments made into a wide breadth of sectors from the banking industry (having bought stakes in Deutsche Bank) to electronics (having taken over Ingram Micro). Such aggressive buying has rendered that outbound M&A approval is now subject to investigations by Chinese regulators into the relationship between the

---

[151] Shanghai Daily, Vera Ye, *Culture Clash cited for M&A Failures*, (November 2013).

acquiring and acquisition company; to assess whether proposed investments are strategic (in consolidating a company's existing portfolio), or aimed purely at aggressive diversification.

"The level of inquiry has gone a lot deeper than the past - who you are as a buyer and what you are buying are of important focus."[152]

The policy changes are much welcome in that they impress upon Chinese companies the need for outbound M&As to be precedent as long term investments, necessitating that strategic planning takes into account both the pre and post-merger stages. Therein, the role of synergy plays a vital role in post-merger success, recognising the need for solid integration mechanisms to ensure stability and growth. However, problems of synergy do not only arise in situations where the industry focus is misaligned between the acquirer and the target firm. Rather companies within the same or similar industry sectors can also face problems where effective internal integration mechanisms are missing.

Take for instance BenQ's acquisition of Siemen's mobile phone division in 2005. Herein BenQ, unlike HNA and Wanda, strategically identified an industry-compatible M&A target operating in the same telecommunications sector. The deal showed promise that the expertise of BenQ in the manufacture and supply of mobile phones may be able to help the struggling Siemens division, which had been making losses of approximately USD 1.5 million a day prior to acquisition.[153] Yet, in just over one year following the takeover, it became apparent that the entire transaction had been a complete failure when BenQ was forced to file for bankruptcy protection.

---

[152] Reuters, Kane Wu and Sumeet Chatterjee, *Exclusive: China Regulators Plan to Crack Down Further on Overseas Deals,* (August 2017).

[153] EE Times, Blog, *Comment: BenQ gets hard lesson in brand building,* (September 2006).

A study examining the case, published by the International Journal of Business and Social Science[154], identified that the core reasons for such failure was the inability of BenQ to adequately secure cultural integration following the takeover. Herein the problems faced by the acquisition started with the intrinsic differences that exist between different cultures; an obstacle that any company shall face when dealing with cross-border M&A. The cultural disparity herein existed with Siemens possessing a strong cultural affiliation to European business practices, and BenQ (a Taiwanese company) a strong affinity to Oriental norms.

In appreciation of this inevitable culture clash, BenQ decided to retain the chief executive of the newly acquired Siemens mobile division as the chief executive of the new venture. It was hoped that by doing so, as well as retaining a large number of the original employees, the transformation of the acquisition company could be gradually implemented with a longer transition period for adjustment. However, the basis of this decision has since been attributed to BenQ drawing from its Oriental values; focusing its attentions on maintaining stable relationships. This standpoint clashed with the more individualistic business culture of Siemens, in which European business focuses more heavily on uniform standardized procedures and rules. Hence, whilst the European expectation following takeover is to establish an entirely new precedence in terms of business management and structure, BenQ tackled the situation in the exact opposite, trying to maintain stability by sticking with the old.

Notwithstanding cultural differences, the use of a gradual approach was somewhat ill-advised in light of the financial context of the Sie-

---

[154] Shuhui Sophy Cheng, Matthew W. Seeger, *Cultural Differences and Communications Issues in International Mergers and Acquisitions: A Case Study of BenQ Debacle*, Int'l Journal of Business and Social Science, Vol.2: No.24 [Special Issue: December 2011].

men's division too; whereby time really was of the essence. In such a scenario, it was necessary to provide clearer indications of how the acquisition aimed to tackle the mobile subsidiary's financial situation and establish a clear course of action therein. This is owing to the fact that the sensitive situation, coupled with the unavoidable communication problems that arise following M&As, would have established an environment of greater uncertainty for those further down the management chain; exacerbated by the fact that no real change would be immediately noticeable at post-takeover stage. Herein, implementing a more diverse management team from the very beginning may have been better suited to navigating initial culture clashes. This in turn would have enabled problems to be resolved in a much quicker and more efficient manner, with the benefits of speed useful in eliminating workplace tensions surrounding the acquisition's severe financial pressures.[155]

In fact, it is recommended from the outset that companies engaged in M&A fully equip themselves with a specialised team within the Human Resources department, tasked with cultivating culture alignment and synergy. This shall ensure from the pre-merger stage, that the company has fully prepared itself with internal mechanisms needed to handle post-merger complications. Within such a role, the importance of communication channels capable of piercing the entire management structure are pivotal for post-merger integration, enabling the acquisition company to clearly relay its intentions for the new venture. This requires clear communication of new business goals, core values and processes relating to management, workplace productivity, accountability and discipline. In turn uncertainties may be eliminated and greater stability secured within the new organisation. Indeed, even where such internal processes remain unaffected following the takeover, there is still a need to communicate this fact down the corporate structure; synergy cannot be achieved where communication is utterly absent.

---

[155] Supra note 32, Shuhui Sophy Cheng, Matthew W. Seeger.

The importance of strategic communication mechanisms both pre- and post-takeover are thus iterated by the case. In depth dialogue exchange ought to have been conducted between the management teams of the acquiring and target company during the entire M&A process. This is not only from a conscious due diligence perspective, in recognizing and identifying challenging areas for successful integration; but from a synergy perspective, in enabling both companies to familiarize themselves with the cultural and communicative differences between them, drawing from their own practical experience when interacting. Indeed, in the case of BenQ, the company's sole reliance on due diligence checks without actually visiting Siemen's production lines aggravated the problem. Handling the acquisition as an arms-length transaction meant that the very initial relationship between the two companies started from a point of distance; a stance non-conducive to synergy. Some scholars cite the Pollyanna Principle for the negligence of communication both internal and external, where people are susceptible to what's known as the tendency to overrate positive memories and discount negative ones.

In turn, favouring an arms-length approach over a hands-on one, exacerbated uncertainties in the already pressurized situation of the Siemens mobile division. With BenQ failing to ensure it had allocated enough resources to enable stronger communication at all levels of the corporation and all stages of the M&A, the entire governance structure became more and more disassociated with the reasons and aims underpinning such drastic change in ownership; not to mention BenQ's plans for the future of the company. The net effect resulted in a number of senior management leaving shortly after the takeover; a factor noted to have caused further instability. After all, maintaining key members of staff from both the acquiring and acquisition company is integral to ensuring cohesion. This is in appreciation of the role that directors, senior managers and other long standing members in the corporate governance structure, can play to integration. Possessing key knowledge and insight into the operations, structure, procedures and consumer market of the company, such personnel provide a bedrock upon which the precariousness that is bound to follow a takeover can be quickly stabilized. Consequently, their knowledge is key to ensuring effective ongoing integration, such that the M&A continues to strengthen and develop following the takeover.

Indeed, it is important to remember that M&As do not solely require input and focus on the transaction itself, but on the future development and projects of the new venture that has been established post-transaction. In this respect, synergy is key to securing the long term success that Chinese public policy advocates; essential to establishing a new, stronger and well integrated business with its own unique policies, practices and culture.

2.3 Conclusion

All in all, the future for Chinese outbound M&As appears much brighter regardless the expedient punctuation in policy introduced in 2017. By promoting more mature and strategic outbound investment at government level, and by overcoming the learning curve at corporate level, they it is hoped the general reputation of Chinese companies will see steady improvement internationally.

As a matter of fact, recent years have demonstrated that this shift in approach and thinking is not purely policy driven, but has also been practically applied and promoted by some of the more experienced Chinese companies investing overseas. With greater focus on transparency, due diligence and synergy for ensuring long term integration, companies such as Alibaba[156] and Lenovo[157] have demonstrated the success that

---

[156] Technode, Piet Walraven, *A brief history (and future) of Alibaba.com,* (January 2009).

comes when more sophisticated and strategic long term business plans are used to smooth transitions and ultimately establish successful global ventures. Nonetheless, as recent setbacks encountered by Fuyao Glass investing in Ohio demonstrate, there is still room for improvement. More strategically, with the OBOR initiative roaring in, Chinese ODI either in the format of greenfield operation or M&A, is likely to meet tougher challenges not only because of the vast cultural differences between home and host countries, but also because of the huge development gap and insufficiency of rule-binding cooperative structure.

With this in mind, it is necessary for future outbound M&As to consider the lessons learnt from the aforementioned cases - the relationships between: 'transparency and trust'; 'due diligence and decision making', and 'synergy and success.'

2.4 Questions for Thought

1. Diversification is often a primary reason for a company to enter into an M&A. How may the desire for diversification and the need for synergy be reconciled?
2. Is there an imbalance in the level of due diligence expected of the acquiring vs. target company? Should there be?
3. M&As should not underestimate the importance of synergy to success. However, does this apply differently to acquisitions than it does to mergers?
4. Are the 2017 policy changes aimed at curbing "irrational" investments, too stringent?

---

[157] Fortune, Caroline Fairchild, *Lenovo's Secret M&A recipe,* (October 2014); Bloomberg Business Week, Steve Hamm, *Lenovo and IBM: East meets West, Big-Time,* (May 2005).

5. How to successfully roll out communication strategy with stakeholders other than host government and corporate management of the target company?

2.5 Appendix

Exhibit 2.6 China 2016 Surge in M&A Outbound Transactions

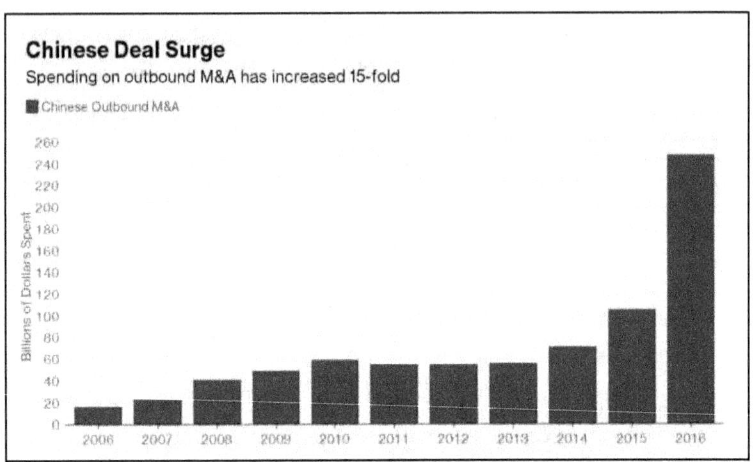

Source: Bloomberg Markets, Sarah Syed, Chinese M&A Scrutiny Helped Void Up to $75 Billion in Deals, (2017).

Whilst the sudden surge resulted in China overtaking the U.S. for its volume of outbound M&As, it also resulted in a dip in Chinese Foreign Reserves (see Figure 2).

Exhibit 2.7 China Foreign Exchange Reserves

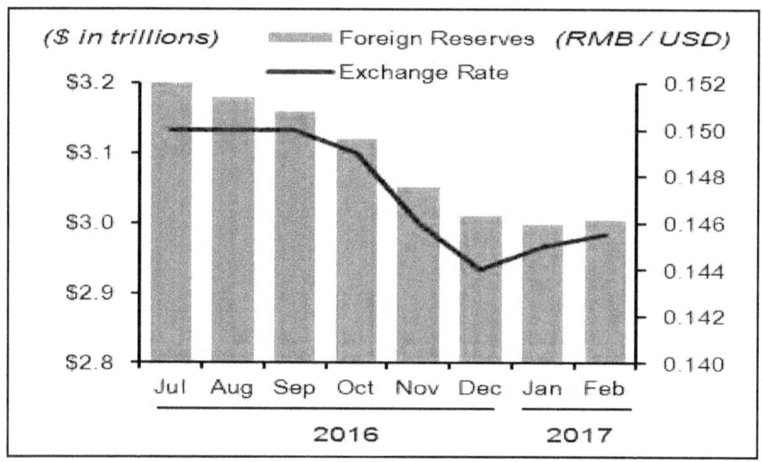

Source: Robert W. Baird & Co. Will Stricter Chinese Regulatory Controls Impact Outbound M&A? (March 2017).

The sharp decline of foreign exchange reserves in December 2016 will have likely prompted the 2017 regulatory changes for tighter control over outbound investment, particularly M&A activity.

Exhibit 2.8 Notice of the General Office of the State Council on Forwarding the Guiding Opinions of NDRC, MOFCOM, PBOC and MFA on Further Guiding and Regulating the Direction of Outbound Investments (2017)_Unofficial English Translation

No. 74 [2017] of the General Office of the State Council
[August 4, 2017]
**Guiding Opinions on Further Directing and Regulating
the Direction of Overseas Investments**

... In order to: strengthen the macro guidance of OI; to further guide and regulate OI; to facilitate the continuous, orderly and healthy development of OI; to effectively guard against all types of risks; and to better meet the needs of national economic and social development, the following guidelines are issued thereinafter:

1) Guiding Principle

The guiding principle is – to comprehensively implement: the take-aways from the 18th National Congress of the CPC and the Third, Fourth, Fifth, and Sixth Plenary Sessions of the Party; the series of important speeches and new concept, thinking, and strategy of governance formulated by Xi Jinping (General Secretary of the Communist Party of China); and decisions and arrangements by the Party Central Committee and the State Council, *"Five-in-One"* and *"Four Comprehensives"* overall strategic planning. Emphasis should be placed on: people-oriented development; the overall theme of steady progress; the concept of innovative, harmonious, green, open and shared development; the strategy of opening-up for mutual benefit and win-win; continuous efforts to build a more comprehensive, in-depth, and diverse environment for opening-up; and the supply-side structural reform as the underlying theme. "Belt and Road" development should be used as guidance to: deepen the reform mechanism of OI by Chinese enterprises; to further guide and regulate OI; to facilitate the orderly and rational development of OI; to prevent and address OI risks; to promote sustained and healthy development of OI; and to achieve win-win and shared development with investment destination countries.

2) Basic Principles

Emphasis on Enterprises as the lead. In the areas of OI: give full play and decision-making power to the market in terms of resources allocation; improve the role that governments play; enable enterprise-led OI, oriented by the market in accordance with business principles and international practice. Enterprises under the guidance of the government, shall independently make decisions and assume sole responsibility for its profits or losses at their own risk.

Emphasis on deepening reforms. Facilitate the innovation on governance systems and mechanism, enhance the convenience of outbound investment, promote the reform for streamlined administration and delegation of powers to lower levels, integrate the benefits of power-delegation and supervision, optimize reform of services, take the file system as the main measures to manage outbound investment, implement market-oriented management mechanisms within capital accounts, guide and regulate outbound investment within the model of "Encouraged Development + Negative List"

Emphasis on mutual benefit and win-win. Guide enterprises to fully consider the specific conditions and actual needs of recipient countries, prioritizing mutually beneficial cooperation with local governments and enterprises to bring about sound economic and social benefits, whilst promoting mutual benefit and win-win cooperation.

Emphasis on risk prevention. Adhere to the overall tone of pursuing steady progress; align with overall economic and diplomatic strategy of the country; adhere to laws and regulations; ensure the pace and focus of OI remains rational; proactively carry out supervision before, during, and after OI; and effectively guard against all risks.

3)   Overseas Investments to be Encouraged

[Purpose:] support competent and well-positioned Chinese enterprises to actively and steadily carry out OI activities; promote the "Belt and Road" construction; deepen international capacity cooperation; drive export of advantaged capacity, high quality equipment, and applicable technologies; enhance China's technology R&D, and manufacturing capabilities; eliminate China's shortage in energy resources; and promote the upgrade and quality improvement of related industries in China.

(1) Focus on promoting overseas infrastructure investment that facilitates the "Belt and Road" construction and the interconnectivity of peripheral infrastructure.

(2) Steadily carry out OI to promote the export of superior production capacity, high-quality equipment and technical standards.

(3) Strengthen investment cooperation with foreign high-tech and advanced manufacturing enterprises, and encourage the establishment of R&D centres abroad.

(4) On the basis of prudent assessment of economic benefits, steadily participate in the exploration and development of overseas oil and gas, minerals and other energy resources.

(5) Expand cooperation on agriculture with other countries, and carry out mutually beneficial and win-win investment cooperation in: agriculture, forestry, animal husbandry, fishery and other areas.

(6) Facilitate OI in: business and trade, culture, logistics and other areas of services in an orderly manner. Support qualified financial institutions to establish branches and service networks abroad, and ensure that business is conducted in accordance with laws and regulations

4)   Overseas Investments to be Restricted

[Purpose:] Limit domestic enterprises from engaging in OI that are not in line with the country's foreign policy on: peace and development, strategy of mutual benefit and win-win, or the country's macro-control policies. Includes:

(1) OI in sensitive countries and regions that China has not established diplomatic ties with, are in war with, or are restricted by bilateral or multilateral treaties or agreements of which China is a signatory.

(2) OI in real estate, hotels, film studios, entertainment, sports clubs and others.

(3) Overseas establishment of equity investment fund or investment platform without actual, specific industrial projects.

(4) OI using outdated production equipment that does not meet the technical requirements of the investment recipient country.

(5) OI that does not meet the environmental protection, energy consumption and safety standards of the recipient country. Among them, investments of the first three categories are subject to the approval of relevant OI authorities

5)   Overseas Investments to be Prohibited

[Purpose:] Prohibit domestic enterprises from participating in OI that endangers or may endanger national interests or national security. Includes:

(1) OI involving the export of core technologies or products belonging to the military industry without the approval of the Country [China].

(2) OI involving the use of technology, techniques or products that are banned from export by the Country [China].

(3) OI in industries such as gambling and sexual services.

(4) OI that is banned by international treaties concluded with or signed by China.

(5) Other OI that endangers or may endanger national interests and national security.

6) Safeguard Measures

(1) Implement category-based guidance. For OIs that are to be encouraged, further improve the level of services in terms of: taxation, foreign exchange, insurance, customs, information and other aspects, in order to create more favourable conditions for the convenience of domestic enterprises. For OIs that are to be limited, guide companies to invest in a prudent manner, and give necessary guidance and reminders based on each specific situation. For OIs that are to be prohibited, take effective measures to ensure rigorous management and control.

(2) Optimize the mechanism of management. Strengthen the review

for the authenticity and compliance of OI to prevent false investment behaviours. Establish an OI blacklist and jointly prevent and penalize non-compliant investment behaviours. Establish an information-sharing system across sectors. Guide domestic enterprises to: strengthen supervision and control of OI under their management; to establish and improve OI decision-making, financial management and non-compliance accountability systems. Establish the state owned enterprise OI capital system. Improve the OI auditing system of state-owned enterprises and safeguard overseas state-owned assets.

(3) Improve level of services. Develop and improve OI management practices. Guide enterprises to: establish and improve the overseas business compliance risk review, control and decision-making system; to establish in-depth understanding of OI cooperation policies, regulations and international practices; and to comply with local laws and regulations in their business. Strengthen institutionalized cooperation with related countries in: investment protection, finance, personnel exchanges and other aspects, to create a favourable external environment for companies carrying out OI. Support the development of related intermediary organizations, such as: domestic assets assessment, legal services, accounting services, tax services, investment consulting, design consulting, risk assessment, certification and arbitration. Provide companies with market-oriented, society-based and international business consulting services within OI, and reduce the risks they face in overseas investment and operations.

(4) Strengthen security safeguard. Regularly publish the *"Report on Investment and Operation Convenience Level by Country."* This is to: strengthen guidance and supervision for enterprises involved in investment in high-risk countries and regions; to timely flag and report major political, economic and social risks of relevant countries; and to propose response plans and preventive measures to safeguard the legal rights and interests of our enterprises abroad. Urge enterprises to: carry out safety risk assessment on overseas projects, ensure safety risk forecast and response readiness, establish and optimize the security system, strengthen security training, and enhance the safety risk prevention capabilities of enterprises in their investments abroad.

Translated by: Mingtiandi.com [with alterations from the Author]

Exhibit 2.9 2017 China Tightened Control over ODI_ Classification System Summarised

Source: South China Morning Post, Wendy Wu, Overseas Real Estate and Soccer Clubs in Crosshairs as China Ramps up Invest-ment Clampdown, (August 2017).

3

INTEGRATION OF LOCAL EMPLOYEES

3.1 Case Background

Economists view land, capital and labor all as factors of production. Thus, managers are responsible for allocating these factors for productivity to the society and profitability to shareholders. Nonetheless, Carl Marx among other classical economists discover that the value of economic output - commodities – is denominated by a series of "socially necessary abstract labor" embodied therein. Labor is the sole dynamic force that transforms the objects (materials) with the instruments (capital) into utility. He draws a distinction between labor power and labor done. While the former is just a stock of ability to work, only the latter is the service actually delivered.

Managers today can derive important inspirations from Marxist labor theory. While human resource manager gathers labor power through an institutional process of planning, recruiting, budgeting and evaluation, it is the frontline manager's job to translate labor power to labor done through tasking, motivation and supervision. To maximize performance level, managers at all levels have to be acutely aware of the intrinsic value and dynamism in the workforce. A core issue is to regard each of them as an individual human being with different personality and preferences rather than a lump of raw materials or machineries. Their physical and mental contribution to the production process and output quality depends not only how well they are organized, but rather how well they are respected as equal peers. Cultural differences that lead to whopping misconceptions add further complications to business operations in a foreign land. In addition to compliance with those explicit labor rules, inadequate understanding and appreciation of local conditionality that is subtle and trivial, may invoke tension and even conflict between managers and workers as well as the community in which business resides. Chinese investors possess strong skills cutting through red tapes and currying favor with bureaucracies - a valuable experience accrued at home, but many are flummoxed with divergent job behaviors among local employees with regard to work discipline and collective bargaining organized by labor union in a foreign land. Some wonder, for instance, why should they ask for an early leave for bonfire parties or decline lucrative overtime workload ignoring the recourse to save their family from chronically necessitous conditions.

3.2 Background Context

Towards the latter end of the 20th Century, the 'Made in China' reputation cultivated by a surge in foreign investment into the country's newly opened doors, saw China transformed into the world's number one industrial powerhouse. Today, China is the only country that owns the most sophisticated industrial structure with 39 categories. Having surpassed the United States as the largest manufacturer of goods in 2011, the country's economy next to doubled, allowing it to rapidly grow into the world's second-largest economy.[158] In addition to global trade, the growing industrial might propels the pusuit of market expansion through direct investment and localized operation by Chinese companies, rendering China the 2nd largest source of ODI (EXHIBIT 3.1).

---

[158] McKinsey & Company, Karel Eloot, Alan Huang and Martin Lehnich, *A New Era for Manufacturing in China*, McKinsey Quarterly, (June 2013).

Exhibit 3.1 Top 10 Global Investors (Unit: Billion USD)

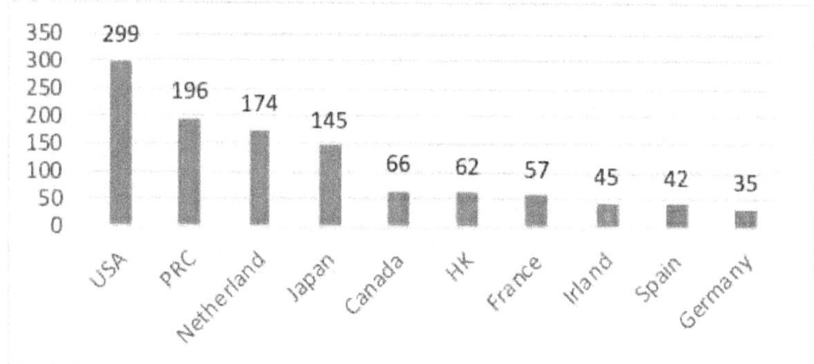

Source: Statistical Communique of Chinese ODI – 2016, MOFCOM, State Statistical Bureau and State Administration of Foreign Exchange; World Investment Report - 2017, UNCTA

According to the product life cycle (PLC) theory developed by Raymond Vernon, the locus of production will shift internationally depending upon the stage of product life cycle in search of continued cost advantage. For a large portion of its open-door process, China's success shaping itself as the world manufacture hub is attributed to its internalization advantage primarily drawing on its abundant supply of cheap labour, lower environmental standards and policy incentives attracting foreign investment into various development zones. Now that increasing number of industries in the country is entering maturity stage of their PLC, when confronted with fierce competition and rising labour cost at home, production relocation will follow the same waterfall pattern flowing into lesser developed countries. With rising per capita income, a steadily expanding middle class and improved quality of life, Chinese policymakers are resolved to transform their industrial structure phasing out low value-added manufacture toward a more sustainable innovation driven economic model. This is figuratively described as "emptying the case for new birds". As a result, both domestic and foreign invested firms are seriously looking for new opportunities in lesser developed world such as south and central Asia, Africa and Latin America for renewed cost advantage, amongst which, Vietnam, Ethiopia and Bangladesh have become the hot spots (EXHIBIT 3.2).

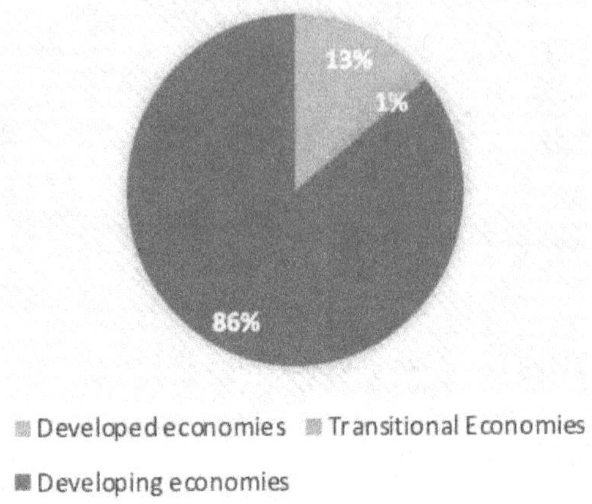

Exhibit 3.2 Chinese ODI in different economies
Source: 2017 Statistical Bulletin of China's Outward Foreign Direct Investment

3.2.1 The Melody

However, this is not to say that China no longer has a place in the manufacturing sector. Rather the first-hand experience of Chinese factories is welcomed, in effectively managing manufacture and production hubs in less developed climates. After all, China is no stranger to setting up and running successful factories in a developing country.

As companies such as Huajian International Shoes demonstrate, a lot can be gained on both sides from Chinese companies engaging in such ODI. Huajian Group, headquartered in Dongguan, a manufacture hub in Guangdong Province, established in 1996, specializes in the production and sales of leather shoes. Its president Zhang Huarong, has established himself a reputation in Ethiopia since relocating part of his production line to the African country back in 2012. The company, which produces shoes for well reputed brands such as Guess, Nine West, Tommy Hilfiger and Calvin Klein, established a factory on the outskirts of Ethiopia's capital city, Addis Ababa, in light of the rising costs such as labour, land and raw materials faced back at home. It is revealed by New York Times, the intensification of labour relations in which many workers complaining about excessive hours and seeking higher pay constituted the major driver for the factory owner to send their jobs to Ethiopia. Three labour activists from China Labour Watch who scrutinized undercover the factory were reportedly detained by Chinese authorities.[159] Based on this observation, it would be naturally deduced that Huajian would transmit this allegedly harsh labour conditions to the factory in Ethiopia. However, the localized factory has been considered by many to be a rather good example of how mutual cooperation and understanding of both employer and employee needs, which has laid the foundation for long term success.

According to World Bank data, per capita income was USD468.51 in Ethiopia as compared to USD6,337.88 in China when Huajian began to set foot on this north-eastern part of African continent, popularly known as the Horn of Africa. Massive unemployment has long been a malignant plight in this country, particularly among the youngsters, with a rate that averaged 19.88 percent from 1999 until 2015.[160] The establishment of Huajian Factory has not only been able to maximize on profits through the lower labour costs in the second-most populous nation in Africa with 92.44 million inhabitants, but has also exalted in local popularity by providing them with stable, dependable incomes and opportunities for future career and skill development.

---

[159] Keith Bradsher, Chinese Maker of Ivanka Trump's Shoes Looks for Cheaper Labor, The New York Times, June 1, 2017

[160] The Problem Of Youth Unemployment In Ethiopia, Dec 1, 2017, https://www.ethiopiaprosperous.com/2017/12/problem-youth-unemployment-ethiopia/

"The work is good because I pay my rent and I can look after my-self...It has transformed my life."[161]

--Employee at Huajian, Addis Ababa factory

Such success has since been attributed to the fact that development of the factory's production line focused on the importance of localization to long term sustainability.

As a result of such an ethos, the factory has steadily been growing in profitability, efficiency and output. Able to obtain local media support coupled with developing strong relationships with the Ethiopian Government, it has since worked closely at a ministerial level with the development of Addis Ababa more generally.[162] It has been so successful that Huajian has recently negotiated with the Nigerian Government on a USD 1.5 billion deal to expand over in Aba, Nigeria; in recognition of the company's success in fostering mutually beneficial relationships.[163]

As illustrated in this case, effective localization is central to ODI operations in a foreign land. This not only enables business ventures to withstand and overcome the inevitable obstacles at the entry stage, but also to grow and expand in line with local conditions. Localization is not confined to local hire, the role of local procurement therein, embodies a most effective way to integrate with the local business community. On this point, Huajian's position is very clear:

---

[161]Bloomberg, Kevin Hamlin, Ilya Gridneff and William Davidson, *Ethiopia Becomes China's China in Search for Cheap Labour*, (July 2014).
Please note: the 2017 controversies concerning Huajian International Shoes factory and the manufacture of Ivanka Trump's brand line of shoes, is solely regarding the company's domestic factory in Dongguan, China. No mention of unethical practices in the Addis Ababa factory have been voiced as of yet.
[162] Fana Broadcasting (Popular platform for Ethiopian news and culture), *Chinese Shoe Factory Huajian Now Employs 3,200 People,* (September 2014).
[163] Press Reader, Melanie Peters, *Ivanka's Shoes to be Made in Nigeria Factory,* (April 2017).

"One thing in my strategy is very clear: that I don't want to compete with locals...I want to help them grow because when local producers grow, the whole market is growing."[164]

--Helen Hai (Vice-President, Huajian Group)

This is by virtue of its ability to continuously maintain ongoing relationships with local communities. To secure a firm foothold within a host territory, benefits can be reaped by: a). employing locals, b). developing collaborative relationships with local businesses, and c). actively contributing to the development of a skilled local workforce.

One would wonder why going all the way to Ethiopia when neighbouring countries such as Vietnam, Cambodia and Myanmar are able to offer the same cost advantage? In fact, Huajian's first move for globalization was targeting Vietnam as early as in 2004. Unfortunately, they had to pull out 4 years later for a number of reasons. "It is very troublesome; their labour force is incompetent to meet our high quality standard, and many raw materials have to be shipped from China because of the gap in the supply chain," said Liu Yikong, vice president of Huajian International. Lack of in-house expertise to effectively communicate with the host government, and ill knowledge of local regulations also accounted for their setbacks in a number of labour disputes.

Huajian's globalization ambition dwindled quite a while after their Vietnam misgivings. It was until 2011 when an invitation from Ethiopian prime minister arrived, they began to deliberate on investment in this country. In addition to 1/10th of labour cost at home, abundant supply of leather, they found that the country had enjoyed over two decades of social political stability free from civil wars and social upheavals, and the host government offered a basket of preferential policies and ser-

---

[164] The Guardian, Elissa Jobson, *Chinese firm steps up investment in Ethiopia with 'shoe city',* (April 2013).

vices for foreign companies that were able to provide job opportunities and earn foreign exchange via export from the country.

Many Chinese companies have recognized the benefits of both a) and b), having employed and worked alongside local workers when operating abroad [Table 3.1]. This has been the case even where the company's transition into overseas territories was not motivated by the consideration of labour cost.

Table 3.1

Country	Project	Year	Local Laborers	Chinese Laborers
Mozambique	Stadium	2010	1,000 (67%)	500 (33%)
Angola	Stadium	2010	250 (26%)	700 (74%)
Angola	Railway	2010	300 (50%)	300 (50%)
Republic of Congo	Dam	2010	2,000 (83%)	400 (17%)
Zambia	Coal Mine	2010	855 (93%)	62 (7%)
Kenya	Mombasa Harbor	2011	1,371 (97%)	45 (3%)
Rwanda	Roads	2011	2,000 (95%)	110 (5%)
Rwanda	Housing	2011	300 (86%)	50 (14%)
Rwanda	Conference Center	2011	500 (78%)	140 (23%)
Rwanda	Hospital	2011	150 (81%)	35 (19%)
Benin	Textile Factory	2011	1,100 (99%)	5 (1%)
Zimbabwe	Diamond mine	2011	1,490 (88%)	210 (12%)

Source: John Hopkins University-SAIS, Professor Deborah Brautigam Blog, "China in Africa: The Real Story." Data as of 2010-2011

To skeptics, the sun rarely shines over a cause of greater worth. Despite criticism that Chinese firms heavily depend on Chinese labor, for example, most infrastructure projects are completed primarily by African workers, with Chinese nationals in management or technical positions. A comprehensive 2017 McKinsey report on Sino-African economic relations reported that Africans comprised 89% of labor on the projects surveyed. Local content and job training are regularly included as part of contract negotiations between African countries and Chinese investors.[165]

For instance in extractive sectors, where the impetus for ODI lies in access to raw materials as opposed to cheaper production and manufacture, trends demonstrate a persistent focus of Chinese corporations on local procurement within their overall workforce. As such, initial contentions voiced by NGOs and the academic community against Chinese companies utilising Chinese labourers over local human resources, are no longer as pressing a concern.

Even in situations where this has been the case, it is generally noted that the motives of such decisions primarily lies in necessity; with particularly high level positions carried out by more experienced Chinese employees who possess the technical skills needed to perform said duties. This is especially worth consideration when the net effect of the Chinese company's presence is to introduce a relatively novel industry to the operating areas, i.e. in situations where the local workforce is more in tune with industries such as farming and agriculture, and therefore lacks the expertise to take on high-level management and industrial positions.

Nonetheless, whilst in some situations necessity dictates the use of Chinese employees for higher-level positions, this should remain true only for the beginning of an endeavour. Following on, the need for gradual localisation by proxy of training and apprenticeship schemes ought to allow higher skilled positions to be passed onto local workers. In this way technology and knowledge transfer can be ensured.

However, it is exactly this notion that highlights the crux of the problem. Despite the fact that Chinese companies are employing locals, a key issue arises with respect to the manner in which they are being

---

[165] Dispelling the Dominant Myths of China in Africa, Aubrey Hruby, the Atlantic Council   https://www.weforum.org/agenda/2018/09/three-myths-about-chinas-investment-in-africa-and-why-they-need-to-be-dispelled/

hired, highlighting that the issue now lies in the application of c). actively contributing to the development of a skilled local workforce. It is noted in a number of circumstances that a large proportion of local workforces in Chinese enterprises, are denied of their legal rights under local labour laws as a direct result of casual, non-contractual based employment.[166] In other words, despite collaborating with locals, companies are doing so in an unorthodox way which enables basic employee welfare standards to be circumvented; providing a somewhat unilateral relationship which fails to recognize, balance and ultimately align the needs and interests of local employees with those of the company.

"Many workers are not formally employed and are not represented by trade unions, so they have little recourse when fired unexpectedly."[167]

One potential reason for this behavior has been attributed to inherent obstacles in hiring local community members with different economic needs and cultural outlooks. In appreciation of differences in culture and work ethic, there have been contentions from Chinese employers that the ability to protect workers' rights by entering into official employment contracts is not always a viable option. Issues are raised that local workers can be "lazy" with respect to their duties and obligations, and are not consistent nor dependable enough to be formally hired.[168] It was ob-

---

[166] All Africa, Edwin Okoth, *Kenya: Chinese Firms Hire More Locals Than Foreigners –Report,* (March 2016).

[167] Prosper, Ariel Gandolfo, *Chinese Investment in Africa – Where Do the Jobs Go?,* (June 2015).

[168] The Globe and Mail, Geoffrey York, *For South Africa's Workers, A Chinese-supplied job comes at a price,* (December 2010); Howard French, *China's Second Continent; How a Million Migrants are Building a New Empire in Africa,* (Alfred A Knopf Publishing, 2014); The China Africa Project, Eric Olander & Cobus Van Staden, *Why do Chinese bosses think African workers are lazy?,* Blog, (May 2016).

served in one instance, that workers had a tendency to skip work after receiving their previous month's wages, sporadically returning only once they were in need of further income. This spontaneity left the Chinese employer with little choice but to pay local staff on a casual basis; awarding wages for performance and contribution on the days that the employees actually attended work.[169]

However, whilst cultural differences are inescapable and give rise to such challenges; it is crucial to administer effective communication in order to mitigate such obstacles in a proactive and mutually beneficial manner. The first challenge in this regard is the existence of language barriers existent in many overseas companies, preventing any real means of interaction between Chinese employers and local staff. The importance of this cannot be overstated, as before dialogue exchange can even take place with local employees, it is necessary that there exists a common language in the workplace by which to communicate. Yet certain cases have highlighted an absence of such an environment, automatically rendering it nigh impossible for the needs and interests of local employees to be voiced, and more importantly heard.[170]

Even where this first step has been resolved, further procedural and structural challenges arise. After all, communication barriers do not simply extend to sharing a proficiency in a particular language, but further extend to the manner of speaking and the lines of interaction available between employers and employees. Take for instance the aforementioned examples concerning cultural differences, in which the observation of local employees as "lazy" has generated prejudice. In this respect, it is important to recognize that prejudicial attitudes are non-conducive to mutual development. Rather the essence of empathy becomes key; truly attempting to understand the differences that exist. In

---

[169] The China Africa Project, Zhicong Deng, *Chinese Companies' Labour Dilemma in Kenya,* (June 2014).

[170] Supra note 9, The China Africa Project.

such a scenario an empathetic attitude shall recognise that the cheaper labor costs within certain host countries, are in part down to the lower skill level and experience that local community members possess in such fast-paced, modern industries. Deeper understanding that comes from this perspective increases the likelihood of finding a pragmatically amiable solution.

Rather than blaming these challenges upon a singular party, it is to be recognised that there will always exist learning curves in the overall aim of aligning local behavioral and cultural differences with a company's ethos. In appreciation that this cannot be achieved overnight, building a cohesive campus culture helps foster a productive workforce. Through implementation of appropriate training and development programmes, companies can strengthen mutual understanding, reinforce mutual objectives and benefit employee-employer relationships in the long run. More generally speaking, training and development programmes are even an avenue for promoting stronger, more integrated relationships with the local community as a whole.

One example of how such integration might be achieved lies with the aforementioned case of Huajian Shoes Factory, where a particularly direct approach to overcoming obstacles of communication and culture was adopted. Drawing the lesson of fallout in Vietnam, training program was carried out a year before production was formally launched on January 5, 2012. It recruited 200 college graduates from Ethiopia to receive training in China with programs in Chinese language, shoe-making skills and operations management. The average pay level for ordinary workers at the equivalent of a little more than RMB300 is currently comparable to that of a public servant, in addition to free meals and routine transportation. At a result, applicants lined up for various positions which quickly boosted their workforce from 500 to nearly 6,000. Among them, only around 160 are expatriates from China who are primarily technicians. At present, the factory is able to produce 3 million pairs of shoes. By the end of 2016, it has accumulated US$8 million for the host government via export.[171]

An example showcased by the Africa-China Project follows the experiences of a factory employee: Demis Degef. In it, Mr Degef shares that his experiences at the Huajian factory provided him with long term training, and the opportunity of actually travelling to China to gain practical insight into Chinese business culture. This exchange of knowledge not only allowed Demis to learn the Chinese language, but to better understand the cultural differences between Chinese and African business ethos. In recognition of the fact that effective communication transcends language, such hands-on experience provided a platform for deeper two-way understanding of cultural differences.

Following his exposure to Chinese business values, Mr Degef voiced his new outlook on working at the factory, as he became able to take advantage of his new skill sets and experiences, tripling his salary from 2,000 to 6,000 Birr a month. Crucially, the experience paved the way for a new sense of improved job satisfaction, whilst providing him with opportunities for career progression in assuming more senior responsibilities at the factory.[172] The hands-on approach thus strengthened the relationship and loyalty between employees like Mr. Degef and the Huajian factory, overcoming concerns that development and training projects for local employees can lead to a high turnover, by which em-

---

[171] China Economic Daily, *the Trick of Win-win by Huajian's Investment in Ethiopia*, May, 2, 2017, http://intl.ce.cn/specials/zxgjzh/201705/02/t20170502_22474093.shtml

[172] Africa-China Reporting Project, Zhang Zizhu, *Inside the Chinese Factory in Ethiopia where Ivanka Trump places her Shoe Orders*, (January 2017).

Further reading for additional accounts from Huajian factory workers: Tang Xiaoyang, *Does Chinese Employment Benefit Africans? Investigating Chinese Enterprises and their Operations in Africa*, African Studies Quarterly Vol. 16, Issue 3-4, (December 2016).

ployees leave the company for a more profitable alternative. Indeed, to overcome this challenge, it is essential that companies establish a well-developed career development programme, clear in its structure and well communicated to employees so that they may better understand the scope of their job prospects in remaining at the company.

With regards to Huajian, it was both the company's training scheme in allowing Mr Degef to travel to China, and the follow up mechanisms by which he was then able to hone in on his experiences by assuming higher level positions, that created mutual benefit. The aftermath enabled Demis to strengthen his job security at Huajian, whilst Huajian was equally able to secure a long term, loyal and dependable member of staff. In turn the company was able to secure more effective localization, whilst ensuring higher level positions for local workers that would help mitigate the likelihood of encountering cultural and communicative problems in the long run.

Exhibit 3.3

Source: Courtesy of CNN

In fact Huajian's focus on strengthening relations with local employees, and establishing effective synergy in its multicultural workplace, has even prompted the company to display its central business philosophies on the factory floor in all relevant languages [Exhibit 3.3].[173] This ensures that the goals and ethos of the company may be appreciated by all employees: Chinese and locals alike. Other companies may consider utilising similar techniques, as such a simple yet effective mechanism offers a clear, visible and accessible means of communication that helps to establish a more united workforce. Indeed, if nothing else, such an act communicates to local employees that the company understands, appreciates and is willing to cater for their language, their needs and their voice to be heard; establishing open lines of communication.

Despite their attentiveness to local conventions, the factory's operation still encountered labour disputes in this regard. A large chunk of local festivals and celebrations are concentrated in September which can last several days, based on either Christian or Islamic faiths - Meskal that marks the finding of the True Cross in Christianity, local Kiddus Yohannes (New Year's Day) that signifies the end of heavy rain and beginning of spring, as well as 'Id Al Fatr which celebrates the end of Ramadan within Muslin traditions, to name a few (Exhibit 4). Muslim holidays are designated on the lunar calendar and fall at different times each year. The month is devoted to the revelation of the Quran to the Islamic prophet Muhammad by fasting during the daylight hours from dawn to sunset. Intriguingly, Huajian's manager noted that some seasonal festivals are related to the appearance of the moon which is subject the weather conditions; holiday is due for the next day when the moon is full and bright, otherwise, no break is expected. Ignorance of this social custom in work scheduling caused protests. In response, the factory deployed weather forecast to support proper arrangement of work shift.

---

[173] Financial Times, Katrina Manson, *The Ethiopia Paradox*, (July 2015).

Table 3.2 Ethiopian Holidays 2019 by approximation of Solar Calendar

Date	Festivals	Holiday
January 7	Ethiopian Christmas Day	Public Holiday
January 20	Epiphany	Public Holiday
March 2	Adwa Victory Day	Season
March 21	March equinox	Public Holiday
April 26	Ethiopian Good Friday	Public Holiday
April 28	Ethiopian Easter Sunday	Public Holiday
May 1	International Labor Day	Public Holiday
May 5	Freedom Day	Public Holiday
May 28	Derg Downfall Day	Public Holiday
June 21	June Solstice	Season
August 12	Eid-al-Adha	Public Holiday
September 12	Ethiopian New Year	Public Holiday
September 23	September equinox	Season
September 27	Meskel	Season
November 10	The Prophet's Birthday	Public Holiday
December 22	December Solstice	Season

Source: Edited from https://allaboutethio.com/tholidays.html

Based on the learning and trust building process during the past 3 years, Huajian launched a decisive move to deepen its cooperation with this host country by constructing a park of light industry with a total investment of RMB3.2 billion covering an area of 126 hectares with multiple functions. It is expected to generate 30,000 job opportunities upon its completion by 2020.

As a matter of fact, Huajian is not alone for its massive operation in Ethiopia. Riding on the wave of the Belt and Road Initiative and favoured by the country's policy package to allure foreign investment, another four industrial parks have taken shape respectively focusing on pharmaceuticals, garments, equipment manufacture and processing of agricultural products attracting a slew of Chinese investors. And they all constructed by Chinese engineering firms.[174]

Open lines of communication are fundamental to resolving disputes and mitigating the risk of misunderstandings in future. In building such channels, it is recommended that Chinese companies recognize the benefits that can be had in establishing mediating bodies within the corporate structure. By this, it is suggested that local employees are not simply hired for baseline jobs, but that their potential to help in the management and localization of the company is also recognized, as was the case with Demis. For instance, job roles such as: interpreters/translators, human resource managers, supervisors and welfare support officers, may be well suited to locals; if not jointly held by Chinese and local personnel alike. This would help prevent segregation and discord between sub-groups of employees, establishing stronger synergies which ultimately enable the company to continue raising its own awareness of local cultures, thinking and practices.

"[H]ire a local HR manager and avoid direct conflicts with the local employees. The local HR manager is more familiar with local employees and it's easier for them to communicate to avoid misunderstanding and conflicts."[175]

3.2.2 The Elegy

In fact another mechanism that ought to be utilized to aid communication is that of Trade Unions. Not only do such institutions form an integral part of labour protection based on collective bargaining in many countries, but they are primarily concerned with offering a platform for effective dialogue between employers and employees. Unfortunately however, not all companies have come to recognize this, and thus per-

---

[174] MOFCOM, Exchange Bureau, Envoy to African Union, 2017-11-13

[175] Supra note 9, The China Africa Project.

ceive of labour unions as a general hindrance. As a result, some companies fail to make use of the lines of communication that unions open up to them; not only with respect to communicating with employees in understanding their needs and concerns, but also in deepening the company's own understanding of local labour laws and standards.

This in turn has led to a growing distrust in Chinese enterprises amongst local staff members, exacerbated by serious underlying problems relating to employee welfare standards in a handful of cases. It has been noted that whilst some companies do make use of local workforces, it is not necessarily in the interests of localisation that such decision have been made. Rather, in the absence of adequate employee protection standards and enforcement of employee welfare in certain overseas territories, the unethical exploitation of local employees may be witnessed. Such situations have arisen regardless of whether the locals are employed on a casual basis or one of formal contractual employment, given that the ability to unethically exploit workers arises from contextual factors of the host country, e.g.: weak governance; lack of effective enforcement mechanisms; non-comprehensive labour protection laws etc. In some instances violation of labour standards within ODI does not occur with ill intentions, but rather as a direct result from a company's lack of knowledge on domestic regulations. In either case, the use of trade unions is pivotal to pre-empting and mitigating problems.

However, failure to recognize the true potential of mutual development, and the role that labour unions play in achieving this goal, has led to a series of past failings and controversies; many of which focus on the persistent exploitation of local workforces within ODI. The cumulative effect hinders long term development and estrange links with local Governments, ultimately provokes a number of problems with Chinese companies operating abroad. In some cases, such outright denial of employee welfare has even resulted in aggressive protests; disrupting company operations, squandering resources, and in especially serious cases, even risking the safety of staff members. In 2012, Wu Shengzai, a Chinese manager, was killed and another was injured on spot by a coal trolley by strikers in Sinazongwe, 200 miles south of the capital Lusaka, Zambia, as several Zambian miners, after strike in protest against delays in implementing a new minimum wage erupted into violence. The miners were on strike because their wages were lower than a new minimum wage of £205 a month paid to shop workers. There was also attempted murder case in the same Collum mine miners were fired during a separate wage dispute in the previous year.[176]

In such situations, it is not only the importance of adhering to local welfare protection standards that is being overlooked, but notably the importance of labour unions in mitigating hostilities.

Exhibit 3.4 Myanmar's Clothing Export, 2010-2015

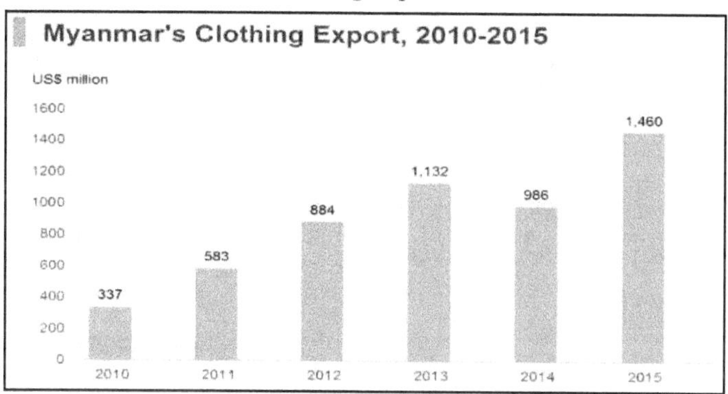

Source: World Trade Organization, Myanmar Garment Manufacturers Association Via Hong Kong Trade Development Council, Winnie Tsui, Myanmar Rising: The Garment Sector Takes Off, (2016).

Two recent cases of Chinese ODI best illustrate this. The first concerns recent protests in January 2017, at the Hangzhou Hundred-Tex Garment factory in Myanmar. The factory, like many other garment

---

[176] The Telegraph, *Zambian miners kill Chinese manager*, 05 Aug 2012, https://www.telegraph.co.uk/news/worldnews/africaandindianocean/zambia/9454001/Zambian-miners-kill-Chinese-manager.html

factories, turned to Myanmar for its cheaper labour and production costs [Exhibit 3.4]. Since 2014, it has been manufacturing clothes in Yangon for the leading fashion giant H&M. However, as brought to attention in 2016, it has since faced problems concerning the distribution of wages to local employees. Workers demanded: to be paid wages owed for overtime work; wages in accordance with local laws, and requested the establishment of a workplace coordination committee.

In line with such needs the company entered into an agreement in December 2016 with the local employees' Trade Union (backed by the Confederation Trade Unions of Myanmar). However, in mid-January heated protests broke out when the Trade Union President, *Ko Thet Paing Oo*, who had been instrumental in establishing the agreement; was dismissed. The basis of his dismissal was attributed to having taken a 2 week unapproved absence from the factory; however it was argued, that the time taken was actually a pre-agreed sick leave on the recommendation of his doctor that he had measles, evidenced by a medical note.

"Factory officials were not happy with me because they had to compensate about K70 million to the workers when we demanded our rights according to the law. They fired me because they were not happy that I supported the strikers. They admitted as much"

--Ko Thet Paing Oo[177]

Despite the agreement which had been reached to resolve internal labour issues little over a month before, protests still broke out. In mid-January 2017 workers began a 3 week-long strike against the company, demanding that it not only honour the agreement that had been established back in December, but that it further: implement a better performance review system; provide healthcare coverage, and immediately

---

[177] Myanmar Times, Zaw Zaw Htwe, *Garment Factory Closes after Attack by Workers,* (February 2017).

reinstate Ko Thet Paing Oo.[178] In essence, the new demands directly corresponded to the purportedly unfair dismissal of the factory union President.

After 3 weeks of no avail, the protest quickly escalated into a riot. On February 9th 2017, approximately 300 employees entered the factory with force: smashing factory doors and windows; damaging facilities; destroying surveillance cameras and even detaining 7 Chinese managers. One news report further announced the existence of video footage showing several female workers physically attacking a Chinese manager,[179] although it has since been denied that any of the factory workers assaulted anyone nor broke industrial equipment.[180]

The strike has been referenced by the Guardian Newspaper as: *"one of the most violent labour disputes in the country in many years."*[181] As a result, operations at the factory have been severely impacted. Not only does the company now have an estimated damage cost of US$75,000, but crucially, its contract with H&M has since been suspended. The impact of such mounting employee dissatisfaction on wider business relationships is thus noted, affecting fundamental revenue streams.

The case illustrates a pressing need for Chinese companies to recognize the importance of ensuring *genuine cooperation* with Trade Unions; crucial in establishing stronger relationships and trust amongst employees, and in ultimately mitigating workplace tensions before they escalate out of control. Whilst it may appear that Trade Unions are purely one-sided in acting as an employee safety net, in reality they provide both

---

[178] South China Morning Post, Kinling Lo, *Strike at Chinese Factory in Myanmar another bump along 'One Road'*, (March 2017).

[179] Reuters, Shwe Yee Saw Myint, Yimou Lee, *H&M supply factory in Myanmar damaged in violent labour protest*, (March 2017).

[180] Supra note 15, South China Morning Post.

[181] The Guardian, Shwe Yee Saw Myint, Yimou Lee, Anna Ringstorm, *H&M supply factory in Myanmar damaged in violent labour protest*, (March 2017).

employer and employee with a great service: balance and harmony. By ensuring that employee rights and interests are appropriately protected, and simultaneously managing employee expectations; job satisfaction is secured and company's prevented from losing face in light of public protests and negative limelight in international media.

Notably, both sides are further protected from the dangers and disruption caused by protest-turned-riots, fuelled by anger. Indeed the case concerning the Collum Mine in Zambia, highlights just how badly situations can spiral out of control when sensitive labour related issues have been handled independently. I.e.: when employees feel that they have no other choice but to take matters into their own hands.

Contextually speaking, locals employed at Chinese mines in Zambia have been known to voice concerns with regards to:

"curtailment of union activity: [whereby] several Chinese operations suppress workers' right to join the labour union of their choice and retaliate against outspoken union representatives."[182]

It has been noted that despite the Zambian labour law allowing workers the freedom to be represented by unions of their choice, Chinese companies have displayed passive aggressive acts in attempting to deter employees from taking part in trade unions, or at the very least limiting the scope of their options therein. Prejudicial treatment of employees based on union association was amongst the problems most associated with company behaviours.

Failure by said companies to abide by national laws and recognise the importance of safeguarding employee welfare, has resulted in uneth-

---

[182] Human Rights Watch Report, *" 'You'll be Fired if you Refuse' – Labor Abuses in Zambia's Chinese State-Owned Copper Mines"* (November 2011) <https://www.hrw.org/report/2011/11/04/youll-be-fired-if-you-refuse/labor-abuses-zambias-chinese-state-owned-copper-mines> [accessed on 3rd May 2017].

ical working conditions. In turn, this has generated unrest amongst local citizens, giving rise to problems of protests, official complaints and general prejudice against Chinese companies and their operations. Most notably, refusal to comply with labour protection standards along with other relevant Zambian laws, led to a series of dramatic events in the case of the Collum Mine. The case received worldwide attention from leading newspapers for its rapid downward spiral into violent protests.

The privately owned coal mine located in Sinazongwe Zambia, was established back in 2000 by five brothers from Jiangxi province, China: the Xu family. The mine was known to have been riddled with a number of employee welfare problems relating to: health and safety; long working hours; no breaks; inadequate wages and so on. In fact in 2010, aggressive action was taken against the company when hundreds of miners gathered together in protest, demanding higher wages. It was alleged that when employees began throwing rocks, two Chinese supervisors retaliated by shooting in open fire, leaving at least 11 miners wounded.[183]

Whilst it is still uncertain why the Chinese supervisors had been armed, the animosity that existed between employees and employers was clearly strong enough to have left both sides feeling that they were physically threatened. Indeed just a few months before, rumours spread that when 22 local miners were seriously injured in a gas explosion caused by inadequate health and safety measures, a Chinese national had to quickly escape "lynching by an angry mob."[184] Zambian media reports of previous labour disputes even suggested incidents of mine workers throwing '*missiles*' at Chinese managers;[185] demonstrating the

---

[183] The Telegraph, Aislinn Laing, *Zambian Miners Shot by Chinese Managers,* (October 2010).

[184] CNN, Eve Bower, *Zambia Mine Shootings Raise Tensions with China,* (November 2010).

[185] Supra note 21, CNN.

severity of hostilities that had already been steadily growing in serious-ness and scale, prior to the 2010 incident.

Despite these telltale signs that an intermediary may be necessary to help resolve disputes between employers and employees, it was noted that the "Collum managers [still] avoided meeting with union leaders…" and had inherent problems with miscommunication and bad labour cul-ture.[186] Ironically, the very matter of contention in the 2010 protest (i.e.: higher wages), had already been previously settled between the company and the miners' Trade Union. However, failure to implement effective lines of communication within the corporate structure meant that this information went crucially unnoticed. As a result, the protest commenced despite the fact that the nature of the problem was on its way to being resolved.

Exhibit 3.5

Source: Courtesy of LusakaTimes

Even following such protests, little changes were made to improving the workplace environment. With rising distrust and an increasingly divided workforce, tensions escalated further in August 2012, leading to

---

[186]The New Yorker, Alexis Okeowo, *China, Zambia and a Clash in a Coal Mine,* (October 2013).

the accidental death of a Chinese manager when a protest turned particularly hostile. The protest once again concerned the issue of wages, and prompted approximately 12,000 workers to gather outside the mine [Exhibit 3.5]. Seeing the protestors, Chinese managers residing in settlements built onsite, left their homes to enter the mine for protection. A series of events eventually culminated in the release of a one-ton trolley which was pushed into the mine and inadvertently injured two Chinese managers, whilst killing a third: Wu Shengzai. The situation had gotten so out of hand, it was noted that several protestors did not even know that somebody had been killed until much later on.[187]

In view of its history of conflict, building an honest and genuine relationship with the miner's Trade Union ought to be placed as a top priority. With such a high level of existing animosity between employees and employers, there existed a clear need for the company to take account of an independent third party perspective; especially when it was clear that conflicts could not be amiably resolved between the two parties alone. Efforts taken in order to demonstrate to employees that the company was actually attempting to rectify the working environment, would have further aided in dissolving conflict. However, in the case of the Collum Mines, it appears that there was very little intention on behalf of the company to resolve rising tensions, at least this was certainly the message portrayed to local employees and local communities at large.

The case highlights the importance of channels of communication in stabilizing situations, particularly where tensions and emotions run high. In situations of conflict, it is clear that there is no use in trying to "sweep it all under the rug"; rather dialogue exchange and the use of mediators such as local labour NGOs and Trade Unions, should be utilised to deal with the matter at hand. Indeed, enterprises such as the Collum Mine ought not to underestimate the importance of all stakeholders, both in-

---

[187] Supra note 23, The New Yorker.

ternal and external. Herein it is emphasised that a company does not necessarily have all conflicts under its control purely because those conflicts are within the realms of the corporate structure. Certain situations may warrant that to properly manage relationships, even with internal stakeholders such as employees, a company has to rely on more than just its internal processes and structures; the use of a third party may be essential. In this way, companies may better manage their relationships utilising the help and expertise of institutions trained in conflict resolution, and ensure that they have fulfilled their duties in conducting diligent risk management.

Developing honest relationships with trade unions will thus go a long way to maintaining a stable and dependable workforce, securing the company's presence and reputation long term. Where such mechanisms go unnoticed, the likelihood is that Chinese companies shall experience heated protests, which as demonstrated by the previous factory cases in Myanmar and Zambia, can quickly turn riot.

3.3 Conclusion

The above cases emphasize that operating in different territories ultimately necessitates that traditional business views and cultures be adapted in light of the needs and interests of local workforces. It is no longer enough to simply hire local labourers; company's need to proactively work towards developing an operational, efficient and well integrated unit.

In attempting to balance employee-employer interests to create such a dependable multi-cultural unit, it is to be remembered that this is an ongoing process. As such, money, time and planning must be invested into developing training and integration programmes to help local workers assimilate to their work standards and protocols, whilst in turn helping the company to assimilate to the new culture standards and laws of their overseas market.

3.4 Questions for Thought

1. Companies have their own standard of protocol and work ethic. To what extent should these be upheld, despite cultural and behavioural differences in overseas territories?

2. Are Trade Unions really impartial institutions?

3. What types of training programmes may be most useful in developing the skill set of local employees who lack exposure to modern industries such as: factory production; advanced mining etc.?

4. "Employees will always naturally segregate into cultural subgroups" – Do you agree?

5. "Employees will always naturally segregate into cultural subgroups" – Do you agree?

3.5 Appendix

Domestic Manufacturing Industry: China Today

Exhibit 3.6 China as the World's Manufacturing Base Source: Thomson

Reuters and Economist Intelligence Unit

Via The Economist, The Future Factory of Asia: A Tightening Grip, (2015).

Exhibit 3.7 China Manufacturing Wages_Increase Year on Year

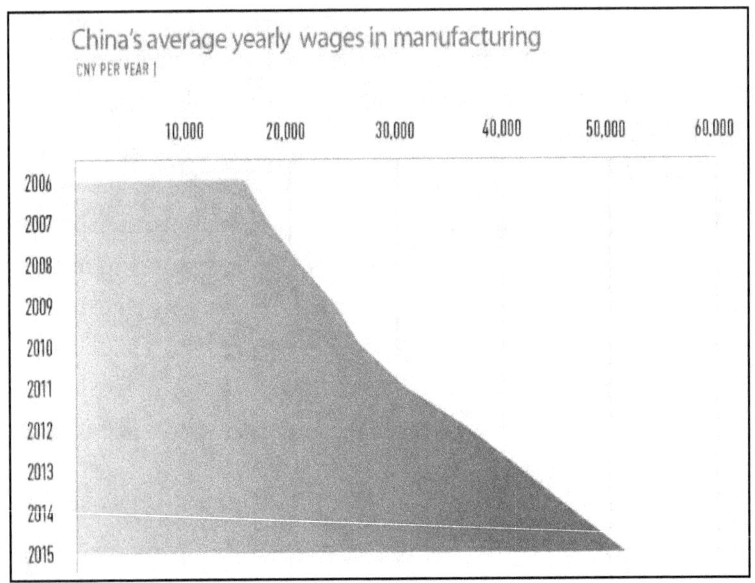

Source: Trading Economics Via World Finance, Matt Timms, A Tough Road Ahead for China's Manufacturing Industry, (2015).

The steady increase in wages for the average Chinese factory employee has made countries such as Thailand, Philippines, and Myanmar more attractive for lower-end manufacturing, owing to the cheaper labour costs in these areas.

Chinese Investments in Africa

Exhibit 3.8 Chinese ODI_Africa

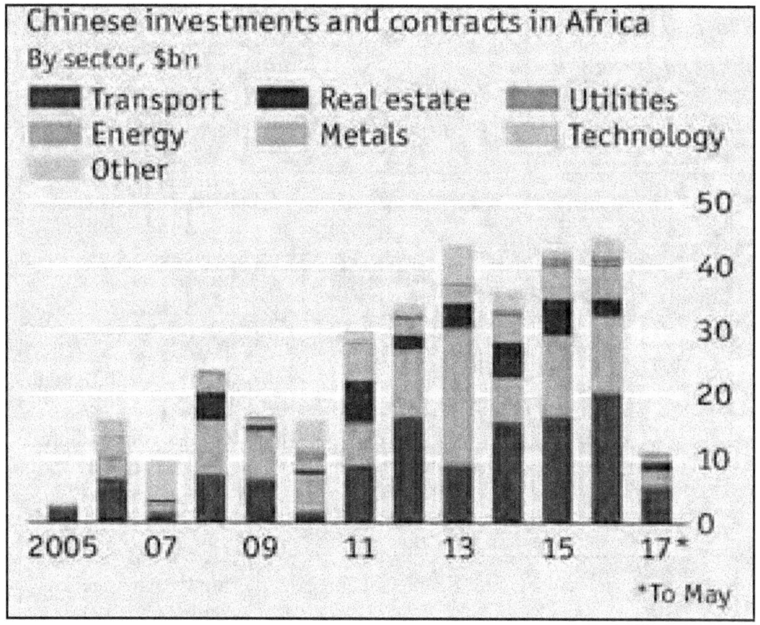

Source: American Enterprise Institute Via The Economist, A Thousand Golden Stars: China goes to Africa, (2017).

Exhibit 3.9 Distribution of Chinese Employees in Africa

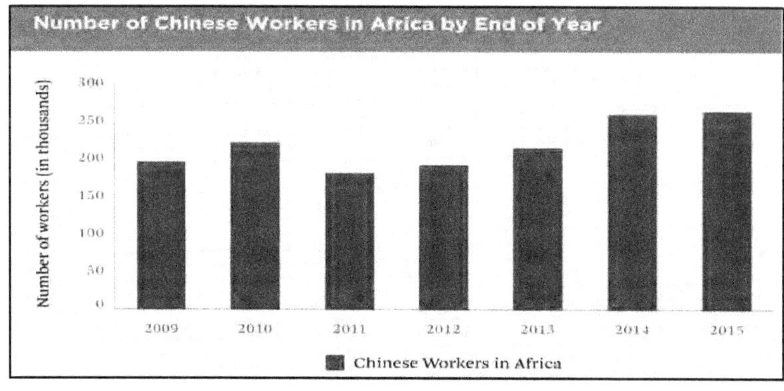

Source: China Statistical Yearbook, National Bureau of Statistics, China Annual Bulletin of Statistics of Contracted Projects, Labor Cooperation with Foreign Countries, Almanac of China's Foreign Economic Relations and Trade Via: China Africa Research Initiative

Exhibit 3.10 Local Procurement_ Chinese Companies in Africa

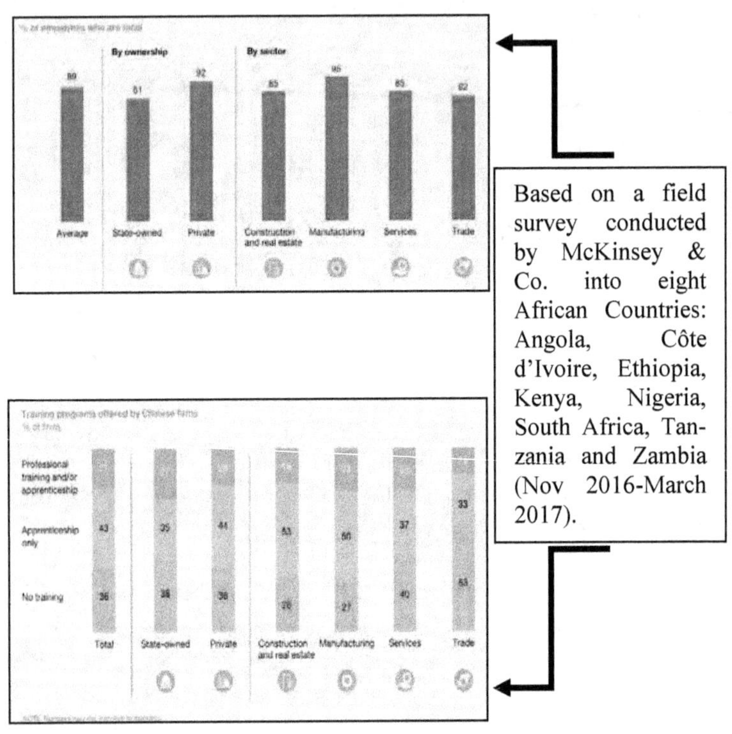

Based on a field survey conducted by McKinsey & Co. into eight African Countries: Angola, Côte d'Ivoire, Ethiopia, Kenya, Nigeria, South Africa, Tanzania and Zambia (Nov 2016-March 2017).

Source: McKinsey & Company, Irene Yuan Sun, Kartik Jayaram Omid Kassiri, Dance of the Lions and Dragons, (June 2017) p.41.

Table 3.3 Comparative Wages of Local Employees_Zambian Copper Industry

Zambian Copper Smelting, Processing and Engineering Companies Comparative Wages for Locals (September 2011)				
Company	Pay Increase in 2011	Lowest Group Monthly Salary Range	Middle Group Salary Range	Highest Group Salary Range
Sino Metals	12%	$101-$118 (5.9% of employees)	$116-$161 (61.4% of employees)	$213-$287 (6.3% of employees)
Chambishi Copper Smelter (CCS)	12%	US$117	$141 to $154 (approx 50% of employees)	$261-$340
Chambishi Metals	9%	$360	$475	$655
Kansanshi	9.9%	$348	$481-625	$1030
KCM (surface)	11.5%	$544-$634	$631-$756	$665-$808
Mopani (surface)	11.5%	$466-$503	$508-$545	$562-$717

Source: Human Rights Watch, Matt Wells, "You'll Be Fired if You Refuse" – Labor Abuses in Zambia's Chinese State-Owned Copper Mines, (November 2011).

Suggested further reading: For a greater understanding of the labour standards in Chinese-owned Zambian copper mines (the backdrop of the Collum Mines), please refer to the stated source: Human Rights Watch.

4

THE CASE OF THE MYITSONE DAM

The importance of acquiring a social license

4.1 Case Background

However thorough analysis has been conducted pertaining to business climate in the host country and feasibility of the target project, market entry decisions, after all, are made by gauging the surface and usually by people sitting in the home headquarter. Only by stepping into actual overseas operations, can gaps begin to unfold between what is painted in feasibility report and the crude reality which also evolves with time. In initiating operations, one of the more notable cases highlighting the complexities that can go amiss when the interests of certain stakeholder groups are unaccounted for, is that of the Myitsone Hydroelectric Dam. This mega project has dragged in troubled waters for nearly a decade and wreckage continues to soak large chunk of money. This case depicts a host of typical greyer areas within corporate social responsibility clouded in geopolitical entanglement.

Indeed, it is still very much an unresolved issue, with the project remaining a source of contention between China and Myanmar (Burma) for the past 7 years. It was an ambitious hydro power project composed of 7 dams in the northern Kachin State of Myanmar. In 2001, 30-year power development plan was drawn by the Burmese government that included 64 hydro and 3 coal power stations. With designed capacity of 20,000 MW, the single Myitsone hydro project would contribute 41% of all power generation facilities to the entire country. Proposed by the Burmese Military Junta (the then ruling government which had been in power since 1962), the project aimed to provide an answer to Myanmar's critical shortage of electricity and aid in the country's overall development. Yet the turbulent political landscape upon which the project unfolded, coupled with a lack of community engagement and disclosure of key project information, escalated in public disapproval and the project's ultimate suspension in 2011, following the country's democratic political reform.[188] As such, the US$30 billion initiative for the building of a hydroelectric dam cluster remains shrouded in uncertainty as to its future, living on as a testimony to the importance of securing a social license in overseas projects.

Initial proposals for the dam's construction were first put forward in 2002 by the Military Junta, who maintained governmental power despite growing public animosity against the party's rule. Indeed, just ten years earlier in 1990, the free election of Burmese citizens demonstrated an 80% majority in favour of Aung San Suu Kyi's civilian led government. However, it was yet unable to prompt political reform in the country.[189]

The project, initiated in the hope of utilizing foreign capital and expertise to expand access to electricity for Burmese citizens, was initially offered to the Japanese Kansai Electric Power Company (KEPCO). Following the withdrawal of a number of potential investors including KEPCO from the initiative, it was eventually pursued as a joint venture between China Power Investment Corporation (CPIC) and Asia World Company, a partner designated by the Burmese government; taking

---

[188] For more information on Myanmar's political history and rise of democracy, see: Council on Foreign Relations Official Website: <<https://www.cfr.org/backgrounder/understanding-myanmar>> [accessed: 3rd March 2017].

[189] International Business Times, Daniel Tovrov, *Myanmar Election Results: Aung San Suu Kyi Victorious,* (February 2012).

account of CPIC's established reputation as one of the five largest energy producers in China.[190]

After a series of initial inspections, a Memorandum of Understanding ("MOU") was eventually signed in December 2006 between the CPIC-Asia World Company joint venture and the newly established Burmese Ministry of Electricity and Energy. The MOU stipulated that the project would adopt a build-operate-transfer (BOT) model to engage in the construction of Myitsone station of 6 MW and Chibwe Station of 3.4 MW. By a contract term of 50 years, 100% ownership of the dam with an expected life span for additional 50 years would pass to the Government of Myanmar permanently.

In the meantime, ownership of the project was to be divided threefold: CPIC and Asia World Company would enjoy ownership in the division of 80% and 5% respectively, whilst the remaining 15% ownership shares remained with the Burmese Ministry. Profits of the dam would be shared disproportionately, with the Myanmar Government receiving 10% of generated electricity for free, literally as tax revenue, along with its 15% combined equity position. By estimation, revenue split, coupled with withholding and export taxes, would provide the Myanmar Government with 60% of total profits over the 50 year contract period.[191]

With this in mind the agreement portrayed a 'win-win' situation for virtually all stakeholders involved. It would be an inexhaustible source of green energy in the region of environmental vulnerability, but critically need for economic growth of Myanmar, a country just ready for in-

---

[190] Journal of Current Southeast Asian Affairs, *"Chronology of the Myitsone Dam at the Confluence of Rivers above Myitkyina and Map of Kachin State dams"* Vol. 31, No. 1, (2012), pp.141-153.

[191] Reuters, *Factbox: Myanmar Suspends Controversial Myitsone Dam,* (September 2011); Burma Rivers Network, *New Light of Myanmar,* Excerpt: *Memorandum of Agreement on N'Mai/Mali/Irrawady Dams Signed,* (June 2009).

dustrialization. The surplus power generated would be sold to neighbouring countries to earn foreign exchange, including China to address the power shortage in its southwest region. CPIC and Asia World Company would enjoy access to Myanmar's rivers as a source of energy production, a beneficial commodity given the rivers' vast potential for creating hydroelectric power. The host government would receive the capital, technology and expertise in order to secure access to electricity for its people. Indeed, given that majority of the project costs were to be covered by CPIC, the Burmese Government's long term investment was secured without the burden of amassing large sum capital on its own. In addition, considering the cultural adjacency between the two neighbours, ensuing operative coordination would be a smooth sailing. As a diplomatic principle, China manifested a strong commitment to refraining from attaching any political conditions for its overseas projects, a notion that has gained popularity among the underdeveloped world.

Exhibit 4.1

Source: Courtesy of Mekong Eye News.

Yet, despite all the explicit benefits that might accrue to multiple parties, the project was instantly met with objection from local people [Exhibit 4.1]. Notwithstanding it's purported aims to provide electricity for local communities, objections were noted on several bases, including: a general distrust of the Military Junta's true intentions; a growing anti-Chinese sentiment; and the intrusion into historical heritage since the Myitsone Dam to be situated in the confluence region of the Mali and N'mai rivers would affect the source of the Ayeyawady River (deemed by many to be the birthplace of Burmese civilization).

As the dam project commenced, further concerns were also raised as to: lack of transparency concerning project details; the availability of environmental and social impact assessments (ESIA); the placement of the dam on an earthquake prone zone; and issues relating to the resettlement of local villages in affected areas. To make matters worse, contentions were voiced against the backdrop of rising political tension between the Military Junta and the Kachin Independence Organization (KIO). The KIO, predominant within the Kachin region, was an organization established in the 1960s as a form of political opposition to the government, which had grown large enough to boast its own army of some 10,000 troops.[192]   Accordingly, it was a prevalent organisation within the very region that the Myitsone dam intended to be built.

All such local concerns and social instability gave rise to large scale controversy and public disapproval surrounding the project, culminating in 2011. Upon political reform of Myanmar as a civilian led State, election winner and newly appointed President Thein Sein, abruptly declared that having been democratically elected:

"We have the responsibility to address public concerns in all seriousness. So construction of Myitsone Dam will be suspended in the time of our government."[193]

Accordingly, the project was indefinitely suspended during his term of office. Even now, following President Thein Sein's replacement with

---

[192]See: Myanmar Peace Monitor, <<http://www.mmpeacemonitor.org/component/content/article/57-stakeholders/155-kio>> [accessed: 14th March 2017].

[193] Eleven Media Group, *President Thein Sein sent a letter to parliament for cancellation of the Myitsone Dam Project,* (August 2011).

President Htin Kyaw and Myanmar's new civilian leader Aung San Suu Kyi in April 2016, it is still unclear whether the project shall be resumed or not. This is such, notwithstanding CPI's legal rights by virtue of the jointly invested project between itself and the former Military Junta.

4.2 Issues of Community Engagement

Suspension of the Myitsone dam, which would have been the largest dam built out of all the proposed initiatives, came directly as a result of local opposition; resulting in its eventual embroilment as somewhat of a political symbol. However, notably of all seven dam projects in place, it was the only one to give rise to such extensive controversy; suggesting that public dissatisfaction surrounding it, did not simply lie with the development of hydropower in Myanmar, but more specifically with the proposal and operations of the Myitsone project itself.

Certainly, prior to CPIs engagement, there existed strong disapproval from Kachin villagers about the very concept of building a dam on the confluence region of the Myitsone. Whilst still under the care of Japan's KEPCO, locals had submitted letters of disapproval to the Kachin Consultative Body and Kachin ceasefire groups against the project's proposal back in 2004.[194] Contentions were raised for cultural reasons, with the Ayeyawady River having long been recognized by the Kachin locals as *"a symbol of our national spirit"*[195]; by virtue of cultural legends and historical evidence in the area. As such the project was instantly criticized not only for its insensitivity, but for its unwise business decision in choosing to *"build [a dam] right where it would be most taboo"*.[196]

---

[194] Supra note 3, Chronology of the Myitsone Dam Project.

[195] China Dialogue, Qin Hui, *Behind Myanmar's suspended dam*, (March 2012).

[196] Supra note 8, China Dialogue (Qin Hui).

4.2.1 Issue One: Social Impact Assessment

Given the backdrop of the project, it thus came as no surprise following it's initiation that strong concerns were voiced by the local Kachin minority. Amongst contentions that the dam would tarnish a powerful cultural symbol, the locals voiced their fears that it would also inevitably result in hydrological changes and potential flooding, affecting their ability to continue farming and fishing. In turn, whilst no commercial fishing activities generally took place by the Kachin locals, their strong reliance on farming for their livelihood, accentuated the perception of the project as a very real threat to the villager's existing lifestyles and future prospects.

The significance of flooding concerns were further exacerbated by the Ayeyawady River's reputation as the country's most important commercial waterway, providing the main means of transporting essential commodities such as rice. This coupled with its status as amongst one of the world's top priority river basins, emphasised the impact of hydrological changes to both the local society, and ecologically speaking, the indigenous biodiversity in the region.[197]

Further concerns were also raised as the proposed dam would be directly positioned on an earthquake prone zone, not more than 100 kilometres away from the Sagaing fault line [Exhibit 4.2]. It was thereby feared by the local community that should the dam collapse, it had a grave potential of endangering the lives of residents living downstream. Of significance was the threat it could pose to the city of Myitkyina; the largest city in the Kachin State and home to hundreds and thousands of residents.

---

[197] Burma Rivers Network, Irrawaddy River, (August 2008) <<http://burmariversnetwork.org/index.php?option=com_content&view=article &id=51&Itemid=48>> [accessed: 5th March 2017].

In response to such concerns CPI had made attempts to mitigate the inherent risks posed by the project. As is commonly noted, one major way in which companies can hope to gain a social license, as well as having obtained a legal and political one, is through the use of apt environmental and social impact assessments (ESIA). In fact, in a number of host countries such a requirement may be mandatory prior to the company commencing its operations; however this may not always be the case in many developing countries, lacking in advanced legal systems. Indeed, back in 2006 upon the signing of the Myitsone Dam's MOU, Myanmar fell within the latter category; whereby the country's environmental and social management frameworks were not introduced until much later on in 2012.[198]

Exhibit 4.2

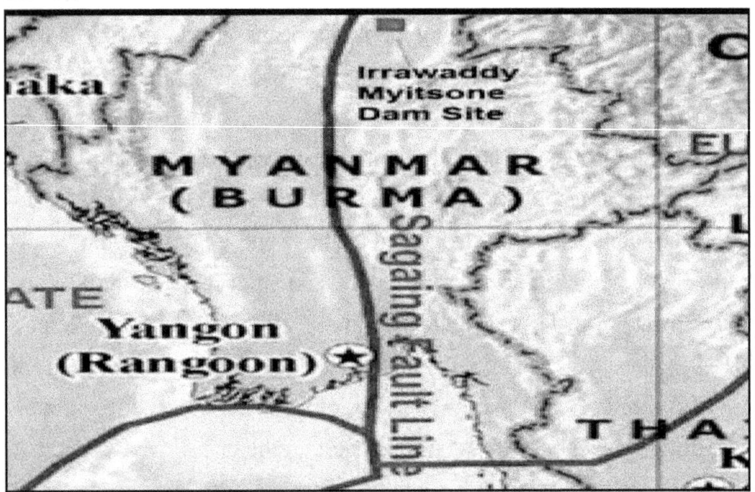

Source: France 24, The Observers, Burmese Villagers forced to move for a Chinese dam, (2010).

---

[198] Myanmar's Environmental Conservation Law (2012); International Finance Corporation (IFC), Hydro Advisory Programme, ESIA Consult Pty Limited. Peter Wulf, *Environmental and Social Impact Assessment Guidelines for Hydropower Projects in Myanmar*, (2016).

Nonetheless, despite a lack of concrete legislation on the matter, CPI had already taken initiative back in 2007 to conduct over 20 topical assessments addressing the impacts of its proposed operations. In order to account for the aforementioned risks associated with flooding, the company ensured that the highest standard for flood control was adopted. Equipped with 23 flood outlets, deemed sufficient in relation to the dam's size, the dam's design thus addressed such social impact issues.

Similarly with regards to concerns about the project's location on an earthquake prone zone, Lu Qizhou (the President of CPI), once again highlighted the preliminary efforts put into the dam's research and conception. As such, the dam had been designed with the capability to withstand an earthquake of intensity 9; which given research undertaken into the zone's 1000 year old history indicating no earthquake over 7 had previously occurred in the area, was hoped to be a sufficient measure to defuse safety concerns.[199]

Indeed further efforts were invested later in 2009, with CPI commissioning an independent EIA by experts from both Myanmar and China.[200] Yet problems arose as to the objectiveness of the assessment, undermining the company's overall attempts to account for the needs of locals. Despite having been conducted by external experts in the field, the determinations drawn by the impact assessment have since been criticized by an independent expert review for failing to accord a long

---

[199] China Daily, *CPI: Mutually Beneficial and Double Winning China-Myanmar Myitsone Hydropower Project,* (October 2011), Interview with Mr. Lu Qizhou (President of CPI).

[200] International Rivers, *The Myitsone Dam on the Irrawaddy River: A Briefing,* (September 2011). Experts consisted of members from: the Changjiang Institute of Surveying, Planning, Design and Research; The Chinese Academy of Sciences; The Ministry of Water Resources; South China Botanical Garden of the Chinese Academy of Sciences, South China Institute of Endangered Animals, and notably Burma's Biodiversity and Nature Conservation Association.

and extensive enough study period to truly determine the environmental and social risks likely to emanate from the dam construction. The independent review contended that the impact assessment:

1). failed to provide a well-balanced and neutral account of proposed operations;

2). that it was based purely on findings obtained over the course of just one week, and

3). that it had failed to account for all reasonable and foreseeable effects of construction on the river.

Notably, the report concluded that despite efforts made it was still left "largely questionable whether and to what extent diverse stakeholders [were] involved in the social impact assessment"[201]; highlighting the assessment's shortcomings in attempting to ascertain the social impacts of CPIs operations without properly engaging in direct dialogue exchange with local communities.

This significantly led to biased findings as noted by the independent review, whereby the handful of social concerns considered, were largely unsubstantiated, oversimplified and overly optimistic. The criticisms indicated that the needs of local communities may only have been superficially considered by CPI, if at all; an outcome that is likely where little to nil direct community engagement has taken place with the stakeholders concerned. To make matters worse, the independent review highlighted indications by virtue of the ESIA's wording that *"the project would proceed or was already on-going regardless of the social impact assessment outcome"*[202]; a notion that is further enforced by CPI's own

---

[201] International Rivers, *Independent Expert Review of the Myitsone Dam EIA*, (Berkeley, CA: International Rivers, 2012) p.20.
[202] Supra note 14, International Rivers, p.22.

actions, in choosing to begin construction of the dam before the ESIA results had even been collated.

In essence, the report's findings suggest that whilst CPI may have attempted to engage in sustainable practices by commissioning impact assessments and conducting its own topical investigations, it did so utilizing a primarily tick-box mentality. By this it is meant that the company did not go far enough to truly determine the needs, opinions and fears of the local people who were bound to be affected by their operations. Resultantly, the company's ESIAs were only able to provide a limited and artificial reflection of the social context underpinning the project, exacerbating the distrust of the local Kachin people towards the proposed dam.

Resolution: Direct Exchange with Locals

Such shortcomings highlight the need for future overseas initiatives to conduct ESIAs in an honest and diligent manner; necessitating the use of open and direct dialogue exchange with local communities, as opposed to generalized risk identification. Such communicative efforts may have dispelled the strong contentions and distrust that the Kachin people held towards CPI's dam operations, alleviating public pressure on the matter and preventing President Thein Sein's later decision to suspend construction.

After all, the decision to build the Myitsone dam within the confluence region of the Ayeyawady River may well be justified from a practical perspective. Given its capacity to produce 3,600-6,000 megawatts of energy, 41% of the total power generated by the seven-dam project,[203] it is no surprise that this wasn't the first attempt to build a dam in the region. Rather, the Myanmar Government had already previously

---

[203] Harvard Kennedy School, David Dapice, *To Build or Not to Build? Designing Sustainable Hydro for Federalism in Myanmar,* (February 2016).

recommended doing so back in 1952, having only failed on the basis of funding.[204]

Taking this into account, the issue at hand does not purely lie with the suitability of the Ayeyawady River for constructing a dam, but on the role of ESIAs in handling the consequences of such a decision through effective community engagement. Whilst the location was particularly controversial from the very beginning, rendering complaints against the dam's initiation easily foreseeable, the company still failed to take proper precautions in safeguarding against the imminent public disapproval that was bound to arise.

The importance of securing a social license within ODI, let alone within a sensitive project such as the Myitsone Dam, simply cannot afford any oversight. In CPI's case, it was thus vital that the expansive concerns and needs of local people be *directly* heard in an attempt to secure their approval, providing an open and accessible means for community members to voice their opinions. Such a dual natured relationship may even have helped CPI in fostering realistic solutions for mitigating potential social impacts.

Nonetheless, even with Myanmar's long standing turbulent political history acting as a reminder that the views and opinions of the public ought to be headed, very few successful attempts were made by CPI to directly engage in effective dialogue exchange with Kachin villagers or even the KIO. Rather the company continued to rely solely on government approval, and the knowledge that legally speaking, they had appropriately abided by all the relevant local laws.[205]

---

[204] Upstream Ayeyawady Confluence Basin Hydropower Co. Ltd, *2010-2012 Social Responsibility Report*, p.10, Timeline.

[205] Global Business Initiative, China Learning Project Report, *"The Corporate Social Responsibility to Respect Human Rights in China Globally"*, (August 2014).

As a result, the quality of ESIAs were gravely undermined; no longer as effective as a tool for exercising greater due diligence in strengthening the company's understanding of contextual factors. Indeed, the effectiveness of impact assessments rests in communication and discussion, as endorsed by the ISO 26000 Standards. Stricter observation of such internationally recognized guidelines would have been beneficial for CPI in overcoming social challenges; especially given the absence of domestic legislation and guidance on how to realistically manage such interests.

Herein, the focus of the ISO standards on risk identification through effective communication are particularly fitting, emphasizing the importance of: stakeholder identification and engagement[206]; consultation with local representative groups[207], and notably, the need to balance conflicting interests in and amongst the community.[208] Such observances may have avoided CPIs oversight of community concerns; whereby the false sense of security enjoyed by virtue of government endorsement, prevented the company from recognising and appropriately balancing the competing views of other actors in the community. Indeed, had CPI appreciated such conflicting interests and taken the time to engage in an objective, well researched ESIA, its understanding of the political context surrounding the project's operations may have better equipped it to foresee and prepare for Myanmar's political reform.

4.2.2 Issue Two: Barriers of Access to Local People

Nevertheless, it is conceded that Myanmar's political and societal situation during the time of this case was especially sensitive. As contended by CPI:

---

[206] ISO 26000 Standards, 5.3.

[207] ISO 26000 Standards, 6.8.3.2.

[208] ISO 26000 Standards, 6.8.1.

"During the period of Military rule in Myanmar, the military government did not allow the company any independent communication with the media or the public beyond a limited scope and content."[209]

In turn, barriers to access may have prevented CPI from securing genuine public recognition of all the benefits the Myitsone project could deliver; leaving the company at the sting of strong local opposition which ultimately led to its indefinite suspension. Indeed, given that the Burmese Ministry for Hydroelectric Power owned a 15% share in the dam, it is likely that the Military Junta had particular power and influence over the project's operations; holding a dual capacity as the host government and a direct shareholder. Such power and influence may well have prevented any in depth dialogue exchange with local communities given rising political tensions in the country.

However, notwithstanding these obstacles, statements made by local NGOs indicate that a number of opportunities for community engagement had still been presented to CPI and yet went unreciprocated:

"villagers at the dam site, numerous political and community organizations, [and] international human rights organizations…attempted to contact CPI and discuss the concerns about the impacts and process of the project [but] CPI never responded to these attempts at dialogue."[210]

--Burma Rivers Network (BRN)

Further purported attempts by KIO to discuss the project's details were also noted to have gone unnoticed, despite KIO's notable presence

---

[209] Global Business Initiative, China Learning Project Report, *"The Corporate Social Responsibility to Respect Human Rights in China Globally"*, (August 2014): CPI Learning Case, *"CPI Yunnan: The Myitsone Dam Project, resettlement and the social license to operate Yunnan, Myanmar."*
[210] China Dialogue, Liao Ruo, *Lessons from Irrawaddy,* (October 2011).

in the Kachin State.[211] As such, despite politically-motivated barriers to access, it appears that CPI's actions were still non-conducive to resolving the problem. With CPI underestimating the importance of more solid attempts by local representatives and NGOs for communication, it is unsurprising that little dialogue exchange was ultimately achieved with locals.

Nonetheless, it is acknowledged that in line with CPI's own topical assessments, a survey of local villagers who had been resettled by the project was successfully conducted; along with 26 interviews with local elders, religious leaders, experts, scholars and officials.[212] However, the outcomes of these interviews and surveys is yet to be publicly disclosed, providing little comfort to the public that whilst the needs of locals may have been heard, they may not have actually been considered. Indeed, this highlights a further issue relating to the importance of transparency – even where barriers to access may have been prevalent.

"Any win-win result has only been for the military and this is resented by the people of Burma. The lack of transparency by the military and foreign investors increases this resentment."[213]

--Burma Rivers Network

Resolution: Public Disclosure of Key Information

Many projects that are bound to a remarkable conjunction of interests extinguish simply because the initiator is disdainful of the myopia of the other parties. Aside from asymmetry of knowledge that can easily amounts to credulity of rumours and fabrications, difference in philosophy and vision presents the hidden defiance to any proposition therein

---

[211] International Rivers, *The Myitsone Dam on the Irrawaddy River: A Briefing,* (September 2011).

[212] Supra Note 22, CPI Learning Case.

[213] Burma Rivers Network, *Burma Rivers Network Response to China Power Investment Corporation comments on Myitsone Dam,* (October 2011).

raised. While it may be impossible to completely synchronize a shared value universe, trust building is always the starting point. Transparency rests in the ethical quality of honesty and sincerity and to be followed by effective communication. This is key to secure local recognition and approval, given its function in earning greater empathy and trust. In the case of CPI, disclosure of key project information concerning the Myitsone Dam may have achieved just this. During the course of the dam's planning, design and construction, very few concrete facts had been shared with the public, or even to local subcontractors on the details of the dam and the relationship between CPI and the Military Junta. The net result was to exacerbate growing tensions and public distrust, giving rise to a number of rumours that were ultimately harmful to the project's operations.

Exhibit 4.3

Source: Courtesy of International Water Cooperation

For example, news circulated around Myanmar stated that whilst the project entitled the Burmese government to 10% of generated electrical output, the remaining 90% would go to China. In fact, many international news reports and discourse written about the case have since circulated this same information. This gave rise to beliefs that the business relationship underpinning the dam conferred unfair benefits to China, at the expense of Myanmar [Exhibit 4.3]. However, it was later argued that this was not actually the case; rather the first claim to the remaining 90% of generated electricity would go to Myanmar at a negotiated price, after which the "remaining power [would] be sold to anyone who wants to buy it, whether it's China or other countries."[214] Indeed it was even stressed that China had no need for additional electric power, with Yunnan province alone possessing a 7000-megawatt surplus in 2015.[215]

The conflicting accounts on vital project information evidence the inexistence of publicly accessible information; fundamentally with regards to the allocation of benefits arising from the project. Benefit distribution is naturally a key consideration for wider stakeholders affected by large scale ODI, and a crucial indicator of the intentions underpinning an endeavour. As such, the perception of civil society will have been greatly influenced by the notion that CPI's plans for the Myitsone dam aimed to reap more than it sowed. In fact, this idea that the distribution of benefits was grossly in favour of China, failed to reflect the aforementioned reality by which the Myanmar Government was actually predicted to enjoy 60% of the project's benefits, and ultimately the full 100% after 50 years. Nevertheless, regardless of the accuracy of such information, such claims caused reputational harm to both CPI and the Myitsone dam project as a whole.

---

[214] Myanmar Times, Ye Mon and Clare Hammond, *CPI pushes for restart of Myitsone Dam,* (June 2015); Upstream Ayeyawady Confluence Basin Hydropower Co., Ltd Website: <<http://www.uachc.com/Liems/esiten/list/desc.jsp?newsType=2355¤tPageNo=1>>
[215] Supra note 27, Myanmar Times.

"NGOs and some civil society groups dictate[d] the media discourse, which was crucial to the project's suspension."[216]

--Bi Shihong

(Professor, School of International Studies, Yunnan University)

With this in mind, it is strongly advocated that companies recognise the importance of adequately disclosing project information from the outset, especially within industry sectors such as mining, hydropower and construction, where general operations inevitably exert lasting ramifications on local communities. Should a company operating abroad manage to luckily skip this process typically relying on the capricious intervention by the host government, they would find themselves embattled in broiling misgivings and prejudices at a later stage. This particularly holds true where the company has already been noted to have resisted open invitations made by the public for open and honest dialogue exchange.

Indeed, even the purported efforts on behalf of CPI to conduct assessments and interviews, were weakened by an inability for the local community to access such data and findings. Key research such as the aforementioned ESIAs had not been, and still aren't, publicly disclosed to the local Kachin people; undermining their overall ability to mitigate the fears and concerns of relevant stakeholder groups.

"The message to the people is clear: "You do not deserve the important information."[217]

--Myanmar Times (2016)

Such a message, be it intended or not, is likely to have fuelled the public opposition against the dam construction, and acts as a continuing hindrance against prospects for the dam to recommence operations. It is

---

[216] Global Times, Yu Jincui, *Dam Politics*, (October 2013).

[217] Myanmar Times, Aung Tun, *Myitsone dam project: The fourth choice, or the fifth one?* (August 2016).

thereby recommended that CPI publicly disclose key Project data, findings and impact assessments sooner rather than later. This is especially given the special commission formed in 2016 by Myanmar's current President Htin Kyaw to objectively assess the merits of the Myitsone Project. After all, the ultimate decision of the committee on whether to terminate or resume the Project, will most likely rest on key findings which require the company to divulge such information.[218]

All in all, the case highlights the general importance of disclosure at all stages of business; acting as a reminder in future ODI for transparency in dispelling rumours and prejudices against large scale commercial projects. After all, there are always two sides of the coin, but without mechanisms for ensuring effective transparency, both sides may not always be seen. Certainly it has been stressed that without projects such as the Myitsone Dam, Myanmar's new democratic government shall face grave obstacles in its aim of transitioning Myanmar into a developed country by 2030.[219] It has therefore been voiced by some that the public backlash to the Myitsone dam may well just boil down to "the pains of growing up".[220] Nevertheless, what remains clear is that without direct communication and proper disclosure, it was always going to be much harder to expect the public to appreciate CPI's side of the story.

4.2.3 Issue Three: Managing Expectations

Indeed, as well as improved disclosure, there are other mechanisms that CPI may have adopted in order to better defend its own actions and

---

[218] Myanmar Times, Ye Mon, *Hydropower Projects in Kachin to be Reviewed,* (August 2016).

[219] Supra note 29, Global Times.

[220] South China Morning Post, Catherine Wong, *Despite Myanmar dam blockage, China confident about ties with Suu Kyi government,* (March 2016); Myanmar Times, Myo Lwin, *China hopes to resume Myitsone hydro dam,* (March 2016).

intentions in preparation for the inevitable opposition against building a dam on Myanmar's cultural bloodline. Take for instance the issue regarding the resettlement of 11,800 people as a result of the project's operations. As with many projects related to hydroelectric power, it was seen that the building of the Myitsone dam came with direct impacts on villagers in the occupying area. In order to build the dam, it was therefore inevitable that a number of locals would be required to relocate to other vicinities, necessitating the relocation of 400 households.

In order to deal with the matter properly and professionally, CPI invested approximately US$25 million into the resettlement of local people; observing both international and national procedures.[221] Drawing from the experiences of alternative resettlement projects such as those of the World Bank, it maintained the motto: *"be able to move people out, be able to keep the situation stable, be able to develop."* Simultaneously CPI applied its own guiding principle:

"After project implementation, the standard of living of the displaced people is to be no lower than it was before and in fact somewhat higher."[222]

Exhibit 4.4

Source: Courtesy of the Upstream Ayeyawady Confluence Basin Hydropower Co.

In achieving such ends, the company ensured that resettlement villages were provided with new hospitals and clinics, educational facilities, administrative institutions and even religious places of worship; keen to respect the human rights of all resettled people. What's more the new houses were of better quality, structurally more stable in utilising brick and wood as compared with the more traditional straw and wood houses [Exhibit 4.4]. The properties came fully equipped with cooking facilities, water supply, electricity and luxury commodities such as TVs. In ensuring that the livelihood and quality of life of villagers would not be undermined, CPI even supplied: grain rations; allowances for living expenses; rice plants; chemical fertilizers, and virgin land to grow new crops.[223]

Nonetheless, a number of complaints still arose criticizing CPI's handling of the resettlements. Since their relocation, it has been contended by locals that: the new towns are incapable of growing crops; that the compensation awarded to displaced people was insufficient, and that the new services available in the villages have been inadequately maintained.[224] Such contentions emerged despite CPI's survey of displaced people indicating that 80% *"expresse[d] widespread support for the Upper Irrawaddy hydroelectricity project"*[225]; and despite trips made to see villagers prior to resettlement, which helped determine community needs. In fact, it was information collected during such trips which ultimately aided in the decision to establish the new towns in Aung Myay Thar and Mali Yang.

---

[223] Supra note 22, CPI learning case.

[224] The Irrawaddy, Seamus Martov, *Myitsone Dam Project on Hold, but far from Dead,* (November 2013).

[225] Supra note 22, CPI learning Case.

It has since been pointed out that in certain instances there has further existed an imbalance in expectations from local people, placing disproportionate burdens on CPI for their well-being and welfare within the new towns. Take for instance complaints that were raised regarding the lack of teachers in new schools. CPI argued in their defence that the introduction of *"teachers are the government's responsibility"* and that the company could not realistically be expected, nor held responsible, for providing such employees.[226] After all, the extent of a company's social responsibilities should still be managed within a reasonable confine that is both justifiable and pragmatic; whilst there is a need to consider the interests of shareholders, the interests of corporations must also be well balanced.

Resolution: Collaborative Agreements

The situation demonstrates the difficulties inherent in situations where the needs and opinions of local communities appear to change over the progression of business operations. Whilst direct dialogue exchange can help to address such changes, there is also a need for corporations to protect themselves, should they become targets of unrealistic expectations.

In this regard, it is recommended that corporations enter into written agreements with local communities in situations of resettlement, presenting a safeguard so that the expectations of such stakeholders may be realistically managed in future. The agreements, be they legally recognizable contracts or MOUs, would need to ensure that they are easily accessible and properly understood by locals prior to their completion. This is so as to prevent any future misgivings about their legitimacy. As such, it is apt for companies to contact local NGOs/civil society organisations possessing better resources and bargaining power to act on be-

---

[226] Myanmar Times, Tim MclaughLin, *Chinese Ambassador Casts doubt on Myitsone resumption,* (July 2013).

half of the affected communities; thus ensuring that the agreements entered into remain fair and impartial. In such circumstances, should negotiations be ineffective, the involvement of a third party independent mediator may also be utilised, as a further mechanism for helping the company to arrive at some general understanding which would ensure that community expectations are fairly and appropriately managed alongside the development of the project.

Indeed, had CPI entered into written agreements with NGOs such as the Burma Rivers Network, rather than simply depending on surveys and interviews alone; the risk of complaints surrounding the resettlement of local villagers may have been mitigated. In turn, the agreements would have provided a more solid basis for presenting both sides of the coin: that the Project not only intended benefits for CPI but for the citizens of Myanmar too.

The need for mutual consensus and cooperation has been emphasized by institutions such as the WWF and Nature Conservancy, who stress that it is the *"unfair distribution of benefits and costs [that] is likely to trigger or aggravate regional conflicts."*[227] Drawing inspiration from such observations, the use of collaborative agreements with local communities would provide the perfect instrument by which the benefits and costs attached to a project proposal may be effectively negotiated and fairly balanced. The drawing up of such agreements would also provide a suitable platform for the opinions of the local

---

[227] United Kingdom's Department for International Development (DFID), The Nature Conservancy, WWF and The University of Manchester, *Improving Hydropower Outcomes through System-Scale Planning: An Example from Myanmar*, (May 2016) p.13.

community to be properly heard and considered, providing a direct channel of communication to foster dialogue exchange.[228]

4.3 Conclusion

The Myitsone case validates the need for community engagement, highlighting that even where legal and political access has been provided for business undertakings, the presence of local society can have a notable effect on the success of an endeavour. Acquiring a social license is therefore necessary, and particularly crucial within the extractive industries, as well as for those projects that predominantly take place in countries of political and/or economic instability.

Nonetheless the case also embodies a keen observation: the need for stakeholder interests to not only be well considered and accounted for, but to be managed such that the responsibilities and burdens placed on companies may also be managed in turn.

To this end, aligning the interests of businesses with local communities is key, and may be best achieved through: direct communication with local stakeholders; prompt public disclosure of key information; and collaborative agreements with local institutions where necessary. Such mechanisms shall safeguard corporations from unforeseen and potentially catastrophic obstacles to ODI, ensuring better integration of stakeholder needs and interests for the present and future.

4.4 Questions for Throught

1. The Myitsone dam was particularly controversial in choosing to build a dam on Myanmar's great cultural relic (the Ayeyawady Riv-

---

[228] It is also worth considering the use of benefit-sharing arrangements, see: World Bank, Daniel Gibson, *Lao PDR Development Report 2010 Natural Resource Management for Sustainable Development,* (Washington D.C., 2010).

er). Was it doomed from the very beginning regardless of the company's actions?

2. Is it possible to balance the interests of local society, the government and political oppositions in a country where there exists political and social instability?

3. In what way does a politically sensitive environment alter the responsibilities of a corporation operating in that territory?

4. How might the current dilemma surrounding suspension of the Myitsone dam be best resolved?

4.5 Appendix

<u>Myanmar: Background Profile</u>

Exhibit 4.5 Myanmar Annual GDP Economic Growth Rate

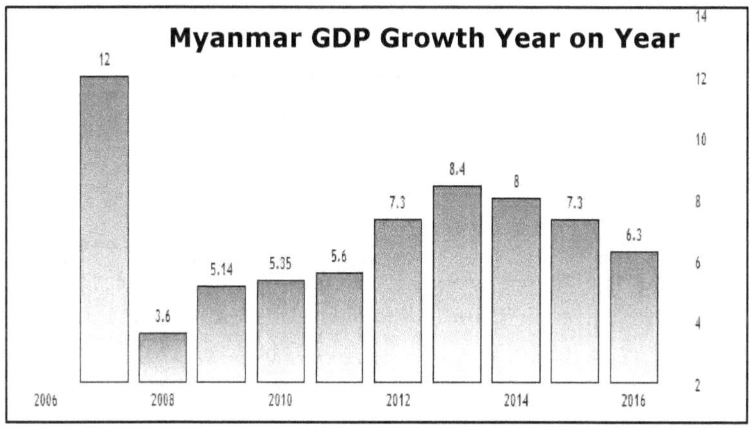

Source:

<<https://tradingeconomics.com/myanmar/gdp-growth-annual>>   [accessed on 20/10/2017]

Exhibit 4.6 Myanmar Access to Electricity Spread (2014 Consensus)

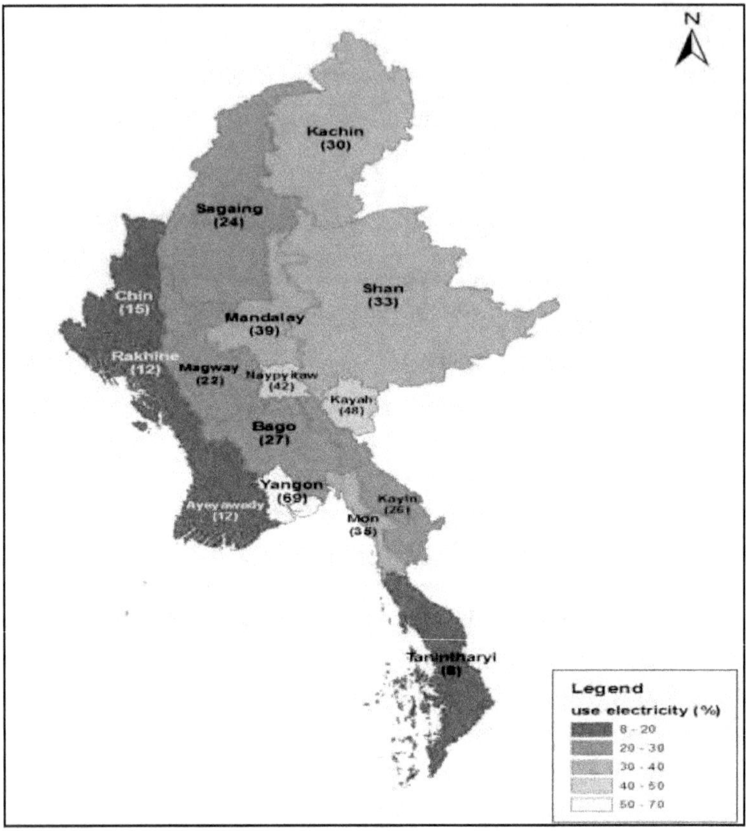

Source: Republic of the Union of Myanmar, Department of Population and Ministry of Immigration and Population, 2014 Myanmar Population and Housing Census: Highlights of the Main Results, Census Report Vol.2-A (May 2015).

Exhibit 4.7 Myanmar Poverty Analysis

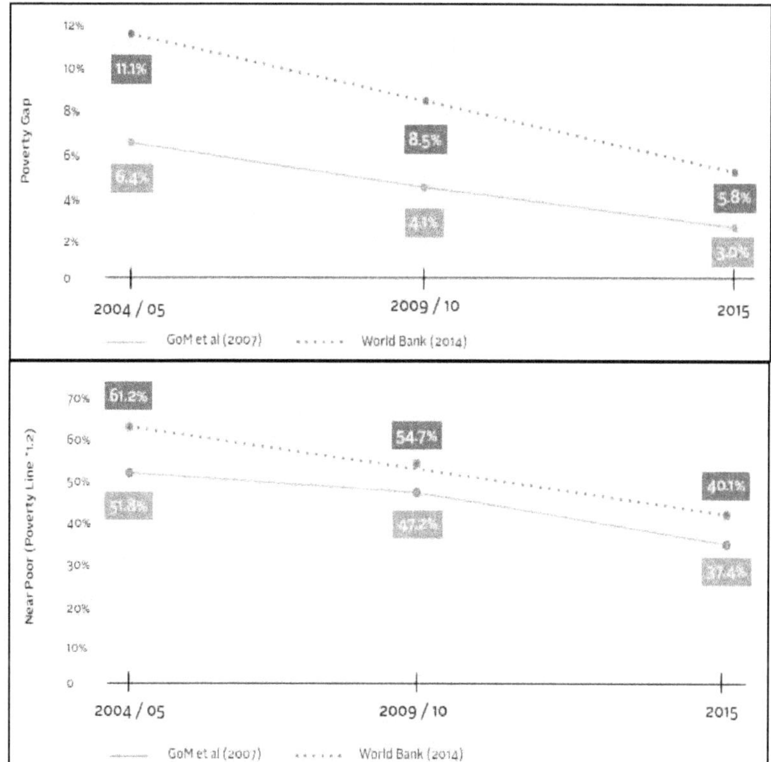

Source: World Bank Group, Government of Myanmar Ministry of Planning and Finance, An Analysis of Poverty in Myanmar: Part 1, Trends between 2004/05 and 2015, (August 2017).

Exhibit 4.8 Myanmar Growth Trajectory of Real GDP to 2030 by Scenario (indexed to 2010 = 100)

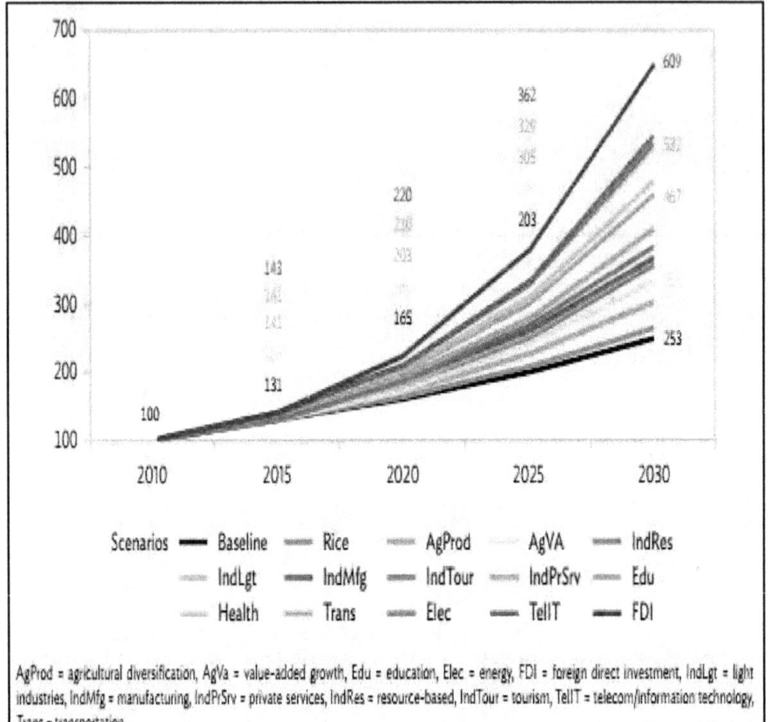

Source: Roland-Holst and Park, Myanmar - Long Term Scenarios for Sustained Macroeconomic Growth. Forthcoming ADB Economics Working Paper Series. (2014)

Myitsone Dam: Timeline and Background Information

Exhibit 4.9 Myanmar Political Reform Timeline

Source: BBC News, Myanmar Profile – Timeline, (October 2017);

1948	• Burma gains independence (Prime Minisiter U Nu in charge).
1962	• Government overthrown by military coup.
1988	• Protests against political oppression and mishandling of the economy. 3,000 people left dead. • Opposition: National League for Democracy is formed.
1989	• Military Junta declares martial law. Country name changed to "Myanmar". • Aung San Suu Kyi placed under house arrest for "endangering the state" (daughter of independence hero Aung San who was assassinated in 1947). • National League for Democracy leaders arrested.
1990	• National League for Democracy wins landside vote in an election authorised by the Military Junta. However results of the vote are ignored.
2003	• Khin Nyunt becomes prime minister. • Proposes to hold convention in 2004 on drafting new constitution as part of "road map" to democracy.
2004	• Constitutional convention begins, despite boycott by National League for Democracy. • Khin Nyunt placed under house arrest.
2006	• Country's capital moved from Rangoon (renamed Yangon) to Nay Pyi Taw (newly built city in the jungle).
2007	• International Committee of the Red Cross take a rare departure from its neutral stance - accuses the government of abusing the Myanmar people's rights. • Aug-Sep = protests. These escalate into the biggest anti-government protest since 1988.
2008	• New constitution allocates 1/4 seats in parliament to the military and bans opposition leader Aung San Suu Kyi from holding office.
2010	• Military Junta changes country flag and national anthem. Solidifies "Myanmar" as official name of the country. • Elections held for ruling government. Outcome = resounding victory for Military Junta. Election labelled a "sham."
2011	• Thein Sein sworn in as president of a new, nominally civilian government. • September: suspension of controversial Chinese-funded Myitsone hydroelectric dam. Move seen as as showing greater openness to public opinion.
2015	• National League for Democracy, led by Aung San Suu Kyi, wins enough seats in parliamentary elections to form a government.
2016	• Htin Kyaw sworn in as president, as Aung San Suu Kyi is still constitutionally barred from presidency. • Democratic movement takes power after 50 years of military domination.

The Guardian, Matthew Weaver and Peter Walker, Timeline: Burma, (May 2008).

Exhibit 4.10 Myitsone Dam Timeline of Events

Source: International Rivers, The Myitsone Dam on the Irrawaddy River: A Briefing, (September 2011).

2005
- CPI and Asia World establish joint venture to build hydropower projects in seven locations along the Mali Hka and Nmai Hka rivers.

2006
- MOU signed for all 7 dams to be built.

2007
- KIO chairman approaches Yunnan Province State Council, Head of State Senior General Than Shwe and Head of Myanmar Military Northern Command in Kachin State with a letter from local villagers.
- Changjiang Survey, Planning, Design and Research (CSPDR) completes planning report for the feasibility of the hydropower projects.

2008
- Terms of Reference for ESIA is completed and approved.
- Yunnan Power Investment Co Ltd is created for the primary purpose of the development, construction and operation of hydropower projects on the Ayeywady
- BANCA (Biodiversity And Nature Conservation Association) and CPI sign an agreement to conduct an ESIA special investigation.

2009
- Special ESIA conducted by Chinese and Burmese experts from:
  - Changjiang Survey, Planning, Design and Research Co Ltd.
  - Chinese Academy of Sciences.
  - Ministry of Water Resources.
  - South China Botanical Garden of the Chinese Academy of Sciences.
  - South China Institute of Endangered Animals.
  - Burma's Biodiversity and Nature Conservation Association
- Aug = CPI website reflect that site management is concerned about an outbreak in armed conflict in parts of Myanmar. Safety measures implemented.
- Oct = baseline ESIA by BANCA is finalized
- Dec = construction begins as does the resettlement of people

2010
- ESIA Report conducted by Chinese and Burmese experts finalised.
- April, four explosions occur at the Myitsone Dam site - 3 at a worksite and 1 at the workers housing area.
- Government declares that despite the 1994 Ceasefire Agreement with KIO, communications and cooperation would be halted. KIO invites CPI to discussion but receives no response.

2011
- The overall ESIA for the hydropower projects is finally concluded.
- June 9th – fighting erupts, affecting the construction site.
- Aug – Aung San Suu Kyi publishes a letter of appeal: Appeal to Save the Irrawaddy.
- Sep = Myitsone dam is suspended.

Exhibit 4.11 Kachin Independence Organisation Fact File

KIO
Kachin Independence Organization
ကချင်ပြည် လွတ်လပ်ရေး အဖွဲ့

Armed wing: Kachin Independence Army
Government name: Kachin State Special Region-2

Founded: 5 February 1961
Headquarters: Laiza, Kachin state
Operational Area: 8 brigades across Kachin State and Northern Shan state
Estimated strength: 10,000 to 12,000
(excluding the KIO's MHH and MKM civilian militia forces)
The KIO's armed wing the Kachin Independence Army (KIA) is the second largest ethnic armed group in Myanmar. The KIO claims to have 10,000 troops with another 10,000 reservists in the civilian population ready to fight. The KIO generates large revenues from its rich natural resources, which has enabled them to create a powerful army and develop trade centers in several cities along the Sino-Myanmar border. e.g. Laiza, Mai Ja Yang A 17-year ceasefire, which for many years was the only written agreement that the government had with any armed group, ended less than 3 months after the nominally civilian government took power in 2011. The contributing factor was the KIO's refusal to join the government's BGF scheme. Construction of the Myitsone dam – that would flood large tracts of land in KIO controlled territories was also a major source of tension. Although the Myanmar state media started referring to the KIO as an illegal organization from 2009-2010, the ceasefire did not breakdown until government troops attacked the KIO's Sang Gang outpost on June 9, 2011.

Leadership:
Chairman of KIO and President of Kachin Independence
Council : Lanyaw Zawng Hra
Vice-President 1: General N'Ban La
Vice- President 2 (KIC): Major Gen Gunmaw
General Secretary: U La Nan
Joint Gen Secretary: Col Waw Hkyung Sin Wa
Commander in Chief: Lt Gen. Gun Htang Gam Shawng
Deputy C-in-C 1: Brig Gen. Yuk Hkayawng Hkawng Lum
Deputy C-in-C 2: Brig Gen. Awng Seng La

Source: International Rivers, Myanmar Peace Monitor
<<http://www.mmpeacemonitor.org/component/content/article/57-stakeholders/155-kio>> [accessed on: 02/11/2017].

Exhibit 4.12 President Thein Sein Decision to Suspend the Myitsone Dam

(…) NAY PYI TAW, 30 Sept-

President of the Republic of Union of Myanmar U Thein Sein

1. I wish the Speakers of Pyithu Hluttaw/Amyotha Hluttaw and all representatives who are putting all their energies into serving the people's interests at the second regular sessions of the first Pyithu Hluttaw/Amyotha Hluttaw physical and mental well-being. 2. The Union government, and region and state governments also are harmoniously placing emphasis on emergence of good governance, clean government, burgeoning of democratic practices, prevalence of law and order, economic reforms and environmental conservation. 3. The common goal of all the national people is to ensure peace and stability of the State and modernization of the nation. As the Union government offered an olive branch to national race armed groups staying outside the legal fold in accord with the wish of the national people for ensuring eternal peace, state level agreements have been reached with Special Region (2) "Wa" Group and Special Region (4) Group. At present, the Union level dialogues are in progress. Moreover, some groups have made contact with state governments concerned for peace negotiations. 4. At the same time, as Myanmar citizens who were abroad due to various reasons are scrutinized with offer of return to their mother country and native places, some have arrived back. The release of prisoners will be conducted within the framework of powers entrusted in accord with the constitution. While the Union government is accelerating its service for the national interest, it is so regrettable to witness attempts of some parties and elements forcing the government into the tight corner and undermining peace and stability. (…) 9. While first phase of Ayeyawady Myitsone hydropower project was implemented with the investment from the People's Republic of China, we noted that there arise the following public concerns about the Myitsone project. (a) natural beauties of Myitsone the gift of nature and a landmark not only for Kachin State but also for Myanmar may disappear; (b) possible loss of livelihood of national races villages due to inundation at the upstream of the river; (c) commercially-grown rubber and teak plantations which are heavily invested by private entrepreneurs may be destroyed; (d) melting ice from snow-capped mountains at the far north triggered by climate change, torrential rains or severe earthquakes may destroy Myitsone dam, claiming lives and property of the people in towns and villages at the downstream of the dam; and (e) there may be a devastating effect on the Ayeyawady River. 10. As our government is elected by the people, it is to respect the people's will. We have the responsibility to address public concerns in all seriousness.

So construction of Myitsone Dam will be suspended in the time of our government. Other hydropower projects that pose no threat will be implemented through thorough survey for availability of electricity needed for the nation. I would like to inform the Hluttaws that coordination will be made with the neighbouring friendly nation, the People's Republic of China, to accept the agreements regarding the project without undermining cordial relations. Thein Sein President Republic of the Union of Myanmar Source: NLM 2011-10-01

Source: Burma Library

<<http://www.burmalibrary.org/docs12/PH,_AH-NLM2011-10-01.pdf>> [accessed on: 02/11/2017].

5

EMPLOYERS, EMPLOYEES & TRADE UNIONS

Local procurement: mechanisms for securing employee integration

Whilst ESIAs are key for securing the receptiveness and trust of civil society within ODI, long term localisation is not just achieved through communication and transparency. The role of employment and building relationships with local workers is also key to acquiring a social license and entrenching ODI at a community level.

Following on from this line of thought, the experiences of Chinese companies operating in Africa provides insight into the problems that may be faced when employing a local labour force, and how such obstacles can be overcome.[229]

5.1 Background Context

With this rapid GDP growth, the role of the country as the world's primary manufacturing base has necessarily shifted. A steadily expanding middle class and improved quality of life, has meant that the country's focus and expectations have turned away from base level production [Exhibit 5.1], in line with more sustainable innovation driven economic models. As a result, lesser developed countries have been able to gain competitive edge with regards to low-end manufacturing in recent

---

[229] McKinsey & Company, Karel Eloot, Alan Huang and Martin Lehnich, *A New Era for Manufacturing in China,* McKinsey Quarterly, (June 2013).

years. Indeed, attention has begun moving away from China and onto countries such as: Vietnam; Ethiopia and Bangladesh, for cheap manual labour.

Exhibit 5.1

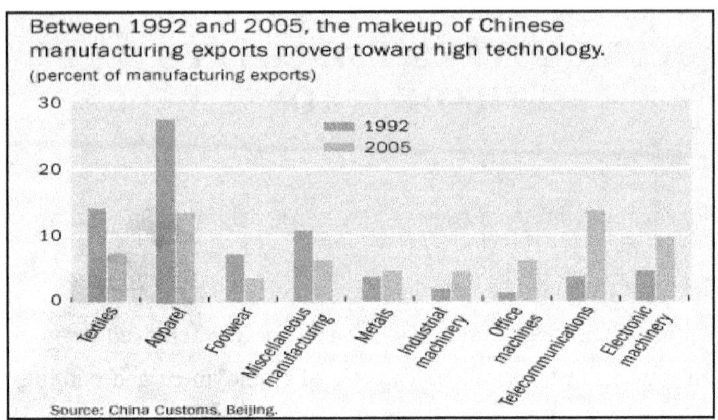

Source: China Customs, Beijing Via International Monetary Fund, Finance and Development, Mary Amiti and Caroline Freund, China's Export Boom, Vol. 44, No. 3, (2007).

5.1.1 The Good

However, this is not to say that China no longer has a place in the manufacturing sector. Rather the first-hand experience of Chinese factories is welcomed, in possessing unique know-how on how to effectively manage manufacturing and production hubs in less developed climates. After all, China is no stranger to setting up and running successful factories in a developing country.

As companies such as Huajian International Shoes demonstrate, there is a lot that can be gained on both sides from Chinese companies engaging in such ODI. Huajian factory's president Zhang Huarong, has established for himself a notable reputation in Ethiopia since relocating part of his production line to the African country back in 2012. The company, which produces shoes for well reputed brands such as Guess, Nine West, Tommy Hilfiger and Calvin Klein, established a factory on the outskirts of Ethiopia's capital city, Addis Ababa, in light of the rising labour costs faced back at home. Since then, the factory has been considered by many to be a rather good example of how mutual cooperation and understanding of both employer and employee needs, can ensure long term success.

As a result, the Huajian Factory has not only been able to maximize on profits through the lower labour costs that Ethiopia has to offer, but has also succeeded in winning the locals favour by providing them with stable, dependable incomes and opportunities for future career and skill development.

"The work is good because I pay my rent and I can look after myself...It's transformed my life."[230]

--Employee at Huajian, Addis Ababa factory

Such success has since been attributed to the fact that development of the factory's production line focused on the importance of localization to long term sustainability:

"One thing in my strategy is very clear: that I don't want to compete with locals...I want to help them grow because when local producers grow, the whole market is growing."[231]

--Helen Hai (Vice-President, Huajian Group)

---

[230] Bloomberg, Kevin Hamlin, Ilya Gridneff and William Davidson, *Ethiopia Becomes China's China in Search for Cheap Labour*, (July 2014).
Please note: the 2017 controversies concerning Huajian International Shoes factory and the manufacture of Ivanka Trump's brand line of shoes, is solely regarding the company's domestic factory in Dongguan, China. No mention of unethical practices in the Addis Ababa factory have been voiced as of yet.
[231] The Guardian, Elissa Jobson, *Chinese firm steps up investment in Ethiopia with 'shoe city'*, (April 2013).

As a result of such an ethos, the factory has steadily been growing in profitability, efficiency and output. Able to obtain local media support coupled with developing strong relationships with the Ethiopian Government, it has since worked closely at a ministerial level with the development of Addis Ababa more generally.[232] Indeed, it has been so successful that Huajian has recently negotiated with the Nigerian Government on a USD 1.5 billion deal to expand over in Aba, Nigeria; in recognition of the company's success in fostering mutually beneficial relationships.[233]

The case acts as an illustration for the benefits that are to be had when effective localization is treated as central to ODI operations; not only to ensure that business ventures are able to withstand and overcome the inevitable obstacles that are bound to arise when entering a new territory, but also to continue growing and expanding in line with local markets. The role of local procurement therein, embodies a most effective way for a company to best integrate itself overseas in the long term. This is by virtue of its ability to continuously maintain ongoing relationships with local communities.

As demonstrated by Huajian, development of local industry in line with Chinese companies is extremely beneficial in ensuring the development of a long term market. In turn the company is better able to secure its foothold within host territories. This requires understanding the benefits that can be had by: a). employing locals, b). developing business relationships with local businesses, and c). actively contributing to the development of a skilled local workforce.

---

[232] Fana Broadcasting (Popular platform for Ethiopian news and culture), *Chinese Shoe Factory Huajian Now Employs 3,200 People*, (September 2014).

[233] Press Reader, Melanie Peters, *Ivanka's Shoes to be Made in Nigeria Factory*, (April 2017).

Indeed, many Chinese companies have recognized the benefits of both a) and b), having employed and worked alongside local workers when operating abroad. This has been the case even where the company's transition into overseas territories was not motivated by cheaper labour concerns.

For instance in extractive sectors, where the reason for ODI lies in access to raw materials as opposed to cheaper production and manufacture, trends demonstrate a persistent focus of Chinese corporations on local procurement within their overall workforce. As such, initial contentions voiced by NGOs and the academic community against Chinese companies utilising Chinese labourers over local human resources, are no longer as pressing a concern.

Even in situations where this has been the case, it is generally noted that the motives of such decisions primarily lies in necessity; with particularly high level positions carried out by more experienced Chinese employees who possess the technical skills needed to perform said duties. This is especially worth consideration when the net effect of the Chinese company's presence is to introduce a relatively novel industry to the operating areas, i.e.: in situations where the local workforce is more in tune with industries such as farming and agriculture, and therefore lacks the expertise to take on high level management and industrial positions.

Nonetheless, whilst in some situations necessity dictates the use of Chinese employees for higher level positions, this should remain true only for the beginning of an endeavour. Following on, the need for gradual localisation by proxy of training and apprenticeship schemes ought to allow higher skilled positions to be passed onto local workers. In this way technology and knowledge transfer can be ensured.

5.1.2 The Bad

However, it is exactly this notion that highlights the crux of the problem. Despite the fact that Chinese companies are employing locals, a key issue arises with respect to the manner in which they are being hired, highlighting that the issue now lies in the application of c). actively contributing to the development of a skilled local workforce. It is noted in a number of circumstances that a large proportion of local workforces in Chinese enterprises, are denied of their legal rights under local labour laws as a direct result of casual, non-contractual based employment.[234] In other words, despite collaborating with locals, companies are doing so in an unorthodox way which enables basic employee welfare standards to be circumvented; providing a somewhat unilateral relationship which fails to recognize, balance and ultimately align the needs and interests of local employees with those of the company.

"Many workers are not formally employed and are not represented by trade unions, so they have little recourse when fired unexpectedly."[235]

One potential reason for this behavior has been attributed to inherent obstacles in hiring local community members with different economic needs and cultural outlooks. In appreciation of differences in culture and work ethic, there have been contentions from Chinese employers that the ability to protect workers' rights by entering into official employment contracts is not always a viable option. Issues are raised that local workers can be "lazy" with respect to their duties and obligations, and are neither consistent nor dependable enough to be formally hired.[236] It was

---

[234] All Africa, Edwin Okoth, *Kenya: Chinese Firms Hire More Locals Than Foreigners –Report,* (March 2016).

[235] Prosper, Ariel Gandolfo, *Chinese Investment in Africa – Where Do the Jobs Go?,* (June 2015).

[236] The Globe and Mail, Geoffrey York, *For South Africa's Workers, A Chinese-supplied job comes at a price,* (December 2010); Howard French, *China's*

observed in one instance, that workers had a tendency to skip work after receiving their previous month's wages, sporadically returning only once they were in need of further income. This spontaneity left the Chinese employer with little choice but to pay local staff on a casual basis; awarding wages for performance and contribution on the days that the employees actually attended work.[237]

However, whilst culture differences are inescapable and give rise to such challenges; it is important that Chinese companies recognize the importance of effective communication for mitigating such obstacles in a positive and mutually beneficial manner. The first challenge in this regard is the existence of language barriers existent in many overseas companies, preventing any real means of interaction between Chinese employers and local staff. The importance of this cannot be overstated, as before dialogue exchange can even take place with local employees, it is necessary that there exists a common language in the workplace by which to communicate. Yet certain cases have highlighted an absence of such an environment, automatically rendering it nigh impossible for the needs and interests of local employees to be voiced, and more importantly heard.[238]

Even where this first step has been resolved, further procedural and structural challenges arise. After all, language barriers do not simply extend to sharing a proficiency in a particular language, but further extend to the manner of speaking and the lines of communication available between employers and employees. Take for instance the aforemen-

---

Second Continent; How a Million Migrants are Building a New Empire in Africa, (Alfred A Knopf Publishing, 2014); The China Africa Project, Eric Olander & Cobus Van Staden, *Why do Chinese bosses think African workers are lazy?,* Blog, (May 2016).

[237] The China Africa Project, Zhicong Deng, *Chinese Companies' Labour Dilemma in Kenya,* (June 2014).

[238] Supra note 9, The China Africa Project.

tioned examples concerning cultural differences, in which the observation of local employees as "lazy" has generated prejudice. In this respect, it is important to recognize that prejudicial attitudes are non-conducive to mutual development. Rather the importance of empathy becomes key; truly attempting to understand the differences that exist. In such a scenario an empathetic attitude shall recognise that the cheaper labor costs within certain host countries, are in part down to the lower skill level and experience that local community members possess in such fast-paced, modern industries. The deeper understanding that comes from this perspective increases the likelihood of finding a pragmatic and proactive solution.

Indeed, rather than blaming these challenges upon a singular party, it is to be recognised that there will always exist learning curves in the overall aim of aligning local behavioral and cultural differences with a company's ethos. In appreciation that this cannot be achieved overnight, it is necessary for companies to take the lead and attempt to foster a more united and productive workforce. Through implementation of appropriate training and development programmes, companies can help to strengthen mutual understanding, reinforce mutual objectives and benefit employee-employer relationships in the long run. More generally speaking, training and development programmes are even an avenue for promoting stronger, more integrated relationships with the local community as a whole.

One example of how such integration might be achieved lies with the aforementioned case of Huajian Shoes Factory, where a particularly direct approach to overcoming obstacles of communication and culture was adopted. An example showcased by the Africa-China Project follows the experiences of a factory employee: Demis Degef. In it, Mr Degef shares that his experiences at the Huajian factory provided him with long term training, and the opportunity of actually travelling to China to gain practical insight into Chinese business culture. This exchange of knowledge not only allowed Demis to learn the Chinese language, but to better understand the cultural differences between Chinese and African business ethos. In recognition of the fact that effective communication transcends language, such hands on experience provided a platform for deeper two-way understanding of cultural differences.

Following his exposure to Chinese business values, Mr Degef voiced his new outlook on working at the factory, as he became able to take advantage of his new skill sets and experiences, tripling his salary from 2,000 to 6,000 Birr a month. Crucially, the experience paved the way for a new sense of improved job satisfaction, whilst providing him with opportunities for career progression in assuming more senior responsibilities at the factory.[239] The hands on approach thus strengthened the relationship and loyalty that existed directly between Mr Degef and the Huajian factory, overcoming concerns that development and training projects for local employees can lead to a high turnover, by which employees leave the company for a more profitable alternative. Indeed, to overcome this challenge, it is essential that companies establish a well-developed career development programme, clear in its structure and well communicated to employees so that they may better understand the scope of their job prospects in remaining at the company.

With regards to Huajian, it was both the company's training scheme in allowing Mr Degef to travel to China, and the follow up mechanisms by which he was then able to hone in on his experiences by assuming higher level positions, that created mutual benefit. The aftermath enabled Demis to strengthen his job security at Huajian, whilst Huajian was

---

[239] Africa-China Reporting Project, Zhang Zizhu, *Inside the Chinese Factory in Ethiopia where Ivanka Trump places her Shoe Orders,* (January 2017).
Further reading for additional accounts from Huajian factory workers: Tang Xiaoyang, *Does Chinese Employment Benefit Africans? Investigating Chinese Enterprises and their Operations in Africa,* African Studies Quarterly Vol. 16, Issue 3-4, (December 2016).

equally able to secure a long term, loyal and dependable member of staff. In turn the company was able to secure more effective localization, whilst ensuring higher level positions for local workers that would help mitigate the likelihood of encountering cultural and communicative problems in the long run.

In fact Huajian's focus on strengthening relations with local employees, and establishing effective synergy in its multicultural workplace, has even prompted the company to display its central business philosophies on the factory floor in all relevant languages.[240] This ensures that the goals and ethos of the company may be appreciated by all employees: Chinese and locals alike. Other companies may consider utilising similar techniques, as such a simple yet effective mechanism offers a clear, visible and accessible means of communication that helps to establish a more united workforce. Indeed, if nothing else, such an act communicates to local employees that the company understands, appreciates and is willing to cater for their language, their needs and their voice to be heard; establishing open lines of communication.

Open lines of communication are fundamental to resolving disputes and mitigating the risk of misunderstandings in future. In building such channels, it is recommended that Chinese companies recognize the benefits that can be had in establishing mediating bodies within the corporate structure. By this, it is suggested that local employees are not simply hired for baseline jobs, but that their potential to help in the management and localization of the company is also recognized, as was the case with Demis. For instance, job roles such as: interpreters/translators, human resource managers, supervisors and welfare support officers, may be well suited to locals; if not jointly held by Chinese and local personnel alike. This would help prevent segregation and discord between sub-groups of employees, establishing stronger synergies which

---

[240] Financial Times, Katrina Manson, *The Ethiopia Paradox,* (July 2015).

ultimately enable the company to continue raising its own awareness of local cultures, thinking and practices.

"[H]ire a local HR manager and avoid direct conflicts with the local employees. The local HR manager is more familiar with local employees and it's easier for them to communicate to avoid misunderstanding and conflicts."[241]

5.1.3 The Ugly

In fact another mechanism that ought to be utilized to aid communication is that of Trade Unions. Not only do such institutions form an integral part of labour protection laws in many countries, but they are primarily concerned with offering a platform for effective dialogue exchange between employers and employees. Unfortunately, however, not all companies have come to recognize this, and there has been a general problem with the perception of labour unions as a hindrance.

As a result, companies are failing to make use of the lines of communication that unions open up to them; not only with respect to communicating with employees in understanding their needs and concerns, but also in deepening the company's own understanding of local labour laws and standards.

This in turn has led to a growing distrust in Chinese enterprises amongst local staff members, exacerbated by serious underlying problems relating to employee welfare standards in a handful of cases. It has been noted that whilst some companies do make use of local workforces, it is not necessarily in the interests of localisation that such decision have been made. Rather, in the absence of adequate employee protection standards and enforcement of employee welfare in certain overseas territories, the unethical exploitation of local employees may be wit-

---

[241] Supra note 9, The China Africa Project.

nessed. Such situations have arisen regardless of whether the locals are employed on a casual basis or one of formal contractual employment, given that the ability to unethically exploit workers arises from contextual factors of the host country, e.g.: weak governance States; lack of effective enforcement mechanisms; non-comprehensive labour protection laws etc. In some instances violation of labour standards within ODI does not occur with bad intentions, but rather as a direct result from a company's lack of knowledge on domestic regulations. In either case, the use of trade unions is pivotal to mitigating problems.

However, failure to recognize the true potential of mutual development, and the role that labour unions play in achieving this goal, has led to a series of past failings and controversies; many of which focus on the persistent exploitation of local workforces within ODI. The cumulative effect has been to hinder long-term development and estrange links with local Governments, ultimately giving rise to a number of problems with Chinese companies operating abroad. In some cases, such outright denial of employee welfare has even resulted in aggressive protests; disrupting company operations, squandering resources, and in especially serious cases, even risking the safety of staff members. In such situations, it is not only the importance of adhering to local welfare protection standards that is being overlooked by Chinese companies, but notably the importance of labour unions in mitigating hostilities.

Two recent cases of Chinese ODI best illustrate this. The first concerns recent protests in January 2017, at the Hangzhou Hundred-Tex Garment factory in Myanmar. The factory, like many other garment factories, turned to Myanmar for its cheaper labour and production costs. Since 2014, it has been manufacturing clothes in Yangon for the leading fashion giant H&M. However, as brought to attention in 2016, it has since faced problems concerning the distribution of wages to local employees. Workers demanded: to be paid wages owed for overtime work; wages in accordance with local laws, and requested the establishment of a workplace coordination committee.

In line with such needs the company entered into an agreement in December 2016 with the local employees' Trade Union (backed by the Confederation Trade Unions of Myanmar). However, in mid-January heated protests broke out when the Trade Union President, Ko Thet Paing Oo, who had been instrumental in establishing the agreement; was dismissed. The basis of his dismissal was attributed to having taken a 2 week unapproved absence from the factory; however it was argued, that the time taken was actually a pre-agreed sick leave on the recommendation of his doctor that he had measles, evidenced by a medical note.

"Factory officials were not happy with me because they had to compensate about K70 million to the workers when we demanded our rights according to the law. They fired me because they were not happy that I supported the strikers. They admitted as much"

--Ko Thet Paing Oo[242]

Despite the agreement which had been reached to resolve internal labour issues little over a month before, protests still broke out. In mid-January 2017 workers began a 3 week-long strike against the company, demanding that it not only honour the agreement that had been established back in December, but that it further: implement a better performance review system; provide healthcare coverage, and immediately reinstate Ko Thet Paing Oo.[243] In essence, the new demands directly corresponded to the purportedly unfair dismissal of the factory union President.

---

[242] Myanmar Times, Zaw Zaw Htwe, *Garment Factory Closes after Attack by Workers,* (February 2017).
[243] South China Morning Post, Kinling Lo, *Strike at Chinese Factory in Myanmar another bump along 'One Road',* (March 2017).

After 3 weeks of no avail, the protest quickly escalated into a riot. On February 9th 2017, approximately 300 employees entered the factory with force: smashing factory doors and windows; damaging facilities; destroying surveillance cameras and even detaining 7 Chinese managers. One news report further announced the existence of video footage showing several female workers physically attacking a Chinese manager,[244] although it has since been denied that any of the factory workers assaulted anyone nor broke industrial equipment.[245]

The strike has been referenced by the Guardian Newspaper as: *"one of the most violent labour disputes in the country in many years."* [246]As a result, operations at the factory have been severely impacted. Not only does the company now have an estimated damage cost of 75,000USD, but crucially, its contract with H&M has since been suspended. The impact of such mounting employee dissatisfaction on wider business relationships is thus noted, affecting fundamental revenue streams.

The case illustrates a need for Chinese companies to recognize the importance of ensuring genuine cooperation with Trade Unions; crucial in establishing stronger relationships and trust amongst employees, and in ultimately mitigating workplace tensions before they escalate out of control. Whilst it may appear that Trade Unions are purely one-sided in acting as an employee safety net, in reality they provide both employer and employee with a great service: balance. By ensuring that employee rights and interests are appropriately protected, and simultaneously managing employee expectations; job satisfaction is secured and company's prevented from losing face in light of public protests and negative limelight in international media.

---

[244] Reuters, Shwe Yee Saw Myint, Yimou Lee, *H&M supply factory in Myanmar damaged in violent labour protest,* (March 2017).

[245] Supra note 15, South China Morning Post.

[246] The Guardian, Shwe Yee Saw Myint, Yimou Lee, Anna Ringstorm, *H&M supply factory in Myanmar damaged in violent labour protest,* (March 2017).

Notably, both sides are further protected from the dangers and disruption caused by protest-turned-riots, fuelled by anger. Indeed the second case concerning the Collum Mine in Zambia, highlights just how badly situations can spiral out of control when sensitive labour related issues have been handled independently. I.e.: when employees feel that they have no other choice but to take matters into their own hands.

Contextually speaking, locals employed at Chinese mines in Zambia have been known to voice concerns with regards to:

"curtailment of union activity: [whereby] several Chinese operations suppress workers' right to join the labour union of their choice and retaliate against outspoken union representatives."[247]

It has been noted that despite the Zambian labour law allowing workers the freedom to be represented by unions of their choice, Chinese companies have displayed passive aggressive acts in attempting to deter employees from taking part in trade unions, or at the very least limiting the scope of their options therein. Prejudicial treatment of employees based on union association was amongst the problems most associated with company behaviours.

Failure by said companies to abide by national laws and recognise the importance of safeguarding employee welfare, has resulted in unethical working conditions. In turn, this has generated unrest amongst local citizens, giving rise to problems of protests, official complaints and general prejudice against Chinese companies and their operations. Most notably, refusal to comply with labour protection standards along with other relevant Zambian laws, led to a series of dramatic events in the

---

[247] Human Rights Watch Report, *"'You'll be Fired if you Refuse' – Labor Abuses in Zambia's Chinese State-Owned Copper Mines"* (November 2011) <<https://www.hrw.org/report/2011/11/04/youll-be-fired-if-you-refuse/labor-abuses-zambias-chinese-state-owned-copper-mines>> [accessed on 3rd May 2017].

case of the Collum Mine. The case received worldwide attention from leading newspapers for its rapid downward spiral into violent protests.

The privately owned coal mine located in Sinazongwe Zambia, was established back in 2000 by five brothers from Jiangxi province, China: the Xu family. The mine was known to have been riddled with a number of employee welfare problems relating to: health and safety; long working hours; no breaks; inadequate wages and so on. In fact in 2010, aggressive action was taken against the company when hundreds of miners gathered together in protest, demanding higher wages. It was alleged that when employees began throwing rocks, two Chinese supervisors retaliated by shooting in open fire, leaving at least 11 miners wounded.[248]

Whilst it is still uncertain why the Chinese supervisors had been armed, the animosity that existed between employees and employers was clearly strong enough to have left both sides feeling that they were physically threatened. Indeed just a few months before, rumours spread that when 22 local miners were seriously injured in a gas explosion caused by inadequate health and safety measures, a Chinese national had to quickly escape "lynching by an angry mob."[249] Zambian media reports of previous labour disputes even suggested incidents of mine workers throwing 'missiles' at Chinese managers;[250] demonstrating the severity of hostilities that had already been steadily growing in seriousness and scale, prior to the 2010 incident.

Despite these tell-tale signs that an intermediary may be necessary to help resolve disputes between employers and employees, it was noted that the "Collum managers [still] avoided meeting with union leaders…"

---

[248] The Telegraph, Aislinn Laing, *Zambian Miners Shot by Chinese Managers,* (October 2010).

[249] CNN, Eve Bower, *Zambia Mine Shootings Raise Tensions with China,* (November 2010).

[250] Supra note 21, CNN.

and had inherent problems with miscommunication and bad labour culture.[251] Ironically, the very matter of contention in the 2010 protest (i.e.: higher wages), had already been previously settled between the company and the miners' Trade Union. However, failure to implement effective lines of communication within the corporate structure meant that this information went crucially unnoticed. As a result, the protest commenced despite the fact that the nature of the problem was on its way to being resolved.

Even following such protests, little changes were made to improving the workplace environment. With rising distrust and an increasingly divided workforce, tensions escalated further in August 2012, leading to the accidental death of a Chinese manager when a protest turned particularly hostile. The protest once again concerned the issue of wages, and prompted approximately 12,000 workers to gather outside the mine. Seeing the protestors, Chinese managers residing in settlements built onsite, left their homes to enter the mine for protection. A series of events eventually culminated in the release of a one-ton trolley which was pushed into the mine and inadvertently injured two Chinese managers, whilst killing a third: Wu Shengzai. The situation had gotten so out of hand, it was noted that several protestors did not even know that somebody had been killed until much later on.[252]

Given the mine's history of conflict, building an honest and genuine relationship with the miner's Trade Union ought to have been a top priority. With such a high level of existing animosity between employees and employers, there existed a clear need for the company to take account of an independent third party perspective; especially when it was clear that conflicts could not be hospitably resolved between the two parties alone. Efforts taken in order to demonstrate to employees

---

[251] The New Yorker, Alexis Okeowo, *China, Zambia and a Clash in a Coal Mine,* (October 2013).

[252] Supra note 23, The New Yorker.

that the company was actually attempting to rectify the working environment, would have further aided in dissolving conflict. However, in the case of the Collum Mines, it appears that there was very little intention on behalf of the company to resolve rising tensions, at least this was certainly the message portrayed to local employees and local communities at large.

The case highlights the importance of channels of communication in stabilizing situations, particularly where tensions and emotions run high. In situations of conflict, it is clear that there is no use in trying to "sweep it all under the rug"; rather dialogue exchange and the use of mediators such as local labour NGOs and Trade Unions, should be utilised to deal with the matter at hand. Indeed, enterprises such as the Collum Mine ought not to underestimate the importance of all stakeholders, both internal and external. Herein it is emphasised that a company does not necessarily have all conflicts under it's control purely because those conflicts are within the realms of the corporate structure. Certain situations may warrant that to properly manage relationships, even with internal stakeholders such as employees, a company has to rely on more than just it's internal processes and structures; the use of a third party may be essential. In this way, companies may better manage their relationships utilising the help and expertise of institutions trained in conflict resolution, and ensure that they have fulfilled their duties in conducting diligent risk management.

Developing honest relationships with trade unions will thus go a long way to maintaining a stable and dependable workforce, securing the company's presence and reputation long term. Where such mechanisms go unnoticed, the likelihood is that Chinese companies shall experience heated protests, which as demonstrated by the previous factory cases in Myanmar and Zambia, can quickly turn riot.

5.2 Conclusion

The above cases emphasize that operating in different territories ultimately necessitates that traditional business views and cultures be adapted in light of the needs and interests of local workforces. It is no longer enough to simply hire local labourers; company's need to proactively work towards developing an operational, efficient and well integrated unit.

In attempting to balance employee-employer interests to create such a dependable multi-cultural unit, it is to be remembered that this is an ongoing process. As such, money, time and planning must be invested into developing training and integration programmes to help local workers assimilate to their work standards and protocols, whilst in turn helping the company to assimilate to the new culture standards and laws of their overseas market.

5.3 Questions for Thought

- Companies have their own standard of protocol and work ethic. To what extent should these be upheld, despite cultural and behavioural differences in overseas territories?
- Are Trade Unions really impartial institutions?
- What types of training programmes may be most useful in developing the skill set of local employees who lack exposure to modern industries such as: factory production; advanced mining etc.?
- "Employees will always naturally segregate into cultural subgroups" – Do you agree?

5.4 Appendix

Chinese Investments in Africa Exhibit 5.2 Chinese ODI_Africa

Source: American Enterprise Institute Via The Economist, A Thousand Golden Stars: China goes to Africa, (2017).

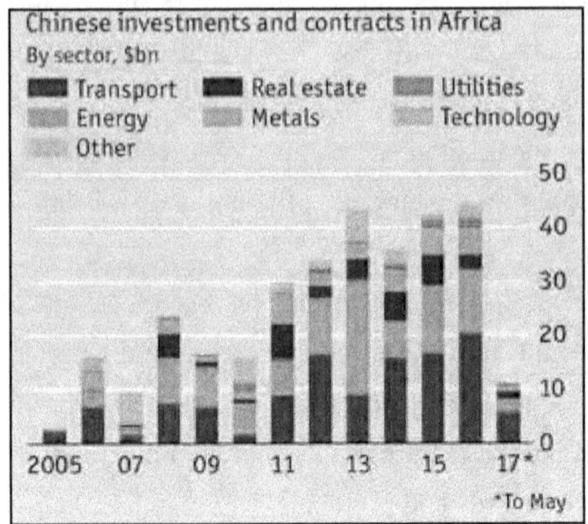

Exhibit 5.3 Local Procurement_ Chinese Companies in Africa and Distribution of training offered_Chinese Companies in Africa

Source: McKinsey & Company, Irene Yuan Sun, Kartik Jayaram Omid

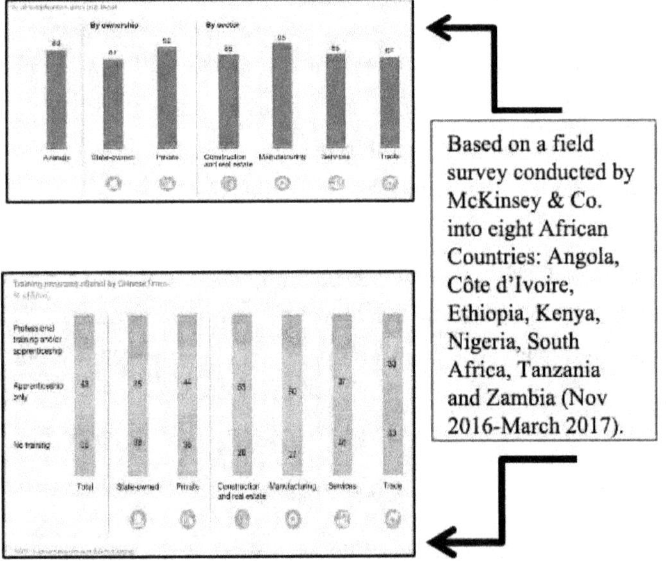

Based on a field survey conducted by McKinsey & Co. into eight African Countries: Angola, Côte d'Ivoire, Ethiopia, Kenya, Nigeria, South Africa, Tanzania and Zambia (Nov 2016-March 2017).

Kassiri, Dance of the Lions and Dragons, (June 2017) p.41.

6

THE CASE OF JIUXING MINES

Corporate responsibility: the need to align stakeholder interests

6.1 Case Background

The final major stakeholder concerned with operating overseas and entwined with securing local support, is that of the environment. The importance of conservation and environmental protection has gained rising significance in both national and international policies within the last few decades. With leading international conferences such as the Earth Summit 2002, and initiatives such as the 2016 Paris Agreement incorporated within the United Nations Framework Convention on Climate Change (UNCCC); there have been more and more dedicated efforts and political commitments made in the global challenge towards environmentally sustainable development.

Such endeavours necessitate joint efforts from all countries worldwide towards improving and re-establishing the world's climate system. In acknowledgement of this fact, coupled with its own reputation as a rapidly developing country with increasing focus on urbanisation and industrialisation; China has taken a more compelling stance, from a once somewhat passive actor, to a driving force in environmental sustainability and the fight against climate change.

As such, the country has placed great emphasis on the importance of environmental protection within many areas of public policy, including Chinese ODI. Along with welcoming major world leaders in 2017 to explore the Belt and Road Initiative, China once again stressed its commitment to environmentally sustainable development with its: Joint Conclusion, "Guidance to Promote the Construction of a Green Belt and Road", formed by the Chinese Ministry of Environmental Protection & Ministry of Foreign Affairs.

The Guidance published in May 2017, reiterates the need to follow:

"The principle of being resource efficient and environment friendly...and incorporate eco-environment protection into all aspects and whole process of the 'Belt and Road' building."[253]

In and amongst such aims, came China's own commitment to, amongst other things:

"Tightening environment management for overseas investment, [and] driving enterprises to voluntarily bear environmental and social responsibilities."[254]

On September 3, 2018, in a keynote speech at the Beijing summit on China-Africa Cooperation, Chinese president manifested his unswerving support to the establishment of Alliance for Corporate Social Responsibility among Chinese companies in Africa, which was subsequently written into the Forum on China-Africa Cooperation: Beijing Action Plan 2019-2021.

In other words, the importance of environmental conservation and sustainable development have been entrenched within China's foreign investment strategies; at a most crucial time, amongst observations of China's rising influence in global affairs and the world's ecosystem:

"No nation has ever changed the planet so rapidly, on such a large scale, and with such a single-minded determination."[255]

---

[253] Government of the P.R.C Official Website, Belt and Road Initiative, *Guidance on Promoting Green Belt and Road,* <<https://eng.yidaiyilu.gov.cn/zchj/qwfb/12479.htm>> [accessed: 18th July 2017]

[254] Supra note 1, Government Website.

Intrinsically linked to China's growing domestic appetite and urbanisation, lies the need for the country to turn outwards, looking to overseas countries for natural resources and minerals in support of its further development. This has inevitably fuelled the export of a large number of extractive, agricultural and construction based industries as part of the country's resource push; most of which, to date, have tended to score rather low on the sustainability front.[256]

The policy changes, strategic in their timing, operate to impress upon companies the importance of environmentally sustainable development, often linked hand-in-hand with the need for protecting society's interests in appreciation of local community needs. As a result, there is a need now, more than ever, for increased capacity building amongst Chinese companies with respect to risk identification and management of environmental and social factors.

In acknowledgement of this fact, the topical case of Jiuxing Mines comes to mind, having recently encountered troubles in the tropical island of Madagascar. The case illustrates the types of environmental and social problems which can emerge in respect to Chinese ODI, particularly when adequate efforts have not been made to appropriately identify contextual environmental risk factors. Indeed, the case has prompted major discussion as of 2017 on all future industry developments in the African country, acting as a warning to future Chinese companies of the kinds of widespread repercussions that irresponsible management of ODI can have.

---

[255] Yale University, YaleEnvironment360, William Laurance, *The Dark Legacy of China's Drive for Global Resources,* (March 2017).

[256] Supra note 3, YaleEnvironment360; The Asia Foundation, Huang Zhen, *Environmental and Social Impacts of Chinese Investment Overseas,* (June 2016); The Wall Street Journal, Te-Ping Chen, *Chinese Companies Named and Shamed on List of Deforestation 'Powerbrokers',* (February 2015).

6.2 Mining in Madagascar

Amongst the countries that have attracted Chinese ODI for their abundant natural resources, is Madagascar [Exhibit 6.1]. Holding the title as the world's fourth largest island, the African country has a particularly interesting geographical terrain owing to the fact that it had historically split from the Indian peninsula. Ecologically speaking, this has thus resulted in the island housing a number of animal and plant species of Asian origin, which have since been able to evolve independently, rendering the island a biodiversity hotspot of particular biological significance.

Exhibit 6.1

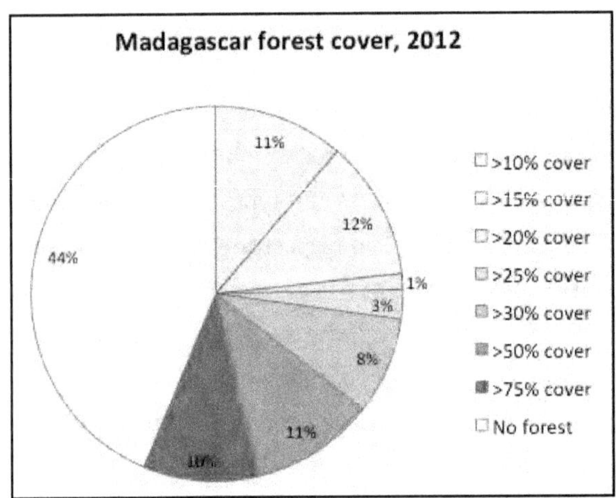

Source: <<http://rainforests.mongabay.com/20madagascar.htm>> [accessed: 16th July 2017].

Owing to its historical origins, the island in turn possesses a vast quantity of natural resources from zinc, iron ore, graphite and even uranium. The wealth of minerals inherent in the country's rich soil has thus caught the attention of many countries, enticing significant volumes of foreign investment from all over the world including China. In fact,

Chinese investment in the country is of particular benefit not only for private businesses, but from a national perspective too; operating as the 'bridge' to Africa in accords with the country's larger foreign investment and macroeconomic strategies.[257]

Exhibit 6.2

Source: Courtesy of XinhuaNet.

Indeed, in April 2017 the Chinese and Malagasy governments came together in a view to bolster investment in the transportation and energy sectors of Madagascar, signing several agreements to such an effect [Exhibit 6.2]. The intended result aimed to increase the already heavy Chinese investment in the country, which as of December 2016 totalled US$740 million, housing more than 800 Chinese companies[258] and an estimated 100,000 Chinese nationals.[259] In the interests of both coun-

---

[257] World Politics Review, Editors, *For 'One Belt, One Road,' China casts Madagascar as a 'Bridge' to Africa,* (May 2017), Interview with Cornelia Tremann [expert on Sino-Malagasy relations].

[258] The Straits Times, Agence France-Presse, *Dominance of Chinese Firms in Madagascar Sparks Social Backlash,* (December 2016).

[259] ChinaFile, *Who Knew? Madagascar Has Africa's Third Largest Chinese Population,* (March 2015).

tries, the agreements hoped to benefit Madagascar with regards to transportation and infrastructure building, whilst acknowledging China's vested interest in the country's natural resources.

More generally speaking, the Malagasy government has even invested its own efforts into establishing an attractive regulatory environment for foreign investment. In order to bolster the country's economic development, the government has thus far focused on:

"the integration of Madagascar into international and regional arenas by integrating trade into the national development strategy and in particular making trade the foundation for leveraging national development".[260]

In alignment with these aims, it is recognised that the country's constitution has long formally and explicitly provided for the rule of law.[261] Theoretically speaking, this adoption ensures foreign enterprises are not only provided with a more predictable and stable environment upon which to root their investments, but are comforted with the knowledge that their investments may also be adequately protected in future. The regulatory backdrop thus establishes an environment conducive to the Malagasy voiced intentions for integrating foreign investment within their developmental policies.

However, with the existence of corruption and bribery as fairly prominent forces still at play within the country's governance structures (as is commonplace in less developed African countries), the extent to which benefits accrued through foreign investment are distributed in the

---

[260] World Trade Organisation, Report by the Secretariat, Trade Policy Review Body, *Trade Policy Review of Madagascar*, WT/TPR/S/318 (June 2015).

[261] Constitution of the Republic of Madagascar, [ADOPTED 19th AUGUST 1992, as Amended 1998], Preamble: *"the founding of a state of law according to which the governing and the governed are subject to the same juridical norms under the supervision of an independent justice."*

aims of national development, are still unknown. In turn, foreign enterprises intending to invest/with investments already in the island, are warned of the lingering socio-political instability that has remained within the country ever since Madagascar's 2009 military coup. In fact, a 2017 report by the International Monetary Fund presents data suggesting that not only is corruption still rife, but that steadily weakening governance indicators directly impact upon the country's macroeconomic stability.[262] In turn, whilst Madagascar's national policies and strengthened relationships with China may pave the way for increased Chinese investment, there is still a need to remain cautious of the contextual risks therein.

Further to these risks, arises the need for ODI projects (particularly those within the extractive industries) to remain sensitive towards environmental concerns. This arises from both an international and national standpoint, given the ecological significance of the country's landscape and rainforests to both local communities and the world as a whole. On the basis of protecting such interests, global and domestic NGOs have secured parameter's around resource rich ground in the aims of biodiversity and forest conservation[263]; with the Malagasy government having stepped up efforts to the same end.[264]

---

[262] International Monetary Fund, *Republic of Madagascar: Selected Issues,* IMF Country Report No. 17/224, (July 2017), Note (p.7): reference to Madagascar's corruption score which was noted to have fallen by 0.9 units in the 10 years between 2005-2015, according to the World Governance Indicators.

[263] World Wildlife Fund, *New Era for Environmental Protection in Madagascar,* (May 2014): WWF and Madagascar National Parks signed a 3 year agreement protecting 17 million hectares of land and marine area (29% of Madagascar's total surface area).

[264] *Office of the High Commissioner for Human Rights (OHCHR), Report of the Special Rapporteur on the issue of human rights obligations relating to the enjoyment of a safe, clean, healthy and sustainable environment, on his visit to*

In short what is presented here, is a current juxtaposition within the country: attempting to capitalise on particularly lucrative resource reserves, whilst recognising the need to preserve priceless, environmentally sensitive and fragile ecosystems.[265] These concerns, coupled with heavy competition between investing nation States, has caused tensions upon the social and environmental landscape of the island. In turn this has resulted in a somewhat critical reception towards ODI; exacerbated by the persistent weaknesses in transparency between the government and its citizens. The net effect is to induce unease and distrust amongst local communities, in view of foreign investments as a purely one-sided interest: that of the government, not the people.

Indeed, whilst Madagascar has attempted to improve such internal issues, having become a candidate of the EITI Standards (Extractive Industries Transparency Initiative) back in 2007; problems relating to weak internal governance and political instability have since hindered such progress. Political tensions surrounding the aforementioned 2009 coup d'état, resulted in the suspension of the country's EITI candidacy for the three years between 2011-2014,[266] evidencing the fragility in trust that has historically existed between different levels of Malagasy society; 90% of which still live well below the international poverty line.[267]

The contextual backdrop renders a need for Chinese enterprises to handle ODI affairs openly, honestly and sensitively; particularly with regards to construction-related or extractive-based industries which

---

Madagascar, Human Rights Council 34th session, Agenda item 3 (27th February-24th March 2017).

[265] BBC News, *Sapphire Mining Threatens the Indri Lemur Species,* (July 2017).

[266] EITI, Christina Berger, *EITI Board Lifts Suspension of Madagascar,* (June 2014); Supra note 8, WTO Trade Policy Review, at p.89, s.4.72.

[267] World Food Programme Official Website: <<http://www1.wfp.org/countries /madagascar>> [accessed: 20th July 2017].

inevitably interfere with the natural environment. However, as the following case demonstrates, not all Chinese companies have recognised the importance of social integration and environmental conservation in achieving successful long-term investments. Such oversight, as evidenced by Jiuxing Mines Company, may ultimately result in financial and reputational detriment.

6.3 Jiuxing Mines Company

Jiuxing Mines S.A.R.L is a Chinese company specialising in the extractive industries. The company, recently known for the problems it encountered with local Malagasy communities, established a gold mine in the Western town of Soamahamanina, Madagascar. The 2016 project, with a total investment of approximately RMB 100 million, hoped to capitalise on Madagascar's extensive gold reserves in order to feed the increasing appetite of Chinese consumers for the commodity [Exhibit 6.3].[268]

The company was granted a 40 yearlong mining license and subsequently began operations in May 2016, despite local controversy raised at the beginning of the year against its investment proposals. However, the company's luck did not last for long when just a few months later in December, it was forced to close amidst local protests. The problem here lay neither with cultural differences nor with issues of local employment; given that the mine had employed 11 full-time members from the local community alongside 20 Chinese employees.

---

[268] Xinhuanet, *Madagascar Gold Export Increases in First Four Months of 2017,* (May 2017).

Exhibit 6.3 China's Huge Appetite for Gold

China's huge appetite for gold

China's gold imports passing through Hong Kong alone

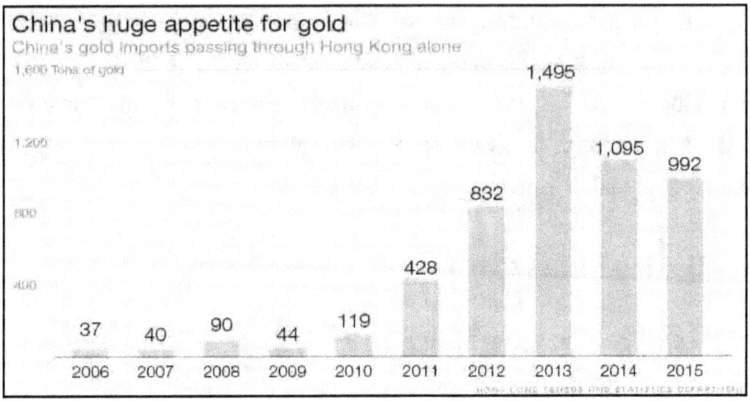

Source: Hong Kong and Statistics Department
Via CNN, Heather Long, China is on a Massive Gold Buying Spree,
(2016).

Rather, local communities were worried that the 7500 hectare project would interfere with agriculture, residences, and even local commodities such as tombs, a church and a school which lay in the wake of the project's proposals. Yet, despite rising angst surrounding the company's project and mining proposals, Jiuxing failed to engage in dialogue exchange with concerned communities, leaving them in the dark about the company's true intentions and plans.

In a similar vein to the Myitsone Dam case, a lack of transparent disclosure thus undermined the efforts that had been made to cater for societal needs: in this case, Jiuxing's commitments towards building roads, water supplies and providing electricity to local communities. Crucially the company's social responsibility was plagued with a larger problem: a failure to properly validate the commitments made, leading to a gap in credibility. Lack of follow-up information delineating the extent of infrastructure to be contributed, left nothing but empty promises incapable of quantification nor enforcement. Accordingly, with no official timeline provided for the commencement of the social projects and no priority order designed for their implementation, such efforts were seen as little more than a simple 'greenwashing' tool: false promises to secure an investment, with no means by which to measure or monitor their authenticity. At the very least, the oversight evidenced poor project management of the company's social responsibility initiatives.

The company's perceived false promises and lack of communication exacerbated tensions surrounding the mine. Tensions truly began to escalate following the environmental permit issued in May 2016, as protestors became angry that the company had managed to secure permission to operate despite failing to enter into any form of prior public consultation with local communities. Given the existence of widespread corruption in the country, it is further likely that the success of Jiuxing Mines to quickly secure a license, irrespective of continuous protests against their ODI proposals, would have created greater hesitancy amongst locals to trust that the company's intentions were pure.

After all previous cases of Chinese ODI have raised suspicion of corruption being used as a means of acquiring mining concessions. One notable example is that of China's third largest steel company, Wuhan Iron and Steel Co. Guanxin (WISCO), and its acquisition of a Soalala iron ore mine in the Boeny region of Madagascar. Although no wrongdoing has ever been noted of the company's acquisition of the mine, the hefty USD 100million fee it paid in May 2010 to the then Rajoelina ruling government for the acquisition of exploration permits would not have gone unnoticed. Especially when the precarious financial situation of the transitional government is considered, along with the fact that WISCO's contribution represented majority of the estimated MGA 291 billion contributed by the mining sector towards the 2010 national budget (1.6% of the country's GDP).[269] The subsequent lack of transparency

---

[269] African Development Bank (AfDB), Organisation for Economic Cooperation and Development (OECD), United Nations Development Programme (UNDP), United Nations Economic Commission for Africa (ECA), *African Economic*

surrounding the transfer ultimately rendered it nigh impossible to discover the ultimate beneficiaries of fees paid.[270] Indeed, speculations of corruption during the transitional government's rule were voiced by the later Malagasy government to have been true.[271]

"Forty years of operation – that is called selling the country...I would like to tell our leaders that the big powers in this world are only turning us against each other to destroy our country."[272]

--Marise-Edine (Malagasy Local)

The absence of transparency and public consultation surrounding Jiuxing's activities led locals to take their own initiative in voicing their concerns against the venture by establishing a Refusal Committee in June 2016. The aim was to provide affected communities with fair representation in the matter.[273] The Refusal Committee and the strong resistance of locals against the project, received outside support from a number of external organisations, strengthening their influence over

---

Outlook, Special Thematic Edition – Madagascar, (2013) referring to the Madagascar, EITI Data Reconciliation Report, 2010; accessible via: <<https://eiti.org/sites/default/files/documents/2010_madagascar_eiti_report_fr.pdf>> [accessed: 11th August 2017].

[270] Freedom House, Jerome Y. Bachelard and Richard R. Marcus, *Countries at the Crossroads 2011 – Madagascar,* (November 2011).

[271] Supra note 12, p.15: *"The Government also stated that officials of the transitional government had engaged in corruption, but it denied that such corruption was a continuing problem. Many other interlocutors, however, told the Special Rapporteur that corruption is still a significant problem, including in respect of mining concessions."*

[272] South China Morning Post, Agence France-Press, *How a gold mining deal in Africa inflamed hostility towards Chinese,* (December 2016)

[273] Mines and Communities, Press Release Appeal to Release the Leaders of Vona Association bringing together the representatives of the local communities opposed to the gold mining project in Soamahamanina – Madagascar, (September 2016).

Jiuxing's activities on the land. As a result, following a letter sent to the President of Madagascar, the mining company had its licenses temporarily suspended in July, with intervention by the Chinese Embassy and Government Council.[274]

Whilst the protestors had succeeded in getting Jiuxing's license suspended, weekly protests still continued, demanding the entire revocation of the company's activity on the land. In response, the company's manner of handling public contentions focused on attempting to drive a greater distance between themselves and local protestors, as opposed to relying on mutual dialogue based communication mechanisms to resolve underlying issues. The effect was to prolong and exacerbate tensions between the company and local society, further provoking the situation.

Heated protests in September 2016 resulted in riot police having been called in to handle the situation, with two particular protests involving heavy use of tear gas to disperse angry locals [Exhibit 6.4]. In addition, hostilities had been further aggravated when two representative leaders of the affected communities were detained. Subsequently the pair, Pierre Robson and Tsihoarana Andrianony, along with three others who had also been arrested, was released in November 2016 with one-year suspended sentences for unauthorised protesting.[275] Using the authorities to deal with public complaints only created further divide, non-conducive to finding a solution. In turn the case drew media attention and international NGOs into the mix, intensifying the negative public image surrounding Jiuxing and its operations.

---

[274] Human Rights Council, 34th Session, Report of the Special Rapporteur on the issue of human rights obligations relating to the enjoyment of a safe, clean, healthy and sustainable environment, on his visit to Madagascar, A/HRC/34/49/Add.1 (March 2017) [Note by the Secretariat] p.15: B. Mining Conflicts.

[275] Supra note 22, Human Rights Council; Front Line Defenders, ANNUAL REPORT on Human Rights Defenders at Risk in 2016, (Front Line Defenders Publishing, Ireland, 2016), p.9.

Exhibit 6.4

Source: Courtesy of Apple Daily <<http://www.appledaily.com.tw/ realtimenews/article/new/20170207/1050408/>>.

Such attempts by the company to remain passive and continue mining notwithstanding local contentions, eventually resulted in it having to stop operations within the Madagascan town altogether. By December 2016, the company acknowledged the need to ultimately abandon the investment project, after it was conceded that the protests were not likely to stop, nor were they likely to improve.

"As a company we think we have the right to stay, but for the sake of social appeasement, we chose to withdraw. We hope to return under new terms, (and) repair past mistakes."[276]

--Ms. Stella Andriamamonjy
(Official Spokeswoman of Jiuxing Mines)

---

[276] Supra note 6, Straits Times.

The key point of note here is the manner utilised by Jiuxing to handle local contentions. Rather than approaching the problem head on, the company's continuing absence and rejection of local concerns only transcended matters from a smaller, community based matter, into a much larger public outcry. Here it is appreciated that this arms-length approach for handling social discontent is in accords with the climate back in China, where social upheaval is regarded as a matter largely for the authorities and government bodies to deal with. However, in countries where government intervention is less prominent, such an approach no longer becomes suitable. In the case of Jiuxing, such a stance allowed external influences to play a bigger role in determining the company's fate; such as Madagascar's political opposition party, who has since been suggested to have prompted ongoing discord against the mine for political reasons.[277]

6.4 Importance of Communication: Risk Identification

The outcome of Jiuxing may have been better managed and even mitigated, had proper risk management mechanisms been put in place. In this regard, it is noted that all risk management strategies require, first and foremost, identification of risks. Indeed, it was at this very first hurdle that Jiuxing failed to adequately prepare themselves for entering the Madagascan market; which had already been noted to have a steadily growing anti-Chinese sentiment, alongside China's continued growth as Madagascar's largest trade partner. The pre-existing climate, along with the rather invasive nature of the extractive industries, should have forewarned the company that social and environmental unease over their mining activities was bound to arise. After all, in majority of cases,

---

[277] Supra note 22, Human Rights Council.

mining operations are frequently met with almost immediate social unrest, irrespective of the country involved.

Nonetheless, Jiuxing's continued behaviour of overlooking locals despite the growing presence of protests, demonstrated its inability in risk assessment; failing to identify the gravity and nature of the social and environmental risks that were facing the company. Here it is once again stressed that during the market entry of an investment project, companies ought to not only scout out an adequate location for proposed ventures from a technical and pragmatic perspective, but need to invest further resources into observing other contextual factors, e.g. biodiversity, ecological niches, local cultures and traditions, social taboos etc. This would have been particularly prudent within countries such as Madagascar, in which a long history of immigration has meant that in many ways the island represents: one country, many cultures. Accordingly, different parts of the island have experienced stronger influences from other countries such as India, Pakistan, Thailand, Japan etc. The net result, is that community needs and cultures are unlikely to be uniform across the entire country, necessitating further efforts of risk identification within ODI.

During operations, had Jiuxing Mines adequately identified the risks it was facing, it would have become clear that one of the major areas of discord with local communities, lay in the lack of discourse between themselves and the company. Such tensions were made clear through official correspondence that had been sent by local communities to the Malagasy government,[278] coupled with their united efforts in forming a Refusal Committee. With this in mind, the arms-length approach utilised by the company was counterintuitive; creating further separation between the local community and the mine. A number of tensions may have been easily diffused had Jiuxing attempted to engage with affected

---

[278] Supra note 21, Mines and Communities.

communities in open dialogue, reconcile the communication gap in the aligned interests of both the company and the locals. Upon doing so, the need to be transparent and respectful would be critical to developing relations and understanding between both parties, cementing their relationship for the future. After all, communication is the first step in helping to uncover overlapping or conflicting interests.

The importance of risk identification in the Jiuxing case was of such gravity, that the incident has provoked changes to Madagascan law. As of February 2017, new policies have been introduced to the country stipulating that a prerequisite for any investment opportunity in obtaining a mining license is for the company involved to first fulfil adequate environmental impact assessments. Within said assessments, it is now legally required for all investing companies to negotiate with local communities on sustainability matters, rendering the discourse between companies and locals as mandatory. Indeed, an entire section of the permit application form has even been dedicated to corporate social responsibility, emphasising the government's strengthened stance on environmental and social protection. The repercussions of such amendments to the law, holds that companies are now obligated to invest the time, money and resources into risk identification of investments, prior to commencing operations.

The drawback here of course, is that even after having undergone these assessment stages, there is no guarantee that the company will actually be granted the permit. The issue here lies in the lack of resource allocation by the domestic government to share the burden of costs that this requirement imposes upon investing companies. As such, foreign enterprises are required to invest significant amounts of their own capital into such procedures, with little to no help from the Malagasy government departments in subsidising the costs incurred. Nonetheless, the legal changes represent a step in the right direction: impressing upon companies the role and significance of risk identification as a crucial step in securing long term ODI. Oversight of this stage can lead to the same troubled end of Jiuxing, which has not only had to abandon its own gold mine, but has also prompted a 2 year suspension on all permits issued to mining concessions, and a complete prohibition ban against mining within a 900km2 radius of Madagascar's capital city centre.

6.5 Aligning Interets

However, it is not just risk management that is a useful tool for localisation. Indeed, risk management is concerned with identifying areas where the interests of an investing company and its stakeholders are likely to *conflict*. However, companies may be surprised at how effective social responsibility initiatives can be, when strategically implemented on the basis of identifying those areas where interests do not compete, but align with one another. For example, one unnamed Chinese gold mining company also situated in Madagascar, has developed its social responsibility by streamlining societal interests with that of its own. As such, in building the infrastructure needed for the mine to maintain its operations, the company considered how the same infrastructure may serve a dual purpose in benefitting local citizens. Roads developed for the transportation of mining equipment to the site, were strategically positioned where they would be of maximum benefit to local communities, who were in need of better transport facilities.

For such an endeavour to be of mutual benefit, it was important for the company to ensure, not only that the *output* of the development project was shared between the company and locals alike, but that the *input* was too. In this way the burdens and risks associated with the initiative could be more equally distributed, in much the same way that the benefits were. Locals were thus entrusted to aid in the design and layout of the proposed road, whilst also providing the manpower necessary for it to be built. In return, the company invested all necessary technical equipment and material resources for the road's construction.

In fact, these kinds of mutually beneficial projects can also help Chinese companies to fulfil their social responsibility with regards to the dissemination of technology and training; providing locals with the skills and experience needed for future employment. At the same time, the role of governments within such projects should not be underestimated. Indeed, government support can help to strengthen the long term goals of development projects in a whole myriad of ways. For instance, in the aforementioned example, host governments could be called upon for the maintenance of the new roads, protecting the project's long term benefits and securing its status as a *sustainable* initiative.

Such a holistic approach to localisation is far more effective than Jiuxing's alleged commitments to build roads, water supplies and provide access to electricity for local citizens. This is because by integrating local communities into the very initiatives designed to aid their development, companies can better ensure that the stated objectives of social responsibility projects meet their intended aims. In turn, the combined efforts of the company and locals in contributing to the initiative, secures it's presence long term, aligns the interests of business and stakeholder, and strengthens the interdependent relationships central to effective localisation. From an economic perspective, the strategy is further advantageous: rather than creating an entirely new commitment on behalf of society, the company strengthens an existing commitment by better integrating it within local needs.

To ensure that the interests of all parties have been appropriately safeguarded, initiatives reliant on shared contributions ought to be clearly outlined by all relevant parties. Accordingly, all meetings and consultations between the relevant stakeholders ought to have accurate minutes, signed by all relevant persons to confirm what has been negotiated and ultimately concluded. The existence of a paper trail provides companies, local communities and host governments, with piece of mind as to what has been established, along with confirmation on the finer details of their business relationship. In this way, the commitment becomes capable of quantification and enforcement, less likely to be regarded as simply *"greenwashing."*

Such an approach is purported by the notion that to aid a local community does not always mean that an investing company has to treat society's interests as independent to their own. Rather it is likely that there exists a common interest, shared between the company, society and government in light of the interdependency between all three. Finding a common aim for the benefit of all, can help companies to better conceptualise their social responsibility initiatives. After all the very process of localisation is the integration of the company into the local eco-system of its host overseas terrain.

In some cases, finding this common interest may not be so easy to achieve. Where this is the case, one recommended method for managing risks, lies in mediation. In fact mediation has been advocated by the United Nations Environment Programme as:

"An underexploited and useful tool that is often well suited to prevent and manage conflicts linked to natural resources."[279]

The process utilises the expertise of a trusted third party, independent actor, to facilitate the establishment of a compromise between stakeholders via rounds of consultation. Whilst this may inevitably require that a Chinese company has to relent on certain factors, the voluntary nature of mediation operates on a consensual basis. As such outcomes

---

[279] United Nations Department of Political Affairs (DPA) and United Nations Environment Programme (UNEP), Series Report No. 6, *Natural Resources and Conflict: A Guide for Mediation Practitioners*, (UN DPA and UNEP, 2015) p.10, s.1.1.

cannot be decided by the mediator but must be jointly agreed upon by all concerned parties.

The notable benefit of this process is to better position a company in identifying the problems at hand. A professional mediator possesses the ability to guide both parties to shift positions and hopefully appreciate the concerns of their counterpart. By providing a platform where issues are discussed with the mutual aim of finding a shared resolution, companies can begin to strategically assess how to manage their interests in the context of local communities. Indeed, the advantage of mediation lies in the balance that an independent actor can bring to the discourse between local communities and companies; diffusing any prejudices or distrust between the two.

6.6 Conclusion

The Jiuxing case illustrates the importance of risk identification with regards to environmental and social concerns. This is especially prominent in countries like Madagascar, which are renowned for their biodiversity and ecological significance. Indeed, this is not to say that particularly invasive industries such as: mining, construction, and agriculture, should not be condoned in said countries, as they can play a significant role in future development. Nonetheless, it provides Chinese companies with even greater cause to respect the landscape upon which they commence such operations; providing reason to ensure that they adequately identify, assess, prepare and manage for the risks that are inherent in such industrial sectors. At the same time, recognising new and innovative means for mutual development through the alignment of stakeholder interests, will help ensure that ODI aids the economic growth of both the company and host country.

6.7 Questions for Thought

1. In industries such as mining, construction and agriculture (where the very nature of operations has an impact upon the natural environment), is it ever possible to secure 100% approval from local communities?

2. Is a company's responsibility towards it stakeholders about balancing competing interests, or building on common interests?

3. How should a company approach local communities (such as in Madagascar), where a history of immigration has led to a cultural mix between people of all different countries?

4. How might existing xenophobia in a country affect the way in which a company approaches the local community? Does the presence of such biases render the project an automatic failure?

5. To what extent does the existence of corruption in a host country alter the dynamics of a company's responsibilities, strategies and ultimate reception?

6.8 Appendix

Madagascar: Background Profile

Exhibit 6.5 2016 Sustainable Development Goal Index_Madagascar Rating

2016 The SDG Index

Rank	Country	Score		Rank	Country	Score
1	Sweden	84.5		127	Sudan	42.2
2	Denmark	83.9		128	Burundi	42.0
3	Norway	82.3		129	Togo	40.9
4	Finland	81.0		130	Benin	40.0
5	Switzerland	80.9		131	Malawi	39.8
6	Germany	80.5		132	Mauritania	39.6
7	Austria	79.1		133	Mozambique	39.5
8	Netherlands	78.9		134	Zambia	38.4
9	Iceland	78.4		135	Mali	38.2
10	United Kingdom	78.1		136	Gambia, The	37.8
11	France	77.9		137	Yemen, Rep.	37.3
12	Belgium	77.4		138	Sierra Leone	36.9
13	Canada	76.8		139	Afghanistan	36.5
14	Ireland	76.7		140	Madagascar	36.2
15	Czech Republic	76.7		141	Nigeria	36.1

... continued

Source: United Nations Sustainable Development Solutions Network and Bertelsmann Stiftung, Leading writers: Jeffrey Sachs, Guido Schmidt-Traub, Christian Kroll, David Durand-Delacre and Katerina Teksoz, SDG Index and Dashboards – Global Report, (2016).

Exhibit 6.6 Madagascar Export Commodities

Madagascar Top 10 export commodities 2014 to 2016

HS code	4-digit heading of Harmonized System 2012	Value (million US$)		
		2014	2015	2016
	All Commodities	2 243.2	2 164.5	2 256.4
7502	Unwrought nickel	601.3	550.6	400.5
0905	Vanilla	118.2	208.5	408.3
6110	Jerseys, pullovers, cardigans, waist-coats and similar articles	139.6	142.1	144.6
0907	Cloves (whole fruit, cloves and stems)	114.2	161.6	149.9
8105	Cobalt mattes and other intermediate products of cobalt metallurgy	87.5	95.2	78.9
0306	Crustaceans, whether in shell or not	98.6	66.1	94.9
2710	Petroleum oils, other than crude	83.7	63.8	55.0
6203	Men's or boys' suits, ensembles, jackets, blazers, trousers	65.6	58.3	66.8
6214	Shawls, scarves, mufflers, mantillas, veils and the like	66.0	38.5	45.8
2614	Titanium ores and concentrates	60.7	32.4	40.3

HS code	Unit value				SITC code
	2014	2015	2016	Unit	
7502	16.6	11.6	9.5	US$/kg	683
0905	50.2	74.7	253.8	US$/kg	075
6110	33.1			US$/unit	845
0907	9.7	7.9	7.2	US$/kg	075
8105	30.1	27.5	24.2	US$/kg	689
0306	9.4	9.3	10.1	US$/kg	036
2710	1.3	1.0	0.6	US$/kg	334
6203					841
6214					846
2614	0.2	0.2	0.2	US$/kg	287

Source: United Nations Comtrade, 2016 International Trade Statistics Yearbook, Vol. 1 p.242 (Madagascar Profile)

Madagascar's exports largely consist of natural resources and the manufacture of apparel.

Jiuxing Mines: Local Community Opposition

Exhibit 6.7 Statement made by Malagasy Civil Society Organisations against Jiuxing Mines Activities

---

THE ENVIRONNEMENTAL PERMIT GRANTED TO THE COMPANY JIUXING MINES S.A.R.L FOR ITS MINING PROJECT IN SOAMAHAMANINA IS NOT ACCEPTABLE

The civil society organisations that have signed the present Declaration express their solidarity with and full support of the rejection by the local population of the gold mining project of JIUXING MINES S.A.R.L. in Soamahamanina, following the meetings and exchanges of their representatives since Tuesday 21 June 2016 with the established Refusal Committee of gold mining by this Chinese company.

For several months, thousands of the residents of Soamahamanina and neighbouring communities have been opposing this project for which an environmental permit for gold mining has just been issued by the National Office for the Environment (ONE) for a duration of 40 years.

The reasons for the refusal of this mining project by the local communities are clear and undisputable.

The first reason is about the complete disregard of the concerned local population by the permit holder and State authorities at different levels: the large majority of the seven (7) communities (fokontany) affected by the mining project has not been consulted, or has refused the project. Threats of repression have been made in response to their demands and expressions of opinion. They strongly suspect that there was corruption among the causes of the current situation and they have filed a complaint with the BIANCO, the entity in charge of the fight against corruption.

These local communities are also opposing the grabbing of their lands and natural resources on which they rely for their livelihoods, along with the loss of the living spaces and food sources of the communities living in the mining concession.

These local communities are also opposing the grabbing of their lands and natural resources on which they rely for their livelihoods, along with the loss of the living spaces and food sources of the communities living in the mining concession.

In addition, the local population affected by the gold mining project strongly object to the disrespect for their cultural and traditional values brought about by the destruction of their tombs. Likewise, they refuse the destruction of the church and school that are enclosed in the mining concession.

Furthermore, the local population is strongly opposed to the loss of the "tapia" forest that is part of a protected area and constitutes a vital source of income for the local silk producers. The concerned communities do not want negative environmental impacts entailed by the use of heavy extraction machinery by JIUXING MINES S.A.R.L., such as water pollution and mudding of rice fields.

Current events together with the actual risks involved clearly demonstrate that the basic human rights of the communities affected by the gold mining project in Soamahamanina and neighbouring communities are seriously endangered.

We, as signatories of civil society, denounce this violation of the basic human rights of the local population, as well as the willingness of State authorities to silence its legitimate opposition by means of the threat of use of repression forces.

We remind the State authorities that they are primarily responsible for the protection and realisation of the rights of all Malagasy citizens, and that they must refrain from using disproportionate means of repression by law enforcement forces to prevent people from claiming their rights.

It should also be noted that granting an environmental permit to projects that destroy the environment and people seems to have become a standard practice of the ONE, as everyone could see in relation to the process of issuing a highly questionable permit to the Toliara Sands Company for ilmenite exploitation in the area of Toliara II.

航企下架去哪儿机票引关注 整治违规机票代理成关键 (2016)

人民网北京 3 月 21 日电 （记者叶欣）

从年初携程的"兑换机票"、"无效电子票号"引发的信任危机，到近日的几大航企从去哪儿网全线下架代理机票，违规机票代理（以下简称"票代"）显然成为了这些事件背后的"罪魁祸首"。如何整顿票代市场，已成为横亘在 OTA 与航企之间的一道坎儿。对票代市场的整治效果，也切实关系到旅客的利益。

票代市场鱼龙混杂、旅客权益难保

据悉，目前国内票代市场鱼龙混杂，除了合法票代外，还充斥着一定数量的"黑票代"，即那些未取得中国航协颁发的票代资质却仍在销售机票的机构。近年来，"黑票代"也开始借助一些 OTA 大平台贩卖机票，甚至通过自行绑定保险产品、收取不合理的高额退改签费用赚钱。

据业内人士介绍，早在 2014 年，南航和东航就曾向一些 OTA 企业下发了一份《关于规范互联网机票销售秩序的通知》，要求"代理人在携程、去哪儿、淘宝上销售机票时，需在订票页面展示其取得航协资质时使用的代理人名称，以及航协资质号"，但此举似乎并未奏效。

近日，南航在要求去哪儿网正式下架所有南航机票产品的公告中也表示，近期公司收到多起旅客在去哪儿网购票所引发的投诉，仅 2016 年 1~2 月累计投诉已达 79 单。投诉主要涉及网络代理违规收取变更退票费用、提供虚假客票、对航班变动未尽通知责任、泄露旅客信息进行诈骗、盗用旅客信息虚占航空公司待销售座位等情况，给旅客造成不同程度的损失，严重损害消费者的合法权益。

而在此前，国航和海航在下架去哪儿网机票产品时，提出的原因也基本相同。

Source: Mines and Communities (2016)

<<http://www.minesandcommunities.org/article.php?a=13444>>   [accessed on 15th July 2017]

Civil Society Organisations comprised of:

1). Centre de Recherches et d'Appui pour les Alternatives de Développement – Océan Indien;

2). RESEAU SOA – Syndicat des Organisations Agricoles;

3). Collectif pour la défense des terres malgaches – TANY. Association MAZOTO – Miaro Aina -Zon'Olombelona sy Tontolo iainana;

4). SeFaFi - Observatoire de la vie publique;

5). Plate-forme de la Société Civile de la Région DIANA;

6). Fédération des Femmes Rurales de Madagascar;

7). Projet TARATRA, and 8). Solidarité des Intervenants sur le Foncier.

Exhibit 6.8 Madagascar Media Coverage Front Page News

Source: Mouvement des Citoyens Malagasy de Paris, Raharimanana Patrick, Orinasa sinoa Jiuxing. Fitrandrahana volamena tsy ankasitrahany vahoaka, Miarinarivo-Itasy, (2016).

Exhibit 6.9 Urgent Appeal for release of Pierre Robson and Tsihoarana Andrianony_Front Line Defenders

27 September 2016

Madagascar – Environmental rights defenders Pierre Robson and Tsihoarana Andrianony arrested and charged

On 23 September 2016, the Court of First Instance at Anosy ordered pre-trial detention for two environmental rights defenders, Messrs Pierre Robson and Tsihoarana Andrianony and charged them on four counts including breach of state security. Their arrest follows a series of mass protests that the two defenders helped to organise against gold mining at Soamahamanina by a Chinese company, Jiuxing Mines S.A.R.L.

Pierre Robson and Tsihoarana Andrianony are the co-presidents of the association VONA, a local organisation that defends environmental rights, and which was one of the main groups organising the recent mass movement at Soamahamanina. VONA is supported by the TANY Collective, a coalition of organisations working to defend Malagasy land and natural resources against land grabbing, and to support development for both urban and rural citizens of Madagascar. The campaign called for suspension of gold mining in the region, amid accusations of irregularities by the defenders and other environmental actors.

On 6 July 2016, the TANY Collective addressed an open letter to the President of the Republic where they requested his intervention to discontinue the gold, zinc, iron, lead and berillium mining at Soamahamanina and in the surrounding area. Among the problems raised to warrant their request were (1) lack of participation and consultation of the population; (2) the lack of respect for the rights of the population that lives at these locations including the lack of respect for their land rights; and (3) degradation of the environment including adverse impact on two rivers, the Ikalariana and the Irihatra, destruction of the tapia forest, and destruction of nearby hills and plains.

On 15 September 2016, the defenders had requested that the government order a permanent shutdown of activities by Jiuxing Mines S.A.R.L. After one week had elapsed without a response to their request, on 22 September 2016, the inhabitants of Soamahamanina went to the streets to protest. The protest resulted in violence as the police released tear gas on the protestors and certain members of the protest threw rocks. Pierre Robson and Tsihoarana Andrianony were not involved in the violence. Later in the day, the defenders were followed by law enforcement officials who arrested them. After a preliminary interview at Miarinarivo, the defenders were transferred to Antananarivo as subjects of an investigation at the court at Anosy.

On 23 September 2016, the defenders were tried in court and charged on four counts. The charges include breach of state security, leading a non-authorised protest, and destruction of common property. The defenders will also be held responsible for a law enforcement official's loss of his gun that disappeared during the dispersal of the protestors at Soamahamanina. After they were indicted, the defenders were taken to a detention center at Antanimora where they await their trial.

Front Line Defenders is sincerely concerned by the arrest and indictment of defenders Pierre Robson and Tsihoarana Andrianony as they are solely motivated by their promotion of and protection for rights linked to the environment. Front Line Defenders urges the authorities in Madagascar to:

1. Immediately and unconditionally release Pierre Robson and Tsihoarana Andrianony;

2. Immediately drop all charges against Pierre Robson and Tsihoarana Andrianony as it is believed that they are solely motivated by his legitimate and peaceful work in defence of human rights;

3. Guarantee in all circumstances that all human rights defenders in Madagascar are able to carry out their legitimate human rights activities without fear of reprisals and free of all restrictions.

Source: Front Line Defenders

<<https://www.frontlinedefenders.org/en/case/tsihoarana-andrianony-released>> [accessed on 24th July 2017].

7

THE CASE OF LENOVO AND SUPERFISH

Supply Chain Management: Adware Turns Malware

7.1 Case Background

Case studies 3-6 focus predominantly on those industry sectors whose international presence requires the export of business operations to a host country. However, in a number of instances, Chinese ODI is driven neither by cheaper manufacturing costs nor by the resources available abroad, but rather on the accessibility of a new consumer market.

In such cases, consideration needs to be paid to respecting the rights and interests of overseas consumers; necessitating an understanding of safety issues, differences in expectations and general consumer rights. Indeed, as the case of Lenovo and Superfish highlights, such matters are important for all companies to heed, even when they already occupy a dominant position in the international market.

Lenovo, a prime example of successful Chinese ODI, is internationally reputed for its well-known brand as one of the leading tech companies around today. Specialising in the sale of electronic hardware, the company has quickly escalated in size, growth and reputation, especially since its successful purchase of IBM's computing division in 2005.[280]

---

[280] Cheung Kong Graduate School of Business, Li Hui, *Chinese Outbound Investment in Technology: Bits, Bytes, and all things Tech,* (November 2014).

The leading brand of Thinkpad acquired that maintains a large number of loyal customers around the globe is expected to exalt the brand equity of the company's entire portfolio onto a new height. In fact, Lenovo is the only accredited Chinese one in parallel to Huawei that has climbed into the top-100 global brands by Interbrand in recent years.

Yet despite its renowned reputation, the company like all others, is largely affected by the rapidly changing market trends within the tech industry. After all, today's market is getting hungrier for new technology, has higher expectations for the integration of new technologies in daily life, and are exposed to greater variety of choice, necessitating that companies need do more to remain competitive. The rapid increase in computers, laptops, tablets, and all sorts of other gadgets and gismos, has left a large proportion of today's consumers expecting electronic products at much cheaper prices.

Exhibit 7.1 Average per-PC Profit for Five Largest PC Manufactuers

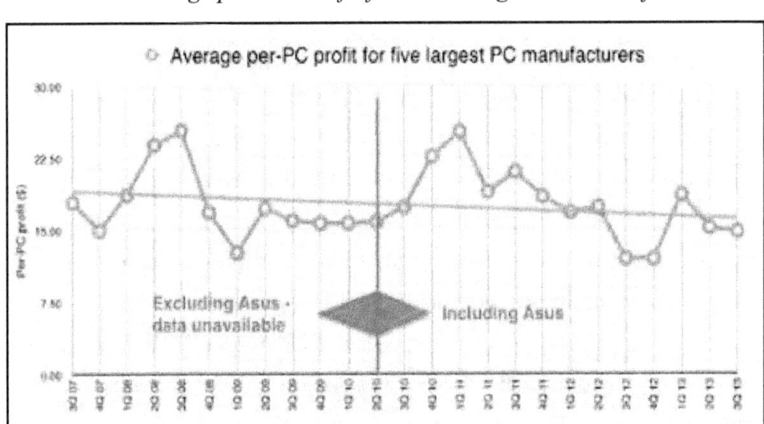

Source:

<<http://bgr.com/2014/01/10/pc-profits-analysis-margins/>> [accessed on 13th March 2017]

Data as of 2014.

As a result, the profitability of computer-based businesses has decreased significantly, with even large companies only enjoying a very small profit margin from the sale of hardware products [Exhibit 7.1]. In order to ensure a more sustainable business model, it has therefore become common practice for companies to gain extra profits through collaborations with software enterprises. Such collaborations take the form of business agreements, by which the hardware company preinstalls software onto its devices for a fee. This enables the hardware company to earn extra profits in exchange for pre-installations, whilst strengthening its competitive advantage over similar third party products. The software company is equally benefitted as a result of increased exposure and consumer access for its software applications.[281] As such the overall integration of hard and software, sold together as one complete package, operates to the mutual benefit of both companies.

7.2 Superfish: "Visual Discovery"

On the basis of such rationale, many leading electronics brands including the aforementioned Lenovo, have begun to preinstall software programmes onto their products before selling them on to consumers. For Lenovo, one of these such software programmes, installed on Lenovo devices towards the latter half of 2014, was "Visual Discovery"; an adware programme developed by a company called: *Superfish.*

The purposes of Visual Discovery (as adware), was to analyse images that a PC user was looking at, in order to inject adverts containing similar images for the user to see. In this way consumers could be enticed to buy products directly suited to their interests; providing a platform for individually tailored advertising. In turn, consumers too would be able to benefit, as such adverts would enable them to see similar

---

[281] The Guardian, Charles Arthur, *Lenovo Demonstrates that Malware is big business,* (February 2015).

products available on the market at more competitive prices; thus widening their scope of choice.

Superfish's unique selling point with Visual Discovery lay in its focus on *image recognition*, differentiating it from other competitors. Whilst other adware companies have previously developed recognition software for the same purposes, monitoring and analyzing the activity of PC users to provide them with more direct and targeted advertising, they tend to do so on the basis of *text based behavioural recognition*. Such programmes operate by identifying the types of interests that a PC user has based on his/her search enquiries, and collating this information to create an online behavioural profile. This in turn enables the software to learn things about users based on their internet search history, online shopping information and so and so forth. For many consumers, this sort of 'online profiling' is uncomfortable from an ethical standpoint, compromising consumer privacy in exchange for profit. At the very least, it is a disconcerting thought that personal computers, a highly integrated part of modern living, are capable of inferring things without its user knowing.

In light of such ethical concerns, Visual Discovery presented an alternative approach to adware:

"purely based on contextual/image and not behavioural. It does not profile nor monitor user behaviour. It does not record user information. It does not know who the user is. Users are not tracked nor re-targeted. Every session is independent."[282]

As such, the software theoretically demonstrated a greater respect for consumer online privacy as compared with regular adware.

Taking this into account, Lenovo entered into contractual business dealings with Superfish to preinstall the software onto its Notebook

---

[282] Timothy Seppala, *New Lenovo PCs Shipped with factory-installed adware*, (February 2015).

products in 2014; with a goal *"to improve [consumer] shopping experience using [Superfish's] visual discovery techniques."[283]* It was stressed here by Lenovo that the primary aim of the pre-installation, lay in improving end-user experience for Lenovo customers as opposed to financial gain.

The software was subsequently preinstalled onto Lenovo Notebooks distributed to customers between September 2014 until January 2015; encompassing a range of up to 52 different models.[284] Yet fundamental problems with Superfish' adware were quickly discovered, relating both to user enjoyment and more pressingly, to problems of consumer safety. As a direct result of consumer apoplexy coupled with severe consumer privacy concerns, Lenovo gummed up the forlorn plight owing to inherent problems with the parasitic Visual Discovery software of its business partner.

7.3 Consumer Protection

Just a few months after Visual Discovery had been distributed through Lenovo notebook sales, customer sparring in December 2014 highlighted problems associated with the adware. Contentions initially arose that the software was interrupting user enjoyment of notebook products as a result of annoying advert pop-ups. However, such concerns quickly grew in both seriousness and degree when fundamental privacy and security concerns were identified. It was noted that the Superfish technology left consumers' confidential online information vul-

---

[283] Lenovo Official Public Statement on the Superfish Matter <<http://news.lenovo.com/news-releases/lenovo-statement-on-superfish.htm>> [accessed on 16th March 2017].

[284] Lenovo Official Website, commenting on the basic facts of the Superfish controversy   <<https://support.lenovo.com/us/zh/product_security/superfish>> [accessed on 17th March 2017].

nerable to malware and malicious attacks,[285] making it surprisingly easy for hackers to obtain personal information such as: passwords; electronic communication; and even bank transactions from unsuspecting users. The safety concern was caused as a direct result of the way in which the software operated, and was thereby an intrinsic flaw embedded within the product itself. As a result, the average Lenovo customer was left unsuspecting that their privacy was at such a risk, leading to consumer outrage at Lenovo for failing to inform them about the preinstalled adware.[286]

The magnitude of the privacy concerns relating to Visual Discovery were particularly severe, infringing upon the legal rights of a vast majority of consumers protected by international and/or national laws. Such laws ensure that goods and services sold to the public in a business to consumer capacity, conform to certain safety and security measures. In this respect, consumer rights extend to the negligent actions of those involved further up in the supply chain, emphasizing the duty of care that is owed regardless of whether a company was aware of the flaws in its product or not. As such, legal issues relating to misrepresentation and product liability, which compromise the integrity of consumer protection, were bound to transpire; and indeed Lenovo found itself almost immediately a target for potential lawsuits from affected customers.[287]

It thereby came as no surprise, that upon learning of the error, Lenovo was quick to act to remedy the situation. By mid-January 2015, the company had already shut down server connections which enabled

---

[285] New York Times, Nicole Perlroth, *Lenovo's Chief Technology Officer Discusses the Superfish Adware Fiasco,* (February 2015) Interview with Peter Hortensius.

[286] BBC News, Jane Wakefield, *Lenovo taken to task over 'malicious' adware,* (February 2015).

[287] Cnet, Lance Whitney, *Lenovo hit by lawsuit over Superfish adware,* (February 2015). For further information regarding the potential illegality of Lenovo's actions as a result of the Superfish controversy, see here:

the Superfish software to run, and released user friendly guides and 'fixes' enabling consumers to independently remove the Superfish application from their products. In acknowledgement that the company had "messed up badly ... [failing to] understand the significant security problem that [Superfish] presented",[288] the company not only publicly apologized for the threat posed by the pre-installation, but recognized the need for a "plan to rebuild [consumer] trust."[289]Accordingly the company promised that in future it would only provide 'clean' hardware, significantly reducing the number of add-ons pre-installed onto its products.[290]

Exhibit 7.2 Laptop Brand Rankings

LAPTOP — BRAND RANKINGS YEAR-TO-YEAR

Rank	2013	2014	2015	2016	2017	Brand	Change
1ST						Lenovo	↑3
2ND						Asus	↑1
3RD						Dell	1
4TH						HP	↑2
5TH						Acer	↑3
6TH						Apple	↓5
7TH						MSI	1
8TH						Razer	--
9TH						Samsung	--
10TH						Microsoft	↓3

*Recent additions: MSI (2015), Microsoft (2016) and Razer (2017)

Source: Laptop, Best and Worst Laptop Brands 2017, (2017)
<< https://www.laptopmag.com/articles/laptop-brand-ratings>>

---

[288] Cnet, Seth Rosenblatt, *Lenovo's Superfish screw-up highlights biggest problem in software,* (February 2015).

[289] Supra note 6, New York Times, Nicole Perlroth interview with Peter Hortensius.

[290] Supra note 10, Cnet.

Despite Lenovo's attempts to resolve the problem quickly and efficiently, the Superfish controversy greatly affected the public image of the corporate giant [Exhibit 7.2]. In the months following the controversy Lenovo received considerably more scrutiny, particularly with regards to its pre-installed applications. For instance, in September 2015, the company was subjected to negative criticisms against its "Lenovo Customer Feedback" software. The software, labelled as 'spyware' on the basis of how it operates,[291] has since been conceded to be no more invasive than those belonging to other tech based companies.

"Had this been any other PC vendor, this might be a triviality. Certainly Microsoft is doing far more tracking in Windows 10".[292]

However the comments related to Lenovo gave more cause for concern; illustrating the lasting impact of the Superfish scandal, in placing the "Lenovo" brand under a more scrupulous eye. Indeed, technology forums indicate a distrust for Lenovo products following the well-publicised Superfish scandal. The company's overall rating as a PC supplier fell drastically in 2015 in the subsequent months.[293] Consequently, whilst the defective software may have been remedied within a matter of months, remedying the damage done to Lenovo's reputation appears as though it will take a whole lot longer.

---

[291]   See: <<http://thehackernews.com/2015/09/lenovo-laptop-virus.html>>   - article written in September 2015 on "Lenovo Customer Feedback software" as spyware.

[292] ComputerWorld, Thinkpad, Michael Horowitz, *Lenovo Collects usage data on ThinkPad, ThinkCentre and ThinkStation PCs,* (September 2015).

[293]   Laptop   Magazine   <<http://www.laptopmag.com/articles/laptop-brand-ratings>> [accessed on 5th March 2017].

7.4 Lessons Learnt

Here it is noted that the Superfish controversy is not an isolated case, and highlights difficulties inherent in most industries, particularly that of electronic goods and technology. Similar scandals have recently come to light in March 2017, regarding leading mobile companies of the likes of Samsung and Xiaomi whose products have also been found to include malware in their operating systems. Whilst these recent examples differ from the Lenovo case, occurring as unauthorised pre-installations and therefore without the mobile companies' knowledge,[294] they reflect the same challenges of supply chain management as faced by Lenovo. After all, maintaining effective quality control standards is much harder in the long supply chains used today, often spanning different countries and continents; let alone for products that are non-tangible.

Indeed, it is acknowledged within the technology industry that the ability to guarantee safety of software is especially tricky as compared with other industrial products, due to the elusive nature of computer code. This is because despite quality control checks conducted to independently verify software as safe, the very nature of computer code means that it may react differently when integrated within other software. In turn, it becomes much harder to determine how the code will behave when installed on different devices with different operating systems. This not only makes it harder for the safety of code to be guaranteed, but leads to more expensive quality control mechanisms. Indeed it has been noted that aviation related software is generally 10 to 100 times more expensive to create than ordinary code, simply because its quality controls need to ensure an even greater level of safety.[295]

---

[294] Checkpoint, Oren Koriat, *Preinstalled Malware targeting Mobile Users,* (March 2017).
[295] Supra note 10, Cnet.

Given that computer products already suffer from particularly narrow profit margins, the burden of maintaining such a high degree of quality control may be impractical from a purely financial perspective. However, notwithstanding these difficulties, it is clear from the controversy raised by the Superfish scandal, that there still exists a need to take added precautions for the sake of maintaining a reliable brand and strong reputation.

7.4.1 Supply Chain Management

"By not properly vetting the Superfish adware, Lenovo became... [Another] unwitting example of broken links in the software supply chain."[296]

Exhibit 7.3 Supply China

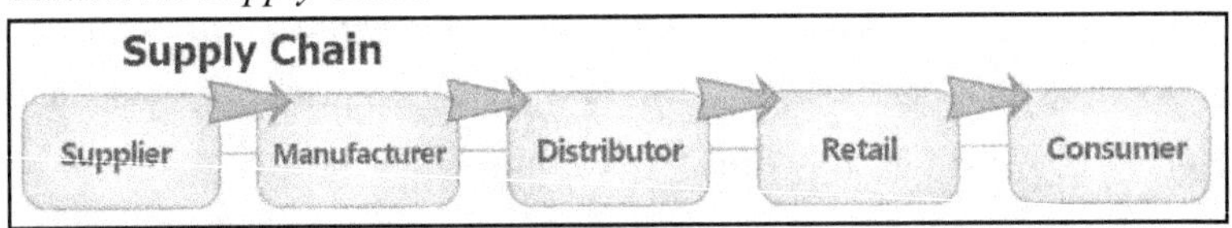

Source: Created by the Author.

One of the primary lessons learnt by Lenovo's misgivings, is the need for corporations in all industries to ensure effective due diligence capable of penetrating long supply chains [Exhibit 7.3]. As highlighted by responses to the scandal, it is no longer possible for corporations to evade responsibility by simply outsourcing from other companies. All laws pertaining to consumer liability dictates recourse to the immediate seller regardless of what contract terms they enter with the supplier. This isn't to say that companies must source, manufacture, distribute and sell products as an entirely in-house operation; but rather to emphasise that a corporation's due diligence extends further than internal processes and production. Diligence needs to be paid to the manner in which outsourc-

---

[296] Supra note 10, Cnet.

ing takes place and the selection process in finding suitable business partners.

After all, as admitted by Lenovo, the Superfish controversy was caused in part, due to the company's own inadequacies in prior research concerning the competences of its business partner. This, coupled with a failure to appropriately vet its products, prevented the risks associated with Visual Discovery from being discovered. In particular, was Lenovo's failure to investigate further along the supply chain, in order to account for the integrity of all aspects of the software.[297] Indeed, later findings discovered that the source of the security flaw could be rooted back to an outsourced company called "Komodia"[298]; an enterprise specializing in network interception. Komodia's programming was directly linked to the security error that had led to fundamental privacy problems within the Visual Discovery code.

It has since been contended that had the relationship and interchange between Komodia and Superfish been adequately investigated into by Lenovo, it may well have been possible for the defect in the Visual Discovery software to be detected much earlier on. This is especially given that the primary business activities of Komodia were to provide technology specifically capable of undermining internet encryption codes, those pivotal in ensuring the internet security of confidential information.

Such contentions reiterate the importance for corporations to ensure that they are made fully aware of all foreseeable aspects of companies with whom they enter into business dealings with, including those third party businesses that may in turn enter the supply chain by proxy. In

---

[297] Supra note 6, New York Times, Nicole Perlroth interview with Peter Hortensius: *"We were told by Superfish that they were using Komodia but we never looked into it...Superfish had a good reputation. But we should have dug in more. I won't debate that."*

[298] Tech Times, Anu Passary, *Worried About Superfish?: Worry more about Komodia SSL Hole and Here Why,* (February 2015).

order to do so, thorough background checks and examinations ought to factor into the decision making process for concluding business related contracts.

Such a need was exacerbated in the case of Lenovo and Superfish, given that the business arrangement between both companies was largely motivated by the way in which Lenovo's well-known brand would help to popularize the lesser known Superfish one. Accordingly, the very nature of the arrangement recognized Superfish as a lesser known, less experienced enterprise; giving Lenovo greater reason to investigate thoroughly into its technological expertise and competences before risking its own reputation by affiliation.

Indeed, years prior to its engagement with Lenovo, Superfish had already received complaints about its software from leading tech companies, questioning the proficiency of its business operations.[299] This coupled with the security problems that had been detected by Lenovo during internal screenings of Visual Discovery,[300] ought to have prompted further investigation into the product prior to its dissemination to the public.

It is noted here that the aim isn't to accuse Superfish for failing to achieve adequate security in its products, but to emphasise the need for corporations to equip themselves with as much knowledge of the supply chain as possible, so that their collaborations with other businesses may be strengthened. Only then may the responsibility for enterprises to engage in due diligence, be secured throughout a product's entire life span. In the case of Lenovo, further investigation and research into Superfish might have enabled the defects in Visual Discovery to be remedied earlier on; establishing a win-win for both companies.

---

[299] Forbes, Thomas Fox-Brewster, *Superfish: a History of Malware Complaints and International Surveillance,* (February 2015).
[300] Slate, David Auerbach, *Are Lenovo and Superfish Evil or Incompetent?* (February 2015).

7.4.2 Consumer Interests

The second lesson learnt from the Superfish controversy, arises with respect to consumer interests. One particular area of contention was the fact that the Lenovo hardware sold to consumers, did not clearly disclose the existence of the pre-installed software. Whilst it has since been argued by Lenovo that consumers could have opted out from using Visual Discovery on their devices by selecting "I don't want to use this" when first installing their PCs; it is clear that a number of consumers were still left unaware of the software's existence.[301]

Given that it is common practice and common knowledge that consumers frequently agree to the generic Terms and Conditions on instalment packages (without ensuring that they properly read through the specifics), enterprises ought to be aware of the risk that whilst this constitutes legally binding notice, in actuality it may achieve very little. In acknowledgement of this fact, it may no longer be enough for companies to convey essential information through such vehicles, without risking the possibility that a large majority of their consumers remain ignorant towards this form of disclosure.

This acts as a reminder of the ever-changing nature of a corporation's social responsibility; intrinsically linked to the development of society. As such, it is of utmost importance that corporations continuously develop new and innovative means for achieving realistic communication with stakeholders, rather than relying on more traditional and outdated methods.

Furthermore, it is emphasized that the focus of such responsibility concerns the greater needs and interests of society, external and above mere legal requirements. As such, whilst Terms and Conditions establish legal agreements with consumers, safeguarding companies from future

---

[301] Supra note 6, New York Times, Nicole Perlroth interview with Peter Hortensius.

legal disputes; the wider purposes of disclosure focus on ensuring greater transparency for fostering stronger relationships and discourse with stakeholders. In accordance with this purpose, it is not so relevant whether consumers 'opted in' or 'agreed' to using Visual Discovery, but rather that enough had been done to make them aware of the pre-installed application on their device. I.e.: that attention was drawn to the existing business relationship held between Lenovo and Superfish.

Another consideration worth taking into account is the fact that even before Visual Discovery's security issue was unveiled, Lenovo's decision to pre-install the software had already received bad reviews. These reviews were specifically targeted against the adware's intended activities, which were seen as an inconvenience to user enjoyment. Customers voiced their anger at the annoying advert pop ups caused by Superfish, questioning Lenovo's true motives behind installing the software.

"[What] are Lenovo doing installing it on new systems? To squeeze a few more pennies out of customers?"[302]

Ironically, Lenovo had defended it's installation on the basis that the pre-installed software would enhance user experience. This contradiction demonstrates that enough research had not been conducted by the company to truly determine the needs of consumers. Had Lenovo conducted prior market research, working with its customers to determine which types of software would be preferable for user experience; the negative repercussions of the controversy might have been mitigated. After all, a company is less likely to be alienated for its mistakes, where consumers can see that the intended objective was in their best interests. However, public backlash was worsened in the case at hand by notions that Lenovo had not only exposed its customers to such security and

---

[302] Lenovo Customer Feedback Forums, pg. 1.
<<https://forums.lenovo.com/t5/forums/v3_1/forumtopicpage/board-id/1104_en/thread-id/79856/page/1>> [accessed 16th March 2017].

privacy risks, but "did it for no good reason"[303]; that "Superfish exist[ed] to help push advertising, not to serve any real consumer need."[304] The knowledge deficit in the company's understanding of modern market needs, highlight a crucial communication gap with its stakeholders, undermining market research and product creation.

Nevertheless, the company's customer feedback channels are praiseworthy in providing the platform upon which Lenovo was able to quickly detect and resolve the situation at hand. By virtue of the company's internal communication mechanisms, in the way of customer feedback forums, end consumers were provided with an easy-to-access, free and efficient manner of communicating their troubles online. Indeed, despite contentions that the problem could have been remedied even quicker had the warnings of experts been acknowledged earlier on, it still stands that through such aftercare efforts, Lenovo was able to discover the critical security risk posed by Superfish much quicker. At the same time, the company utilised the platform to efficiently disseminate quick fixes, mitigating the damage caused by the software.

The need to maintain long lasting communication with stakeholders for the long term interests of the company is thus clear; not only to secure consumer loyalty, but to further strengthen quality control, by providing a platform by which any defects may be identified and remedied at a later stage. In this respect, it is conceded that the company succeeded in securing an adequate and realistic means for maintaining aftercare communication.

---

[303] Supra note 23, Slate, David Auerbach.

[304] Consumer Reports, Donna Tapellini, *How Lenovo's Dangerous Superfish Adware puts its Customers at Risk,* (February 2015).

7.5 Conclusion

The Superfish controversy highlights rather specific practical difficulties that have emerged in the technological sector; dealing with intangible products such as software code. Nonetheless, the case also offers observations and reflections that are suitable to a multitude of industries. With today's commercial enterprises utilizing even longer supply chains than before, the need to improve communication along production and distribution lines has become more important than ever. As such, it is no longer enough for a corporation to focus solely on its own operations when fulfilling its corporate responsibility to stakeholders; there exists a further need to ensure protective mechanisms between its stakeholders and business relations too.

Alongside this greater accountability is the need to recognize the particular focus of commercial law in recent years, for the protection of consumer rights. That being said, it is in the best interests of a corporation to go over and beyond its duties prescribed by law, and ensure higher levels of transparency and communication with its target market.

Indeed, given the susceptibility of technology to hackers, viruses and other forms of malicious attack, it is strongly suggested that all companies within the technology sector commit themselves to cyber security policies, and do so in a way that penetrates the supply chain to ensure the ultimate protection of consumers. After all, it's only a matter of time before cyber security becomes a strengthened legal field in itself, and today's mere "responsibility" transitions to tomorrow's "obligation."

7.6 Questions for Thought

1. Following a high-profile controversy such as the "Visual Discovery" one, what mechanisms may be employed for rebuilding consumer trust?

2. How far back along the supply chain is a corporation reasonably expected to research into? Does this differ depending on the status and size of the corporation in question?

3. How might a corporation ensure that due diligence penetrates the supply chain?

4. If the Visual Discovery adware hadn't caused such serious security concerns, do you think Lenovo's reputation might still have been damaged by pre-installing such software onto its devices with little disclosure?

7.7 Appendix

Discovery: Consumer Safety Concerns

Exhibit 7.4 Customer Feedback Outlining the Dangers of Visual Discovery. Source: Lenovo Customer Feedback Forum

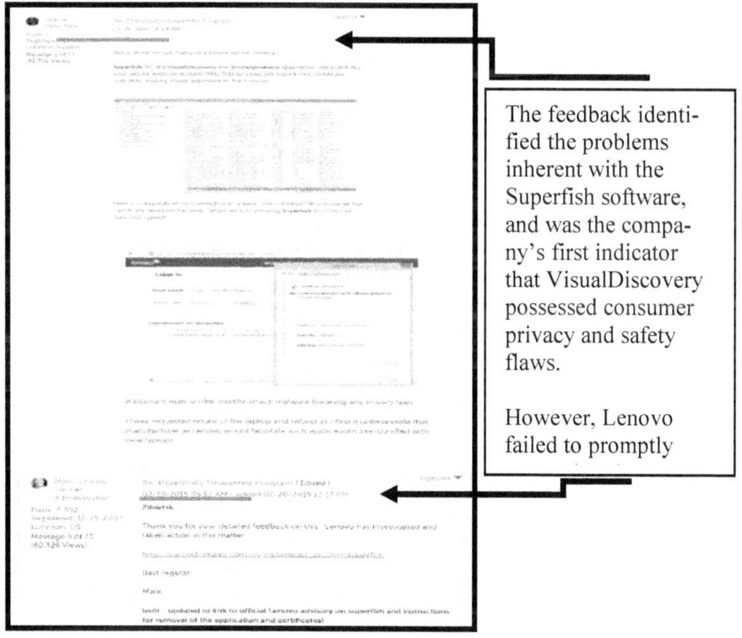

Exhibit 7.5 U.S. Attorney General_Public Announcement of $3.5 million Legal Settlement following VisualDiscovery Scandal [emphasis added]

TRENTON – *Attorney General Christopher S. Porrino announced today that New Jersey has joined with 31 other states in an overall, $3.5 million settlement with Lenovo Inc. that resolves allegations the technology company violated state consumer protection laws by pre-installing software in laptop computers that made users' personal information vulnerable to hackers.* The settlement was negotiated in coordination with the Federal Trade Commission.

"This is an important settlement for New Jersey consumers because it sets down a variety of conditions designed to ensure that, going forward, Lenovo will better protect the personal identifying information of consumers, be more transparent about what software is pre-installed on the products it sells, and *provide consumers clearer and more accessible ways to opt out of having such software activated* – or present on the machine at all," said Attorney General Porrino.

In August 2014, North Carolina-based Lenovo began selling certain laptop computers that contained pre-installed ad software called VisualDiscovery, which was created by the company Superfish, Inc. VisualDiscovery purportedly operated as a shopping assistant by delivering pop-up ads to consumers of similar looking products sold by Superfish retail partners whenever a customer's mouse hovered over the image of a product on a shopping Web site. The states alleged that VisualDiscovery displayed a one-time pop-up window when consumers visited a shopping web site for the first time. Unless consumers affirmatively opted out, VisualDiscovery would then be enabled on their computers.

According to the states, VisualDiscovery operated by acting as a local proxy, or "man in the middle," that stood between the consumer's browser and all Internet web sites that the user visited, including encrypted sites. This technique allowed the software to see all of a user's sensitive personal information that was transmitted on the Internet. Consumer information-- including sensitive communications with encrypted Web sites-- would be collected and transmitted to Superfish.

The states alleged that Visual Discovery created a security vulnerability that made consumers' information susceptible to hackers in certain situations. The states also alleged that Lenovo's failure to disclose the presence of VisualDiscovery on its computers, its failure to warn consumers that the software created a security vulnerability and its inadequate opt-out procedure violated state consumer protection laws.

software created a security vulnerability and its inadequate opt-out procedure violated state consumer protection laws.

Lenovo stopped shipping laptops with VisualDiscovery pre-installed in February 2015, though the states contend that some laptops with the software were still being sold by various retail outlets as late as June 2015.

New Jersey will receive approximately $97,000 from the Lenovo settlement funds. In addition to monetary payment, the settlement requires Lenovo to change its consumer disclosures about pre-installed advertising software, require a consumer's affirmative consent to using the software on their device, and provide a reasonable and effective means for consumers to opt-out, disable or remove the software. Lenovo is also required to implement and maintain a software security compliance program, and must obtain initial and biennial assessments of that program for the next 20 years from a qualified, independent, third-party professional.

"Regardless of the device we're talking about," *Porrino said,* ***"companies who make consumer technology such as personal computers and laptops have a duty not to compromise the personal information of consumers and have a duty to disclose the presence of any software that's been pre-installed on the device. We are committed to protecting the privacy of New Jersey technology consumers, and will hold accountable any companies whose actions jeopardize that privacy."***

Source: The State of New Jersey, Department of Law and Public Safety, Office of the Attorney General, Attorney General Announces $3.5 Million Multi-State Settlement with Lenovo over Hacker-Vulnerable Software, (5th September 2017)

The settlement and findings of the Attorney General highlight the importance of maintaining apt quality control standards along the supply chain, owing to the strict liability that companies may face in situations where consumer safety has been threatened. Chinese companies ought to be aware that consumer safety and consumer privacy concerns are particularly heated in developed countries such as: the United States, United Kingdom, Canada, EU nations etc.

Exhibit 7.6 U.S. Attorney General_Public Announcement of $3.5 million Legal Settlement following VisualDiscovery Scandal [emphasis added]

United States Federal Trade Commission: Lenovo
FILE NO. 152 3134

IT IS ORDERED that [Lenovo], its officers, agents, employees, and attorneys, and all other persons in active concert or participation with any of them, who receive actual notice of this Order, whether acting directly or indirectly, in connection with the advertising, promotion, offering for sale, sale, or distribution of covered software shall not make a misrepresentation, in any manner, expressly or by implication, about any feature of the covered software.

IT IS FURTHER ORDERED that, commencing no later than 120 days after the date of service of this Order, [Lenovo], its officers, agents, employees, and attorneys, and all other persons in active concert or participation with any of them, who receive actual notice of this Order, whether acting directly or indirectly, shall not preinstall or cause to be preinstalled any covered software unless [Lenovo], or the software provider:

    A. Will obtain the consumer's affirmative express consent;

    B. Provides instructions for how the consumer may revoke consent to the covered software's operation, which can include uninstalling the covered software; and

    C. Provides a reasonable and effective means for consumers to opt out, disable or remove all of the covered software's operations, which can include uninstalling the covered software.

    Provided, however, that affirmative express consent will not be required if sharing the covered information is reasonably necessary to comply with applicable law, regulation or legal process. [...]

IT IS FURTHER ORDERED that [Lenovo] must, no later than the date of service of this Order, establish and implement, and thereafter maintain a comprehensive software security program that is reasonably designed to (1) address software security risks related to the development and management of new and existing application software, and (2) protect the security, confidentiality, and integrity of covered information. The content, implementation and maintenance of the software security program must be fully documented in writing. The software security program must contain administrative, technical, and physical safeguards appropriate to [Lenovo's] size and complexity, the nature and scope of [Lenovo's] activities, the nature of the application software, the security policies and practices of the software provider, and the sensitivity of the covered information [...]

Source: The State of New Jersey, Department of Law and Public Safety, Office of the Attorney General, Attorney General Announces $3.5 Million Multi-State Settlement with Lenovo over Hacker-Vulnerable Software, (5th September 2017)

The settlement and findings of the Attorney General highlight the importance of maintaining apt quality control standards along the supply chain, owing to the strict liability that companies may face in situations where consumer safety has been threatened. Chinese companies ought to be aware that consumer safety and consumer privacy concerns are particularly heated in developed countries such as: the United States, United Kingdom, Canada, EU nations etc.

Exhibit 7.7 Consumer Concerns_Importance of Online Privacy

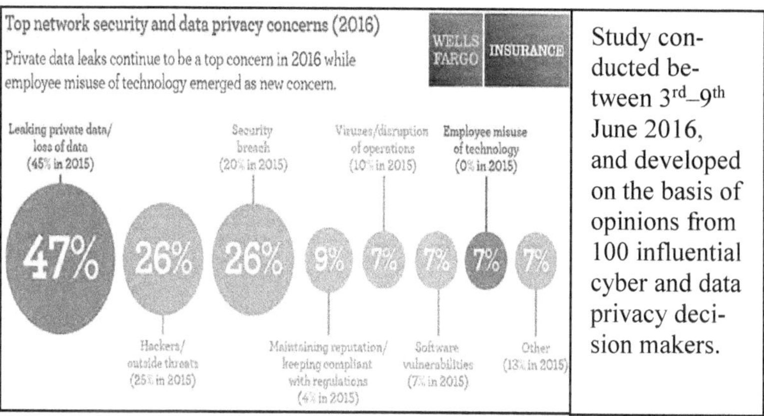

Source: Wells Fargo & Company, Wells Fargo Insurance, 2016 Network Security and Data Privacy Study Via Business Wire, New Wells Fargo Insurance Cyber Security Study Shows Companies More Concerned With Private Data Loss Than With Hackers (2016).

Online Consumer Privacy: Trends

Exhibit 7.8 Consumer Attitudes_Data Protection

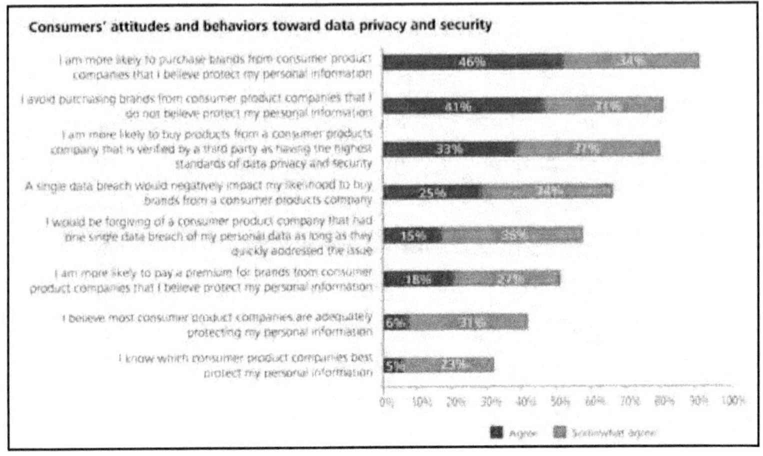

Source: Deloitte LLP, Deloitte University Press, Consumer Re-sponses From the Consumer Product Consumer and Executive Sur-vey on Data Privacy and Security, (August 2014) Via Deloitte Insights, Pat Conroy, Anupam Narula, Frank Milano and Raj Singhal, Building Consumer Trust, (2014). The findings were obtained on the basis of 2 web based surveys conducted amongst 2,001 adult U.S. consumers.

8

RESPONSIBLE ADVERTISING

Accuracy, Sensitivity and Due Diligence

Another factor crucial to maintaining a company's reputation rests in how well it is able to recognise and account for wider consumer interests such as topical social issues. This can be achieved: in the way a company depicts its values to the public, in its advertising strategies, and in any marketing campaigns used to promote awareness of a certain cause, value or philosophy. In turn, advertising is paramount to defining corporate image, building a reliable brand affiliated with greater causes and thus entrenching it further within society.

In fact, consumer advertising is a core aspect of all commercial enterprises specializing in the sale of goods and services to certain consumer groups within the general public. As an area of business management fundamentally concerned with ensuring effective communication between the company and its target market, it aids in building a consumer base and keeping the public updated of what the company has to offer.

Within such a capacity, it is critical for businesses to recognize the existence of the ethical dimension that comes with disseminating information in a public sphere, especially given that the application of advertising lies in its ability to influence consumer decisions and market trends. As such, inherent responsibilities arise in ensuring that the needs and interests of differing consumer groups, alongside public interests, are appropriately taken into account and safeguarded in and amongst a company's drive to further promote its products.

However, a multitude of factors can make such a task increasingly more difficult, especially where a company decides to expand overseas; as introducing an entirely new target market brings with it additional considerations in determining how the wider social concerns and interests of new consumers, may fit in amongst existing ones. Herein, a further challenge arises due to the increasing dependency on technology as an instrument for corporate expansion overseas [Exhibit 8.1].

Exhibit 8.1 Online Ad Spending by Region

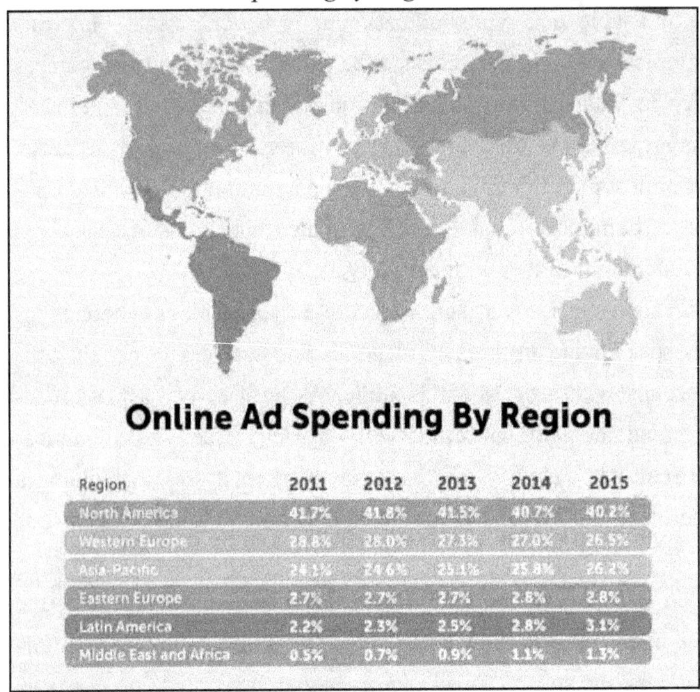

Region	2011	2012	2013	2014	2015
North America	41.7%	41.8%	41.5%	40.7%	40.2%
Western Europe	28.8%	28.0%	27.3%	27.0%	26.5%
Asia-Pacific	24.1%	24.6%	25.1%	25.8%	26.2%
Eastern Europe	2.7%	2.7%	2.7%	2.8%	2.8%
Latin America	2.2%	2.3%	2.5%	2.8%	3.1%
Middle East and Africa	0.5%	0.7%	0.9%	1.1%	1.3%

Source: Online Marketing Trends
<<http://www.onlinemarketing-trends.com/2012/11/global-comparison-in-2012-online-search.html>>

Whilst the speed and extent to which information travels online can aid in a corporation's ability to make information accessible to wider audiences, there is a growing need to ensure that information communicated maintains its accuracy, authenticity and security. This is especially so given the prevalence of less regulated internet and social media platforms to cross-culture, long-distance advertising and communication.

Such concerns are amplified by the dual nature of today's world as both growingly technologized and interconnected; the net effect of which is to widen the sphere of influence that corporations have upon the general public. Indeed the following cases demonstrate that even Chinese corporate giants of the likes of Huawei, Air China and Baidu, have fallen short of securing responsible advertising and effective communication to their own detriment. In particular, key areas of concern consist of:

1. Accuracy in advertising
2. Sensitivity when handling social concerns, and
3. Due diligence in international management: the dissemination of online adverts/sponsorships.

8.1 Accuracy in Advertising

One primary function of advertising lies in its role as a communication mechanism, enabling a company to circulate information to a wide range of consumers. As such, advertising enables businesses to not only highlight the benefits consumers may enjoy from using its products, but to further reflect the company's own mission statements and brand values. Simultaneously the mechanism allows up to date information on new products and services to be relayed on time, in and amongst marketing strategies.

However, given that advertising focuses specifically on persuasive communication, intended to influence buying behaviours, companies need to maintain caution that they do not compromise the accuracy of information advertised. This is especially noteworthy when an advert hopes to utilise irony, sarcasm or melodrama to attract an audience.

Where this occurs, either intentionally, accidentally or as a result of oversight, negative repercussions may ensue. These can take the form of severe legal recourse or loss of consumer faith and loyalty, under the perception that the company has attempted to fool or deceive the public.

A case in point is that of Huawei, who demonstrated that no matter the size and affluence of the company involved, inaccuracy in advertising may be sure to, at the very least, have a notable impact upon corporate reputation. The company, one of the largest leading electronics manufacturers in the world and one of China's most successful companies operating overseas, was caught in controversy over an online advert publicised in July 2016.

Exhibit 8.2

Source: Courtesy of Android Police
Original photo from official Huawei social media accounts.

The advert was aimed towards promoting the company's new Huawei P9 mobile phone range. In acknowledgement of the phone's special photographic abilities, the company posted a photograph of a woman, that had been supposedly taken using the phone [Exhibit 8.2].

Posted on social media channels, the image was accompanied by a caption that read:

We managed to catch a beautiful sunrise with Deliciously Ella. The #HuaweiP9's dual Leica cameras makes taking photos in low light conditions like this a pleasure. Reinvent smartphone photography and share your sunrise pictures with us. #OO[305]

Whilst not a traditional platform for advertisement, the public promotion was widely criticized due to its misleading use of the photo, which had been taken from a Canon EOS 5D Mark III DSLR Camera. Within a mere matter of days it had already become a topic of much conversation, as it implied that the new range of P9 mobile phones were capable of taking photos, that in actual fact, could only be achieved with a proper DSLR camera.

Although Huawei had never directly stated that the image used for the advert was taken by the Huawei P9 itself, it's actions in taking a photo from another company's product without a clear indication of this fact, was enough to spark controversy amongst the online community; giving rise to ridicule from professional photographers and everyday people alike. Comments directed at the company voiced contentions that: the company was *"willing to put blurred lines ahead of customer experience"*[306] and that it had *"stretched the truth by a big margin while advertising the camera"*.[307]

Whilst such criticisms may not have been too severe, they highlight the manner in which advertising mistakes may compromise the integrity and professionalism of a company as a whole. Indeed, many comments

---

[305] Business Insider, Rafi Letzter, *Huawei used an image taken with $4,500 worth of camera gear to promote its smartphone camera,* (July 2016).

[306] Gearburn, Andy Walker, *Gorgeous 'Huawei P' image actually taken using R48k Canon DSLR,* (July 2016).

[307] Tech Times, Horia Ungureanu, *Huawei Responds After Implying A Photo Taken with a $4,500 Canon Setup was Shot with P9 Camera"* (July 2016).

have since teased Huawei for making such a blunder, whilst others remain sceptical that the company had intentionally attempted to fool its consumers[308]: *"It's a little embarrassing that Huawei would pretend."*[309]

In response to contentions, Huawei acted quickly, removing the advert and posting an official apology for the confusion caused as a result.

"We recognize...that we should have been clearer with the captions for this image. It was never our intention to mislead. We apologize for this and we have removed the image."[310]

--Huawei Official Statement

However, in much the same way that the advert hoped to publicize the new P9 by exploiting the dynamism and rapid dissemination of information that online platforms provide, the nature of the internet as a platform for social exchange, made the flaw in Huawei's advert quickly known to many. As such, despite the company's quick actions in identifying and remedying the problem, the advert had already turned 'viral', with many photography enthusiasts, consumers and general members of the public aware of the blunder. Not only does this highlight the heightened risk involved in utilising online methods of advertising, but it demonstrates the unlikelihood for misleading advertisements to go unnoticed in modern society where access to information continues to strengthen.

Rather, the repercussions of knowingly or unwittingly misleading the public are likely to become more and more widespread in future. The internet's ability to circulate information at alarming rates, can work

---

[308] Android Police, David Ruddock, *Update: Huawei removes photo, responds] Huawei publishes implied P9 camera sample, but EXIF data reveals $4500 camera took it,* (July 2016).

[309] Supra note 1, Business Insider.

[310] Supra note 1, Business Insider.

both for and against corporations, dependent on their own ability to communicate effectively, honestly and responsibly.

In some cases the consequences of inaccurate advertising may even reap more serious outcomes; whereby the scope of a company's legal duties extend to ensuring that information communicated, remains clear and precise so not to cause any confusion on behalf of consumers.[311] This is worth bearing in mind for Chinese companies operating in developed host nations, given the large focus of European[312] and American law[313] on concepts such as 'misrepresentation' and misleading advertisements. Such concepts have given rise to greater consumer expectation for adverts to be truthful in Western countries, increasing public interest in the importance of accuracy in advertising.[314]

Indeed, even where this is not the case, there exists a growing social and ethical responsibility for corporations to ensure clear and explicit communication to their consumers. The use of misleading advertisements will only undermine the ability to manage consumer expectations, leaving consumers from any host nation disappointed with the overall service of the company. In turn, the company is sure to risk undermining its overall integrity and loyal consumer base. This is by virtue of the fact that an advert itself is a reflection of the company as a whole, and thereby key to brand reputation.

---

[311] Advertising Law of the People's Republic of China (2015) Article 3, 4.

[312] Directive 2005/29/EC of the European Parliament and of the Council of 11 May 2005 concerning unfair business-to-consumer commercial practices in the internal market and amending Council Directive 84/450/EEC, Directives 97/7/EC, 98/27/EC and Regulation (EC) No 2006/2004.

[313] United States Code, 2006 Edition, Supplement 5, Title 15 – Commerce and Trade, § 52 - *Dissemination of false advertisements.*

[314] The Free Library, Edmondson Intercultural Enterprises, *Chinese consumers' skepticism toward advertising.* (January 2012) <<https://www.thefreelibrary.com/Chinese+consumers%27+skepticism+toward+advertising.-a0280092819>> [accessed on 9th April 207].

In Huawei's case, regardless of the company's intention, the main cause for concern lay in the advertising strategy's exploitation of Canon technology for the benefit of its own reputation. Whilst this not only exposed Huawei to potential law suits from Canon in respect of Intellectual Property infringement, it also created doubt as to why Huawei had to depend on alternative means for the promotion of its own products. In turn, consumer faith in the credibility and quality of Huawei products is likely to have been negatively influenced; a consequence that may have been entirely avoided by ensuring clarity and accuracy to begin with.

With this in mind, it is recommended that companies remain diligent in advertising campaigns, to safeguard against any ambiguity in their communication to consumers. Ensuring that advertising procedures are equipped with proper checks and quality control, will help to identify any possible areas of contention or miscommunication that could discredit the company's products and image.

This is particularly pertinent with respect to the widespread use of digital advertisements [Exhibit 8.3], where the risk of inaccuracies are much higher given the ease and speed at which information can be circulated. Incorporating systematic checks of marketing delivered via online platforms (not just within traditional advertising), shall help protect the company from a legal standpoint and further solidify customer loyalty and faith in the company. Such diligence may be best achieved by ensuring that: all essential information on goods and services are properly disclosed by the advert; that pricing is clear; and, that the product's capabilities have been truthfully reflected.

Herein, it is equally important that all language and imagery used in advertising, is accessible to target markets in a way that can be easily understood. Indeed, the advert should be self-explanatory such that consumers do not need to have substantial former knowledge on the company or its products to be able to understand the advert's representations and implications. Such safeguards may enable companies to mitigate the risk of unwittingly becoming associated with misleading the public whilst attempting to reach out to new consumer markets.

Exhibit 8.3 Rising Tide

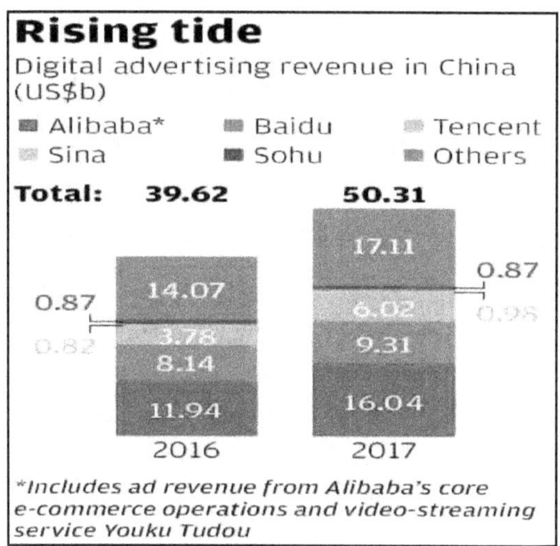

Source: Source: eMarketer and South China Morning Post
Via South China Morning Post, Bien Perez, Alibaba, Baidu, Tencent Dominate China's Red-Hot Digital Advertising Market, (2017)

Then again, it is not only language and imagery that risks giving rise to false advertisement. Similar issues have also arisen with respect to celebrity endorsements for commercial products. Such endorsements aim to widen a company's target market by capitalizing on the reputation of a renowned public figure; the desired result being that the reputation of the company's own products may be improved by affiliation. In essence, the company attempts to evidence its higher quality and benefits over competitors, through recommendations made by well-known celebrities. The celebrity is equally able to capitalize on their own reputation, by earning money through endorsement fees under the arrangement.

However, given that the use of celebrity endorsements works by affiliation and recommendation, there is a risk that a company's reputation may be severely jeopardized where the wrong celebrity is chosen for their advertising campaign. Of equal risk is a scenario where an endorsement has been made, once again, in an inaccurate or dishonest manner. This may be the case where a celebrity selected to endorse a certain product, has never actually used the product themselves, and is therefore unable to vouch for its true quality. In such circumstances, the advertising campaign will have failed to accurately reflect the affiliation that exists between the company and the celebrity in question; misleading the general public to purchase its products on the basis of unsubstantiated claims.

One renowned example involves the promotion of Japanese skin care brand: SK-II, by Hong Kong actress Carina Lau Kar-ling. Herein, SK-II's advert featured the famous actress claiming:

"My facial wrinkles and lines have been reduced by 47 percent after using SK-II for 28 days, and I look 12 years younger."

However, following a health and safety scandal in China associated with the cream, it was discovered that the actress had never actually used the product and could not truthfully vouch for such a claim.[315] Whilst consumer outcry concerning the case predominantly focused on the responsibility of the actress in having made such assertions; the company was also largely responsible in having scripted the claims without ensuring their accuracy. Accordingly, following the controversy Sk-II was fined 25,000 U.S. dollars on the grounds of false advertising, and risked jeopardising their expensive celebrity endorsement. Luckily, Carina Lau Kar-ling continued her support of the skin care product, however given the negative repercussions to both celebrity and company

---

[315] China Daily, Ma Xiaotang, *Actress Accused of False Advertising,* (September 2006).

alike, it would not have been so unlikely for their mutually beneficial agreement to have come to an abrupt end following the scandal.

Public outcry surrounding the advert, along with a series of others, even prompted a change in Chinese law. These changes extended responsibility onto those famous celebrities that had made claims in support of products that they had never actually tried, holding them jointly liable for the false advertising. The changes came amongst the public importance attached within China to accurate advertising, where consumer behaviours are increasingly sceptical of the authenticity of products sold.[316]

However, whilst the inaccuracy of SK-II's advert may have compromised public perception of the company's legitimacy, one of its more recent adverts in 2016, highlighted the mutual benefit that can be established when a company truly considers consumer needs and interests in a honest way. The company's new advert featured in China, centred on a key social concern for the Chinese public: the leftover woman (剩女). The advert aimed to tackle the issue of Chinese women on the familial pressures they face to get married before a certain age, or else be rendered a 'leftover' woman. The approach taken by the company was to reflect actual accounts made by members of the public to truthfully portray the problem at hand. Moving away from the use of celebrity endorsements as a manner of promoting their products, the company thereby chose to feature real life women as part of a campaign to better relate to its target market. This enabled SK-II to more fully understand the needs and concerns of its own consumer base, whilst staying true to its own brand values and motto: *"to inspire and empower women to shape their destiny."*[317]

---

[316] China Insider, Keira Lu Huang, *"Celebrity Endorsements Under Scrutiny as China Steps up Consumer Protection"* (1st Nov 2013).

[317] BBC News, Heather Chen *"Emotional advert about China's 'Leftover Women' goes viral"* (April 2016).

The success of the advert was noted globally, and quickly gained the recognition and approval of the Chinese online community. In turn, the sale of SK-II products soared within China by up to 50% in just 9 months. The advert has since gone viral nationally and internationally, having been watched 46 million times on internet platforms world-wide.[318]

The case demonstrates the changing dynamic of consumer needs, in which honest and open communication enabled the company to reach out to its target market in a more effective manner. Through the power of 'word-of-mouth', which is able now more than ever to reach new heights in light of the surge of online social media platforms, companies may do well to consider wider issues in part of their marketing strate-gies, stimulating public debate and approaching topical concerns. In doing so, the benefits that may be gained when members of a company's consumer base are directly used in advertising, is emphasised: no longer merely as a viewer but also as a contributor. Perhaps future companies may also benefit from a more reciprocal relationship between them-selves and their target market when it comes to advertising and market-ing. This would not only strengthen the relationship between company and consumer, but help to ensure accuracy in advertising: after all, communication is a two-way street.

"Consumers are part of the journey that is changing our destiny as a brand, and that's amazing."

--Kylene Campos (Associate Marketing Director SK-II, P&G)[319]

---

[318] Bloomberg, Carol Hymowitz and Lauren Coleman-Lochner, *"A Skin-Care Ad Tackles Social Taboos in China"* (February 2017).

[319] Eyeka Blog, Yaoqi Lai, *How P&G Uses Crowdsourcing to Build the SK-II Brand #ChangeDestiny,* (November 2015) <<http://news.eyeka.net/2015/11/how-pg-uses-crowdsourcing-to-build-the-sk-ii-brand/>> [accessed on 13th April 2017].

8.2 Sensitive Social Concerns

Indeed, the success of SK-II 's advert was rooted in its ability to relate with key social concerns directly relevant to its target market, building a stronger more current relationship between the company and its consumer base. However, it is noted that in handling social concerns there is a need to carefully consider the sensitivity of advertisements. Tackling especially sensitive and controversial social topics can be either revolutionary or detrimental to a company, depending on how careful they are in approaching the matter.

For instance, an advert for the Chinese company "玖号车汇" back in 2008, received widespread criticism for its insensitivity in promoting its services. The company specialised in offering a platform for the exchange of second hand cars. To promote its services the advert was published on Beijing subway carriage doors, utilizing the slogan: "Crowded? Why not buy a car!" In recognition of social matters, the advert thus attempted to draw upon the experiences of Chinese people using public transportation, particularly during rush hour. However, its oversimplification of the reasons behind overcrowding on subways left a large majority of the public offended that it insinuated people were only commuting to work via public transport as they did not already own a car nor the means of acquiring one. In turn, given the mark of a car to social standing and status within China, it was felt that the advert made insensitive assumptions about commuters, implying that their choice to ride the subway was as a direct result of a lower disposable income. In essence, although the advert attempted to relate to consumer needs and interests, it failed to do so in a sensitive enough manner in appreciation of its target audience.[320]

---

[320] Sina, Sichuan News, Chengdu Daily,卖车广告惹恼北京地铁族 *(Buy-a-car advert annoying Beijing Metro Riders),* (February 2008), accessible via:

Similar problems concerning sensitivity of social issues in advertising, have also been noted amongst well reputed Chinese companies operating abroad. In particular was the 2016 controversy concerning Air China; the international airline operating 98 international routes and recognized overseas as one of China's Top Ten International Brands.[321] An issue here arose with the airline's in-flight magazine: The Wings of China. The magazine, containing travel information for passengers on board their flights, published an article stating:

"到伦敦旅行很安全，　但有些印巴聚集区和黑人聚集区相对较乱。夜晚最好不要单独出行，女士应该尽量结伴而行。"

"London is a generally safe place to travel, however precautions are needed when entering areas mainly populated by Indians, Pakistanis, and black people. We advise tourists not to go out alone at night, and females always to be accompanied by another person when travelling" (Translation).

The article, published by Air China Media Group, was widely criticized for its "racist" implications and offensive comments towards ethnic minorities living in London. Indeed, as a result of its insensitive remarks, not only did Air China find itself the object of much ridicule in international media and online, but it was further requested by official UK Ministers of Parliament (MPs) to revoke the article immediately. The public outrage was such that London based MPs felt the need to invite Air China representatives and Chinese Ambassadors to visit the city and personally verify how safe it is, in an aim to defend the reputa-

---

<<http://news.sina.com.cn/c/2008-02-17/032813422838s.shtml>> [accessed on: 11th April 2017].

[321] Air China Official Website, Company Profile <<https://www.airchina.co.uk/GB/GB/about-us/profile/>> [accessed on 7th April 2017].

tion of its citizens.[322] Rosena Allina-Khan (MP for Tooting) and Virendra Sharma (MP for Ealing) both sent official complaints to the Chinese Ambassador for the offensive comments made.

"I will await their response, and if an appropriate one is not forthcoming I shall feel forced to question whether Air China is a fit company to operate in the UK."[323]

Mr Virendra Sharma (MP for Ealing, UK)

[Comment made following communications

that had been sent to Air China]

In response to the public outcry caused, Air China publicly apologized for the comments published in it's in flight magazine:

"(The article) created a huge negative influence to the operation, image and reputation of Air China. We express our deep apology for this... Air China has withdrawn the magazine on all flights after noticing the problem, and demanded the magazine's publishing house learn lessons and avoid similar problems from happening again."[324]

--Air China Official Statement

Following the scandal, Chinese media and online platforms highlighted strong support on behalf of the Chinese public to defend Air China's actions. It was pointed out that the contents of the article had merely reiterated facts that had been obtained from the UK's own National Statistics relating to the dispersion of criminal activity within London.[325] However, despite such contentions that the company's sta-

---

[322] Straits Times, *Publisher of Air China in-flight Magazine Apologises for 'racist' Article,* (September 2016).

[323] Telegraph, Neil Connor, *Air China Magazine Apologises over 'racist' Article about London,* (September 2016).

[324] Supra note 18, Telegraph.

[325] Times of India, Shailaja Neelakantan, *Chinese Media defends Air China's Racist Travel Tips about Indians, Pakistanis, Black People,* (September 2016).

tistics had been sought from credible sources, the lesson to be learnt from the case lies not so much with the authenticity of published crime rates, but rather with the sensitivity of how such information had been relayed.

Indeed, a corporation's social responsibility focuses on its role in accounting for the needs and interests of wider stakeholders. In this regard, it is conceded that the publication of safety information on tourist destinations, is relevant when accounting for the needs of passengers travelling on board Air China flights. Nonetheless, as an international carrier, Air China not only had the responsibility to account for the needs and interests of its Chinese consumers, but to further recognize the existence of sub-groups that fall within their target market. Given that Air China operates a twice daily direct flight between Beijing and London, the need to take into account the interests of UK citizens (as well as tourists travelling to London), was therefore necessary. To this end, Air China's heated backlash arose in having failed to accord for the ethnic diversity, cultural attitudes and cosmopolitan nature of the UK and its capital city [Exhibit 8.4].

More generally speaking, the company's portrayal of ethnic minorities in London, carried with it racist undertones (intentional or not). The repercussions of the article were not only concentrated to the UK, but spread worldwide. News reports from several other countries, including: America[326], India[327] and Pakistan[328], all expressed shock and outrage at

---

[326] See: USA Today, Louise Watt, *Air China mag warned fliers about minority areas of London,* (September 2016); New York Times, Edward Wong, *Air China Will Fly You To London, and Warn You About Dark-Skinned People There,* (September 2016).

[327] See: Supra note 20, Times of India; Indian Express, *Air China withdraws magazine with racist comments about Indians, apologises for 'editing mistake',* (September 2016).

the magazine's comments; especially in light of growing international social concerns surrounding racism.

Exhibit 8.4 Ethnic Groups, England and Wales, 2011

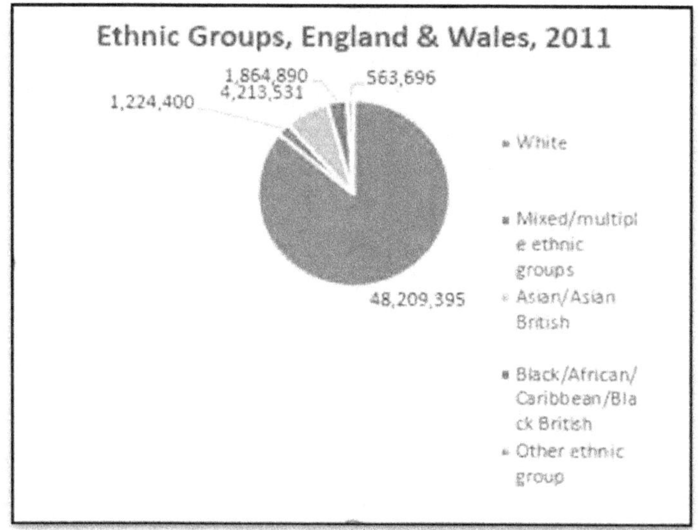

Source: Source: 2011 Census - UK Office for National Statistics.
Note: According to the census, London was the most ethnically diverse area, with the White ethnic group comprising of only 59.8%.

In acknowledgement of the Air China case, it is strongly recommended that Chinese companies engaged in ODI, make themselves aware of sensitive social concerns prior to expansion, both at a domestic and international level. This means recognizing the cultural differences between China and the countries in which Chinese companies operate, so as to better account for the needs and interests of new consumer groups.

---

[328] See: Dawn, *Air China Comes Under Fire for Issuing 'Racist' Travel Warnings,* (September 2016); Dunyan News, *Air China cautions passengers on visiting London areas populated by 'Indians, Pakistanis',* (September 2016).

Here it is stressed, that when implementing corporate responsibility, companies need to recognize the importance of identifying different groups of stakeholders. This requires greater attention that simply categorising stakeholders into the broader terms of: "shareholder", "supplier," "consumer" etc. Rather, it extends to recognizing the existence of sub-groups within those areas. Only then may the company begin to truly understand the different groups affected by their operations, and how to better balance their competing interests in order to effectively communicate in and amongst them.

Whilst doing so, it is further imperative that the company remains sensitive to global concerns such as: anti-discrimination; poverty; human rights; climate change and even political tensions. Given the aforementioned impact of internet technology on the spread of communication, failing to account for such concerns may place a company at risk of damaging its reputation by becoming the subject of international discourse, despite best intentions. This may occur even to domestic companies with no focus on turning international; as demonstrated by the case of Qiaobi.

Qiaobi, a domestic Chinese washing detergent company, released an advert back in 2016 replicated from a former Italian advert televised 9 years before. The Italian version of the advert had depicted a Caucasian man getting thrust into a washing machine with a washing up liquid, only to come out as an African with the tagline: "coloured is better." However Qiaobi, in an attracting the Chinese domestic market, reversed the ad; with an African man entering the washing machine, to come out Asian.[329]

Despite the fact that the company only released the advert in Mainland China, and strictly to its Chinese customers, the age of the internet meant that before long renowned multinational newspapers were com-

---

[329] The Guardian, Emma Graham-Harrison, *Black man is washed whiter in China's racist detergent advert,* (May 2016).

menting on the insensitive racial inferences within the campaign.[330] As a result, the company faced severe backlash for its insensitivity to racial issues and was forced to publicly apologize, stating:

"We express our apology for the harm caused to the African people because of the spread of the ad and the over-amplification by the media...We sincerely hope the public and the media will not over-read it."[331]

The case exemplifies the need for all companies, whether they are operating abroad or not, to take into account key international social concerns. Indeed, it is worth noting that the case is also illustrative of the dynamic nature of social issues, in which a company's *social* responsibility should continue to expand, develop and evolve over time. Accordingly, whilst the Italian advert did not receive any backlash when it was first broadcasted the nature of racial issues and antidiscrimination have evolved such that the market today is much different to that of 9 years ago. In appreciation of this fact, it should have been foreseeable to Qiaobi that problems might arise with such an advertising strategy; highlighting the need for companies to not only make themselves aware of social concerns today, but to ensure that they continuously update their knowledge and understanding of such topics in order to account for society's continuously evolving standards.

A further consideration to be made here regarding the function of the internet, is that even where companies recognize their advertising error and attempt to resolve the situation by removing it from the public arena; it is not possible to completely eradicate the advert from the public

---

[330] See: Aljazeera, *China's Detergent Ad Labelled 'Raw Racism'*, (May 2016); New York Times, Jonah Bromwich, *Chinese Detergent Ad Draws Charges of Racism*, (May 2016); Hong Kong Free Press, Roberto Castillo, *Of Washing Powder, Afrophobia and Racism in China*, (August 2016).

[331] BBC News, *Chinese Firm Apologises over Qiaobi race-row Advert*, (May 2016).

eye. As noted by Qiaobi, there is always a risk of 'over-amplification by the media'; and the rapid dissemination of information online means that despite Huawei, Air China and Qiaobi removing their controversial adverts, it is highly likely that they are still circulating the internet today. It is therefore necessary that companies are more meticulous when advertising, as the lasting implications of advertising scandals are likely to subsist for some time.

8. 3 Due Diligence

Having discussed the need for Chinese companies to ensure accuracy and sensitivity in advertising, additional consideration needs to be paid to companies who specialize as advertising platforms. Accordingly, unlike Huawei, SK-II and Air China who engage in advertising as a business mechanism to promote their goods and services; there exist those companies who engage in advertising as part of their core business operations. Such companies sell their services as a platform for other companies to publicise their adverts on.

In recent years, as technology has continued to rapidly develop, more and more advertising occurs online as opposed to, or at the very least alongside, print media, radio and television. Accordingly, online websites such as YouTube, Facebook and Google have all taken on dual roles as advertising platforms, selling online space for a range of different companies. Within China things are no different, and indeed companies such as Youku, Weibo, and Baidu offer advertising space in much the same way, capitalizing on their well know reputation and large consumer base.

However, given the increased presence and influence of the internet on a large majority of people; there is a need for such platforms to recognize their responsibility to sell advertising space in a diligent manner.

This particular lesson could not be better illustrated than by the extremely controversial case of Wei Zexi and Baidu in 2016.

The case involved a "promoted" search result for the Second Hospital of the Beijing Armed Police Corps and its experimental treatment for cancer. On the basis of a Baidu advert, Wei Zexi, a 21 year old college student from Shaanxi province, received treatment from the hospital for synovial sarcoma. His condition was a rare form of cancer which had failed to be treated successfully through radiation and chemotherapy. Wei and his family, spent approximately 200,000CNY ($32,116USD) on treatments at the hospital, but to no avail. After discovering that the type of treatment had actually been terminated in the U.S. following unsuccessful clinical trials, the student blogged about his ordeal, blaming the hospital and Baidu for advertising false medical information and statistics on the treatment:

"Baidu, I didn't know how evil it is and how it ranks medical information based on a bidding process. We thought: Baidu, a top-ranked hospital...everything must be legitimate."[332]

--Wei Zexi

By the time of Wei's unfortunate death on April 12th 2016, Chinese media had already voiced widespread criticism against Baidu for its failure to ensure due diligence when listing adverts. Before long international media had also got hold of the story, and within weeks following Wei's death, Baidu's share prices had already fallen by 7.92% ($5 billion USD) on the Nasdaq Stock Market; as the engine provider came under official investigation by the Chinese authorities.[333]

---

[332] CNN, Steven Jiang, *Student Death Triggers Probe of China's Baidu,* (May 2016).

[333] BBC, Stephen McDonell, *China investigates search engine Baidu after student's death"* (May 2016).

Public contentions mainly surrounded the manner in which Baidu chose to advertise certain listings over others: choosing to "promote" adverts solely on the basis of the highest bidder. Accordingly, in much the same way that the celebrity endorsement scandals had prompted public anger for failing to accurately reflect the relationship between a company's products and starring celebrities; the issue here lay in the fact that Baidu listings failed to clearly identify "promoted" adverts as ones that had simply been paid for. Rather the term "promoted" implied that Baidu had agreed to endorse said companies as it vouched for their authenticity and good quality. This ambiguity in listing adverts was rendered misleading, actively preventing the public from being able to deduce which adverts had achieved their listing as a result of greater quality and which had simply paid for a higher slot.

Taking consideration of Baidu's financial dependency on advertising, it is conceded that the company may have had little freedom in selecting the goods and services it chose to sponsor. After all majority of the company's revenue from it's free-to-use search engine is generated through advertising.[334] Nevertheless, the dilemma faced by Baidu may have been mitigated had the company taken adequate steps to ensure that the relationship between itself and advert providers was properly disclosed as purely financial; in no way related to the authenticity, reliability or popularity of the products and services advertised. The use of such clear and explicit disclaimers would have ensured that the company was in no way responsible for misleading the public, and may have spared Baidu its integrity and brand reputation.

Notwithstanding these efforts, the repercussions of the case were so immense that they prompted next-to immediate changes in Chinese law. The changes hold that companies like Baidu are now required to review all licenses and claims made by listed adverts, in order to verify their

---

[334] Baidu Official Website, Company Overview: <<http://ir.baidu.com/phoenix. zhtml?c=188488&p=irol-homeprofile>> [accessed on 15th April 2017].

authenticity.[335] In essence, the law aims to heighten the responsibility of advertising platforms to exercise due diligence when offering up advertising space, emphasizing the importance of accuracy in advertising. The legal reform is notable in entrenching a higher degree of responsibility with regards to public communication by corporations. However, it is equally recognized that the ability to verify the authenticity of all contents on the internet is a responsibility that may be too great to presently impose upon companies, in light of practical limitations therein. Indeed such problems are somewhat common place amongst internet-based companies, with other large scale companies like Google facing similar problems, e.g.: the controversy in early 2017 regarding how adverts had been listed on Google's web space.[336]

Still, the need for due diligence ought to have been apparent to Baidu much earlier on, given its substantial market share (close to 80%) within China [Exhibit 8.5]. With an average usage of 660 million people monthly,[337] the company's near-monopoly on internet communication within China, renders it's sphere of influence as especially large. Herein lies the company's proportionally larger responsibility when disseminating information online. Indeed, it goes without saying that the larger your sphere of influence, the greater your responsibility; an intrinsic

---

[335] Advertising Age, Angela Donald, *After New Regulations in China, What's Ahead for Baidu,* (June 2016).

[336] See: Bloomberg Technology, Joe Mayes and Jeremy Kahn, *Google to Revamp Ad Policies After U.K., Big Brands Boycott,* (March 2017); The Guardian, Rupert Neate, *Extremists made $250,000 from ads for UK Brands on Google, say Experts,* (March 2017).

See further, for information on Facebook and problematic advertising: New York Post, Leonid Bershidsky, *Why Facebook is Headed for a Terrible 2018,* (December 2017).

[337] The Guardian, Tom Phillips, *China investigates Baidu after death of student who sought cancer cure on internet,* (May 2016).

notion at the very core of responsible business. This in itself ought to have been sufficient to prompt Baidu into taking extra precaution.

Exhibit 8.5 Search Engine Market Share in China, April 2017

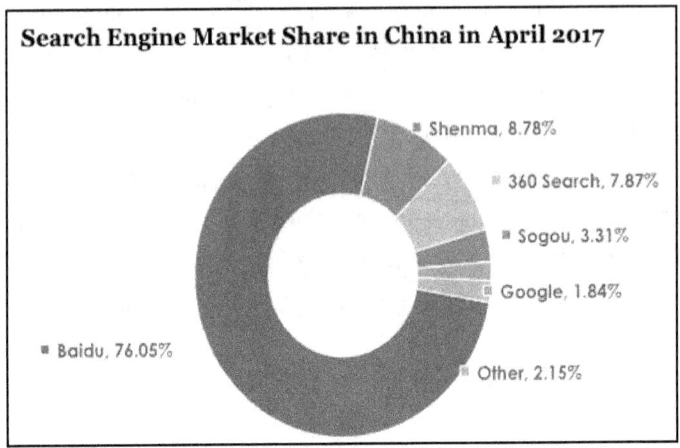

Source: StatCounter, May 2017

Via China Internet Watch, China Search Engine Market Share in April 2017, (2017).

The greater need for due diligence was further prudent when endorsing public services, given the extent of public dependency which currently exists on the search engine.

"Companies that were involved in services that deal with human life should be particularly conscientious of their duties when conducting their businesses. Billions of net users trusted Baidu for their search engine and online forum services, the company is hence responsible for the trust and is obligated to taking up their social responsibilities."[338]

--The People's Daily (official newspaper of the Chinese government)

---

[338] New York Times, Austin Ramzy, *China Investigates Baidu after Student's Death From Cancer*, (May 2016).

Even Baidu's own corporate profile emphasized the need for the company, as a search engine/media platform, to ensure it communicated reliable information:

"We aim to serve the needs of our users and customers with products and solutions that prioritize the user experience and reflect our corporate culture – simple and reliable."[339]

The need to prioritize user experience and reliability, highlighted the internet giant's own internal policies to practice greater due diligence when ranking search results. I.e.: to accord "promoted" internet listings on the basis of more concrete factors than simply bidding.

8.4 Conclusion

The 2016 advertising scandals from Huawei to Air China to Baidu, highlight the importance for all companies to engage in responsible advertising. As telecommunications continue to grow and develop, companies are provided with more and more sophisticated methods of communicating directly to consumer markets and the ability for them to exploit the internet for greater brand recognition is notable.

However, the need for corporations to communicate in an accurate, sensitive and diligent manner is also becoming steadily more and more apparent. Not only is it recognizable at a State level for public security purposes, with cases such as Carina Lau Kar-ling's SK-II celebrity sponsorship and Wei Zexi's experiences with Baidu; but at a private level too, where there exists a growing expectation from consumers for communication to remain open and honest.

---

[339] Supra note 29, Baidu Official Website.

8.5 Questions for Thought

1. To what extent should internet platforms and celebrities be responsible for the adverts they endorse?

2. When do you draw the line between satire and being offensive?

3. Should brands cover social concerns in their marketing campaigns and advertising strategies? If so, how should they choose which topics to engage with?

4. Is there a responsibility for consumers to independently research further into products and services advertised, or should they be able to rely on the face value of a company's adverts alone?

8.6 Appendix

Exhibit 8.7 Global Trust in Advertising Shifting Reliance on Online/Digital Formats

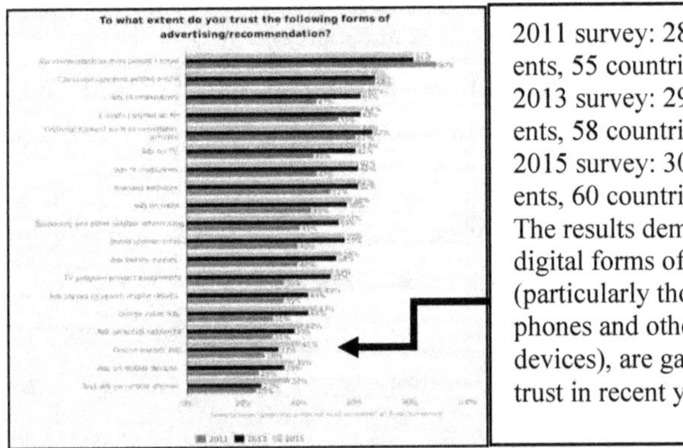

2011 survey: 28,000 respondents, 55 countries.
2013 survey: 29,000 respondents, 58 countries.
2015 survey: 30,000 respondents, 60 countries.
The results demonstrate that digital forms of advertising (particularly those on mobile phones and other handheld devices), are garnering greater trust in recent years.

Source: The Neilsen Company Via Statista <<https://www.statista.com/statistics/222805/consumer-trust-in-advertising-in-north-america/>>

Exhibit 8.8 Chinese Online Advertising Market Share Trends

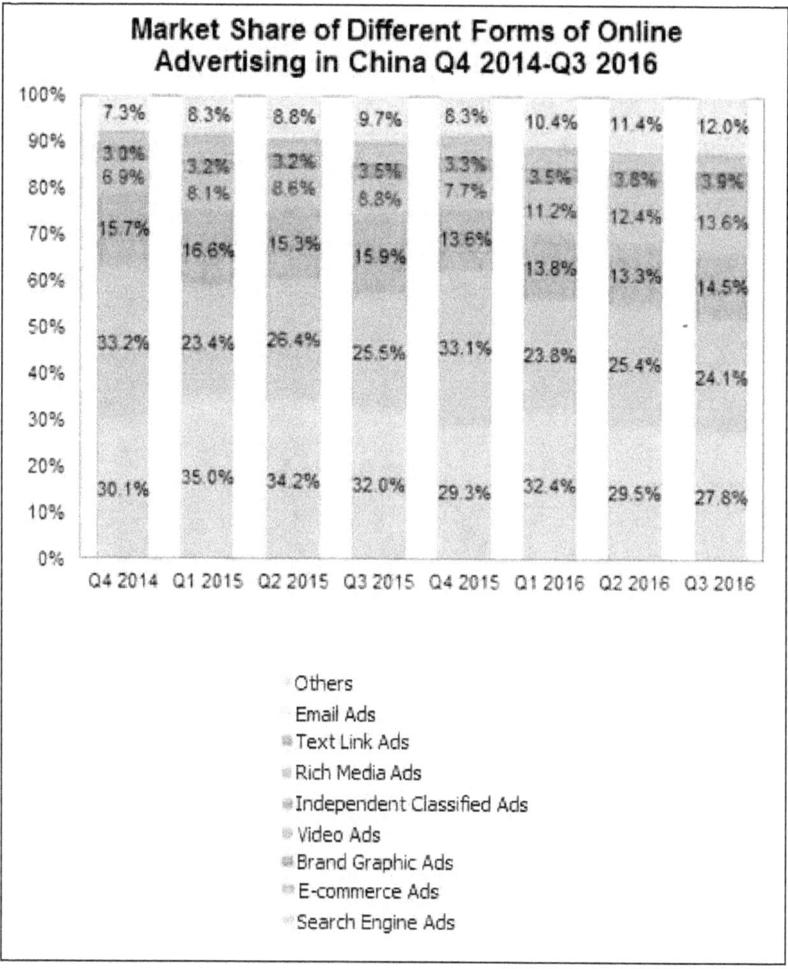

Source: iResearch Global Group, China's Online Advertising Mar-ket Structure Changed Obviously Q3 2016, (2016)

Advertising through search engines such as Baidu dominate the market share for online advertising within Chi-na. As such, it is better understood why the Wei ZeXi scandal prompted such widespread debate amongst the Chinese public, and even influenced cybersecurity policy.

Exhibit 8.9 Social Media Market Share Advertising

Source: eMarketer Via Statista <<https://www.statista.com/ statistics/271408/share-of-social-media-in-online-advertising-spending-worldwide/>>

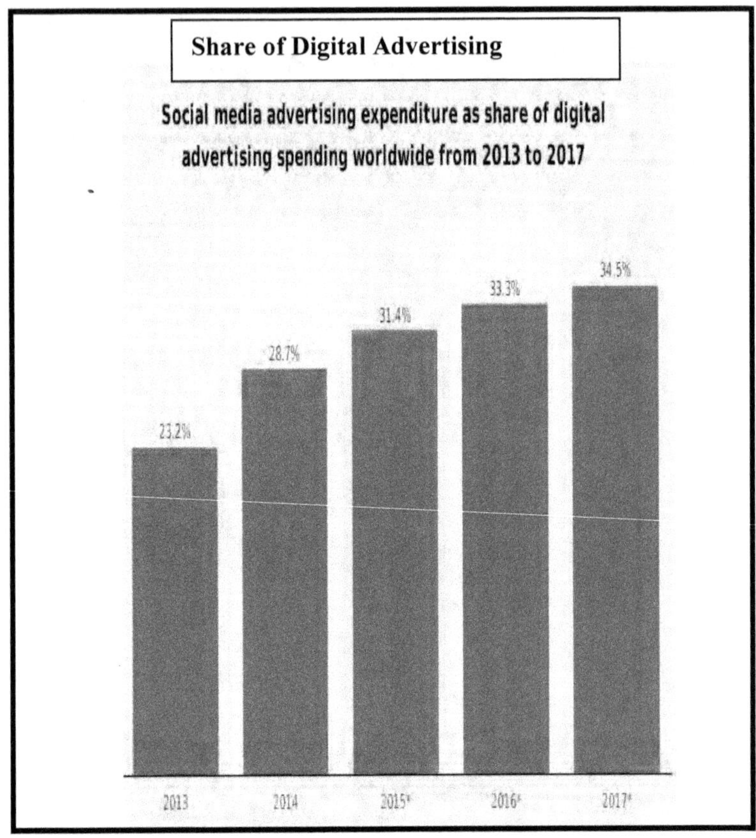

Exhibit 8.10 Speed of Social Media

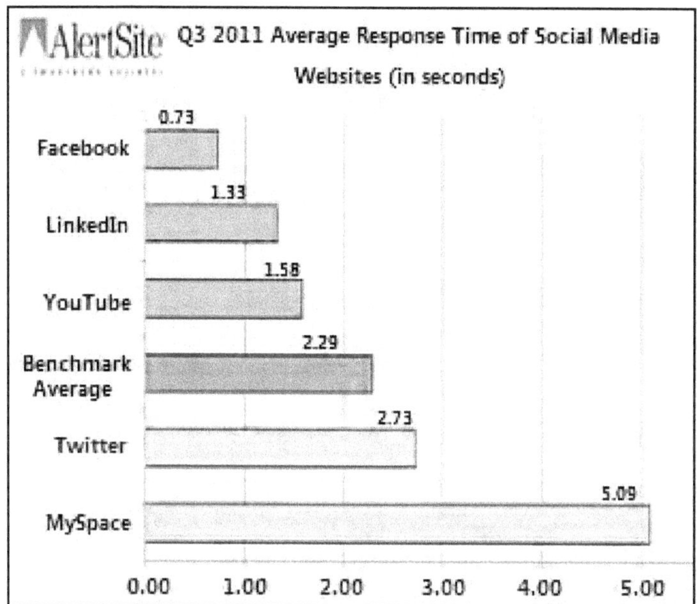

Source: SmartBear Software Com-pany, Web Performance for Social Networks, (2011) Via AdWeek < http://www.adweek.com/digital/ facebook-still-the-fastest-social-network-linkedin-and-twitter-close-behind/

Note: Figure 3 demonstrates the global trend in the use of online advertising through social media platforms. Given the speed at which social media platforms disseminate information (Figure 4), companies exploiting this medium to access their consumer base are reminded of the far reaching consequences that irresponsible/ negligent advertising might have (as was the case with Huawei and it's P9 advert).

Exhibit 8.11 Variance in Advertis-ing appeal Around the World

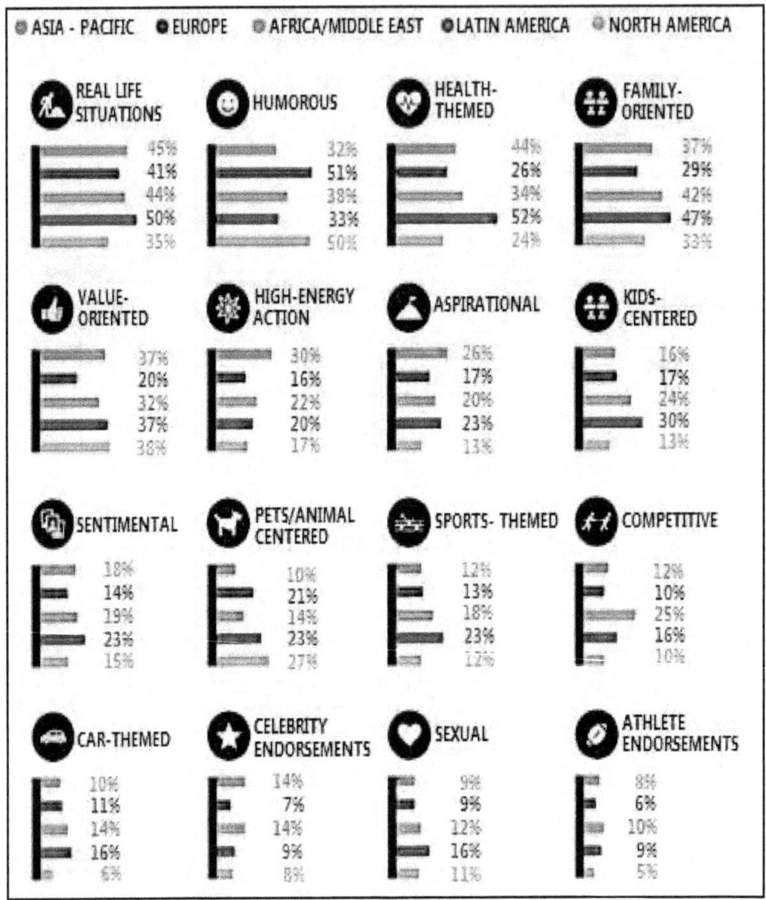

Source: Nielsen Global Trust in Advertising Survey,

Data as of 2015, First Quarter (Survey of 30,000 online consum-ers)

Amendments to Chinese Law: Responsible Advertising
Exhibit 8.12 Current Advertising Law of the PRC_Relevant Articles for Celebrity Endorsement Liability_Official Translation

Presidential Order No. 22 People's Republic of China

<u>Advertising Law of the People's Republic of China (2015)</u>

Article 2. "...Endorser in this Law shall mean natural person, legal person or other organization, other than the advertiser, that recommends and testifies for commodity or service in their own name or image."

Article 16. "The following content is not allowed in advertising for medical, pharmaceutical and medical devices:

... 4) Using Endorser to recommend or testify"

Article 18. "The following content is not allowed in advertising for functional food:

... 5) Using Endorser to recommend or testify"

Article 38. "When an Endorser recommends or testifies for a commodity or service in advertising, he or she should refer to facts, comply with provisions of this Law and other laws and regulations, and should not recommend or testify for commodity or service that he or she has not used....

A natural person, legal person, or other organization that received administrative penalty for recommending or testifying in a false advertising in the last three years should not be hired as Endorser."

Article 56. "In case the false advertisement for a commodity or service that matters to the life and health of the consumers causes harm to the consumers, the Advertising Operator, Advertising Publisher and Endorser should bear joint liabilities with the Advertiser.

In case a false advertisement for a commodity or service other than those described in the above paragraph causes detriment to the consumers, and the Advertising Operator, Advertising Publisher and Endorser knows or should know advertising is false but still designs, produces, acts as agent, publishes, or recommends or testifies for it, the Advertising Operator, Advertising Publisher and Endorser should bear joint liabilities with the Advertiser."

Article 62. "If there is any of the following case for the Endorser, the industry and commerce administration department should confiscate the illegal income, and issue a fine ranging from one to two times of the illegal income.

1. Recommends or testifies in medical, pharmaceutical or medical device advertising, which is in violation of Item 4, paragraph 1, Article 16 of this Law;
2. Recommends or testifies in functional food advertising, which is in violation of Item 5, paragraph 1, Article 18 of this Law;
3. Recommends or testifies for a commodity or service that he or she has not used, which is in violation of paragraph 1, Article 38 of this Law;
4. Recommends or testifies for a commodity or service in an advertising that he or she knows or should know is false.

The new rules were promulgated as a direct response to the problems encountered within China of misleading celebrity endorsements. Several high profile instances of misrepresentation in celebrity endorsements were noted to give rise to the changes in law, not just that of Carina Lau Kar-Ling.

Exhibit 8.13 Action Taken by Chinese Airlines against "Black Market" Online Ticketing

Recently, China Southern Airlines has required that any of their tickets sold by Qunar.com need to be clearly identified as such, given the many customer complaints that have newly arisen against the company: in the first two months of 2016 alone 79 such complaints had already been raised. These complaints have mainly involved violations by online agents: charging additional alteration and refund fees; providing fake tickets; failing in their responsibility to notify of any flight changes, fraudulent disclosure of passenger information, misuse of passenger information accounts for the sale of airline seats, causing varying degrees of loss to passengers, and seriously compromising the legitimate rights and interests of consumers.

The fundamental reasons put forward for Air China and Hainan Airlines' prior decision to shelve Qunar tickets were the same.

Specialised Regulations Launched – Experts: Legal thinking and governance may pave the way

The shelving of tickets on Qunar.com marks but the first step towards remedying the problem with ticketing agents in the airline industry. In February, Air China took the lead with regards to domestic flights, printing the full price of purchased air tickets on boarding passes. As long as the purchased flight number begins with "CA" and Air China is the actual carrier of the domestic flight, the official website of Air China or the Air China wireless client self check-in machines will provide boarding passes containing the ticket price (tax included), showing the full amount of the air ticket including: ticket fares, fuel surcharges and airport construction costs. Recently, some China Southern Airlines boarding passes have also begun [to do the same thing]. The aim of these two large airline providers is to prevent agents from "selling high price tickets" to consumers, whilst enabling the airline provider to better standardise the ticketing market.

> Whilst [Air China] launched the operation, Qunar.com, which suffered continuous encounters with several major airlines for "broken supply," attempted to speed up its "reconciliation" with the airline industry by publishing "Qunar's Notice on Rectifying and Cleaning up the Ticket Agent Sales Market." Here it was stated that [the company] has already implemented a full-scale self-examination, and worked with airline providers to deal with those [ticketing agents] who do not conform to the standard. At present: 91 non-compliant [ticketing agents] have been penalized; 21 agents who seriously fail to comply have been removed from the site and asked to rectify [deficiencies], and two agents who seriously violate the standard with regards to bad customer service, have been permanently removed from the site.

Exhibit 8.14 China New Rules for Internet Search Service Providers Relevant Articles Unofficial Translation

Cyberspace Administration of China
Entry into Force: 01/08/2016

Administrative Provisions on Internet Information Search Services

Article 6. "Internet search service providers shall implement entity liability; shall establish and complete information security management systems such as for information reviews, real-time public information inspections, emergency responses and protection of personal information; and shall possess safe and controllable precautionary measures; so as to provide necessary technical support

Source: Cyberspace Administration of China Official Website
<<http://www.cac.gov.cn/2016-06/25/c_1119109085.htm>>

截至目前已有 9 家航空公司宣布暂停与去哪儿网合作

经济报 2016 年 01 月 07 日 （记者黄荣）

…"2014 年以前，几大航空公司的机票直销比例约为 10%左右，因此不得不对中小代理商的行为'睁一只眼闭一只眼'。"劲旅咨询 CEO 魏长仁告诉记者。随着携程网、去哪儿网等在线旅游网站的兴起，中小代理商也鸟枪换炮，搭上了网上售票的快车。不过由来已久的违规问题并没有因此消失，反而进一步扩大化…

…去年上半年，监管层向"三大航"提出了"双五十"目标：在未来 3 年内，中国三大航空公司的直销比例要提升至 50%，同时代理费要在 2014 年的基础上下降 50%。业内人士告诉记者，虽然直观来看，硬性要求航空公司提升直销比例多少有些"管得太宽"的味道，但实际情况是，两个 50%都是手段，最终的目的是要把机票价格降下来。

一直以来，机票代理公司均给航空公司带来了高额的代理费用成本。某国有航空公司有关负责人向记者透露，其 2014 年代理费用接近 40 亿元。这些成本最终会以机票价格的方式转移给消费者。所以，要给消费者真正的实惠，就必须降低代理费，而要降低代理费，就必须提高直销比例。

事实上，早在 2007 年，国内航空公司就已经开始探索通过提高直销比例，降低企业成本的路径。比如，南航在行业里率先宣布将机票销售的代理人佣金由 1%降为 0。然而，不得不承认，此举整体收效甚微。魏长仁告诉记者，根据劲旅咨询的调查，2015 年末国航、南航、东航、海航四大航空公司的直销比例大概在 20%至 30%之间…

…"航空公司仍然掌握着更大的话语权。作为资源提供方，航空公司出台相应政策对市场的影响还是很大的，用来调节市场的手段也很多。"魏长仁表示，"以往航空公司没有动力去改，能省事就省事，现在有了硬性要求，航空公司做出调整很正常"

Translation from "China Law Translate"

<<http://www.chinalawtranslate.com/searchengineregulation/?lang=en>>

The new rules were promulgated as a direct response to the Baidu controversy concerning Wei ZeXi's death in 2016.

9

THE CASE OF ONEPLUS

Word-of-mouth advertising: How to build a respected brand

9.1 Case Background

Finally, in developing a company's competitive edge over third parties, is the need for innovation in marketing and business strategies. This ensures that companies stand out amongst the variety of brands fighting over the same consumer group. Herein, one particular Chinese smartphone manufacturer has been particularly fruitful in utilising new technologies and approaches to market their products.

Exhibit 9.1 Global Smartphone Shipments

Global Smartphone Shipments (% Share)	2016Q2	2017Q2
Samsung	21.7%	22.0%
Apple	11.3%	11.2%
Huawei	9.0%	10.5%
Oppo	6.5%	8.4%
vivo	4.6%	6.6%
Xiaomi	4.1%	6.3%
LG	3.9%	3.6%
ZTE (excludes Nubia)	4.3%	3.3%
Lenovo (includes Motorola)	3.2%	3.2%
Alcatel	2.1%	1.3%
Others	29.2%	23.4%
Total	100.0%	100.0%

Source: Counterpoint Research, Tarun Pathak, Q2 2017: Chinese Brands Now Contributing to Almost half of Global Smartphone Shipments, (August 2017).

Contextually speaking, Chinese companies have had a fair amount of experience in the industry, holding 4 out of the 6 positions for top smartphone producer in the international market [Exhibit 9.1]. Xiaomi, Huawei, Vivo and OPPO have all steadily grown in both size and reputation, reinventing themselves as respectable brands, both domestically and overseas. In fact the four smartphone manufacturers have seen steady development over the last few years, jointly accounting for 48% of all mobile phone shipments within the second quarter of 2017 globally.[340]

In and amongst their success, two particular companies, OPPO and its sister company Vivo, have been notable in their dramatic surge, rising higher and higher amongst the ranks of competition [Exhibit 9.2].[341] With a shifted focus away from the premium customers of Apple and Samsung, the brands established themselves by tailoring their reach towards consumers based back at home and within emerging markets.[342] Their success can be attributed, by and large, to the business strategy both companies employed in accessing these markets, relying predominantly on offline retail for the distribution of goods.

In acknowledgement of the fact that those in developing countries would likely prefer real life brick-and-mortar stores for purchasing electronic commodities (by proxy of the ability to assess the goods prior to purchase), the companies have maintained themselves as largely offline businesses. In 2016 it was noted by OPPO's Vice President Alan Wu, that only 5% of the company's sales came from online channels; where-

---

[340] Telecom Review Asia, *Emerging Markets: A Gold Mine for Chinese OEMs,* (September 2017).

[341] The Economist, *Beating Apple, Xiaomi and the gang in China,* (February 2017).

[342] Forbes, Casey Hall, *Asian Companies are Dominating Global Smartphone Sales,* (July 2016); CNBC, Arjun Kharpal, *China's Rapidly Growing Smartphone Stars Set Sights on World Domination to Challenge Samsung, Apple,* (March 2017).

by such channels embodied an advertising function over an e-commerce one anyway.[343]

Exhibit 9.2 Opportunity Rings

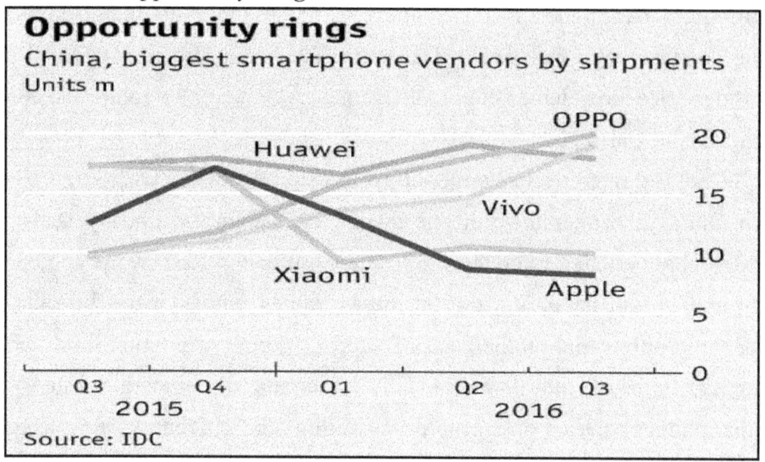

Source: The Economist, Beating Apple, Xiaomi and the gang in China, (2017).

After all, advertising plays a key role for the two smartphone providers, ensuring that their presence does not go unnoticed on their way to becoming household brands overseas. Accordingly, OPPO and Vivo have become known for their large scale capital investments into advertising and celebrity endorsements of new products, securing their position in countries such as India and Indonesia[344]; notwithstanding their online absence.

---

[343] Forbes, Yue Wang, *OPPO Explained: How A Little-Known Smartphone Company Overtook Apple in China,* (July 2016).

[344] Reuters, Eveline Danubrata and Sijia Jiang, *China's OPPO uses sales rep army, ad blitz to leapfrog over smartphone rivals,* (October 2016); The Economic Times, Writankar Mukherjee and Shambhavi Anand, *Revealed: Oppo, Vivo's Rs 2,200 Crore Marketing Strategy to Overtake Samsung in India,* (May 2017).

However, despite the level of success that such an offline, heavy-advertising strategy has brought to both companies, it is interesting that BBK Electronics (OPPO and Vivo's parent company), has one radically different smartphone subsidiary under its name: OnePlus. Interestingly, the company was founded in December 2013 as a project of OPPO's former Vice President, Peter Lau (Chinese Name: Liu Zuohu) and his co-founder Carl Pei.

OnePlus, operates in stark contrast to its predecessors OPPO and Vivo, utilising neither their offline tactics, nor advocating heavy use of external advertising to create a consumer following. Rather, the company employs a marketing and business strategy which operates fundamentally online and on the basis of word-of-mouth promotion. In doing so, the aim of the new brand is to create a competing line of smartphones focused on constant innovation and reinvention, following the motto of "never settle."

"A simple, bold idea: make a better phone...But, not just a better phone – a better way of doing things. A new kind of tech company that works hand in hand with users to do something amazing, something meaningful."

--OnePlus Official Website, "About Us" Section[345]

By proxy of these corporate values, OnePlus has adopted a more open approach, focusing on the power of the internet and social connectivity to raise awareness of its brand and products. As such, majority of advertising employed by the company occurs primarily via internet forums; with the OnePlus official website strongly tailored towards establishing an online community [Exhibit 9.3]. In turn, the company's customer fan base is relied heavily upon for circulating information

---

[345] See OnePlus Official Website: <<https://oneplus.net/about-us>> [accessed on 20th September 2017].

about its new products and developments, helping to define and popularise the OnePlus brand.

Exhibit 9.3

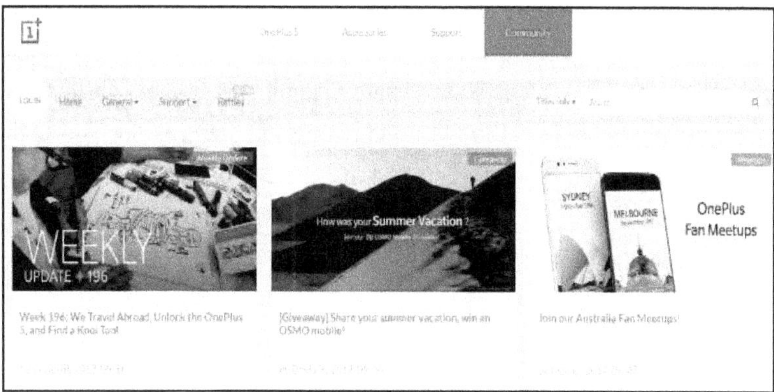

Source: OnePlus Official Website

This social and consumer-centred focus has even been strongly entrenched within OnePlus' business operations, most notably as an essential part of the company's distribution chain. In light of the unique OnePlus "invite" system, only those consumers who have obtained online "invites" from friends and acquaintances are capable of ordering the company's products. Such "invites" effectively operate as a queue, enabling products to be sold on a more controlled supply-demand basis.

The combination of these factors has given rise to a nonconventional growth, promoting the brand's image as one of innovation and novelty. Having never run any traditional or digital adverts in the building of its reputation, the company has relied instead on the exclusivity of its "invites" and the social interaction on its forums to build the brand it currently has today. In turn, this has enabled the company to keep its distribution and marketing costs low; supplying to meet a demand that has already been accurately quantified by the number of "invites", and advertising via the word-of-mouth of its loyal consumer fan base. The net result has enabled the company to sell its products at much cheaper, more affordable prices, giving it the upper hand against its predecessors in emerging markets such as India.

Nonetheless, OnePlus is still yet to have the level of influence that OPPO and Vivo currently enjoy; and indeed it is still a far way off from obtaining the global reputation of the likes of other competing Chinese smartphone brands such as Huawei and Xiaomi. One notable obstacle to such growth, lies in its failure to build a long standing relationship with its consumers; although it is conceded that the company is much younger in comparison to other big name brands. Still, the vast number of controversies that have plagued OnePlus since its fruition, evidence an inability to build trust in its brand. Ironically this is the very make it or break it for the company, given that its current marketing strategy relies heavily on what its consumers think for product advertising.

9.2 Word of Mouth Advertising

Adopting a word of mouth approach, as OnePlus has done, comes with a number of positives and negatives. For one, the technique is useful for newcomers; helping to circulate information and build awareness around those start-up companies that lack funding for traditional advertising. In the case of OnePlus, the use of viral marketing has been the sole source of promotion, which given its next-to-nothing costs, enabled the company to grow despite having a minimal starter marketing budget of just USD$300.[346] On such a small budget, the company's success in selling one million smartphones within its first year of operations is particularly creditworthy[347]; highlighting the advantages of its non-

---

[346] Advertising Age, Angela Doland, *OnePlus: The Startup That Actually Convinced People to Smash their iPhones,* (August 2015); Marketing Week, Jonathan Bacon, *How OnePlus is Taking on the Mobile Giants,* (March 2016).
[347] Forbes, Ewan Spence, *How $300 of Advertising Sold One Million Smartphones,* (January 2015).

conventional approach. In fact the word-of-mouth strategy may be increasingly useful and cost effective in the modern world, making use of the wide range of social platforms that have become an ordinary part of daily life, improving connectivity between people across the world.

On the other hand, the success of such an advertising strategy depends highly on two fragile factors:

1. Creating a hype, and
2. Positive customer feedback.

After all, only where a company has built up enough hype around its products and/or brand, will it be able to grab the attention of consumers in the market, standing out amongst existing competition. This is especially so in the case of OnePlus where no other forms of advertising were initially used to spread the word about the company's existence and products.

However, the problem with hypes is that they are short lived. In order ensure that a company is not only topical today, but remains relevant in the market of tomorrow, a reliable reputation needs to be quickly built. This shall ensure that the company can secure its long term position and competitiveness within the industry, relying solely on word-of-mouth recommendations.

Given that this form of advertising renders the company's reputation at the mercy of its consumers, in order to build a reliable reputation, the company must form meaningful long term relationships with its target market. Only then may it sustain an overall positive public image. As such, the development of a company's brand is not only subject to the corporations will, but also at the hands of customer feedback: how relevant and exciting consumers believe the brand to be; how they respond to its products and services, and the overall critical reception of the company's performance. All such factors place consumers within a more active role in developing and defining the scope of corporate image.

However, OnePlus has experienced problems in both these respects: *"creating a hype"* and *"positive customer feedback."* As a result of controversial marketing campaigns and false promises, the company has since received mixed attitudes and public reception.

"Fame and profits alone seldom equal respect. Respect comes from doing right things the right way and building something that matters."

--OnePlus Official Website, "About Us" Section[348]

Resultantly, whilst the underlying core aims of OnePlus is to provide a better, respectable smartphone brand; insensitive campaigns and improper management has built an inconsistent corporate image and an inability to secure brand trust and affinity long term.

9.3 Creating a Type: OnePlus Invites

Taking the former issue of "Creating a hype" into consideration, OnePlus has become known for its unusual strategy with regards to selling products. Indeed, from the very beginning, the company made it clear that purchase of its devices would be dependent on its novel "invite" system. In essence the company administered a sort of waiting line for the purchase of goods; allowing it to better determine manufacturing and distribution costs in line with a quantifiable demand.

In this way, the company would be better positioned to control and monitor logistical risks; preventing it from falling folly to overproduction problems.

---

[348] Supra note 6, OnePlus Official Website.

"We created the invitation system to manage uncertainty...In the phone industry, failure often comes from overconfidence—producing too many phones in anticipation of high demand"[349]

--Pete Lau (CEO of OnePlus)

However, the strategic merit behind the "invite" system goes much further. Alongside strengthening the company's risk management mechanisms, enabling more efficient stock control by decreasing overproduction losses; the invite system crucially fulfils a dual role, in further encouraging hype around OnePlus products. This is by virtue of the way in which the "invite" system operates, whereby customers wishing to buy a OnePlus product must first receive an invitation from an existing phone owner or from a staff member of OnePlus itself.

Accordingly, the strategy utilises the same principles of viral marketing that helped to widely promote companies like Hotmail, (which initially publicised itself by sending out adverts on the bottom of all emails sent to third parties). The same tactics have even been used for raising awareness around certain causes, with charity based initiatives like the Ice-Bucket Challenge (in which participants were publicly nominated by friends and family on social media, to keep the challenge going).

In fact the hype that OnePlus' invite system gives rise to, is based on the idea of "exclusivity"; building upon the desire of consumers to possess what very few others/a closed circle of individuals are able to possess. In turn it creates an elite social network, operating on an invite only basis. Simultaneously, it acts as a more effective sales technique, as consumers are personally recommended the brand from people they personally know and trust.

---

[349] Forbes, Paul Nunes and Larry Downes, *Disrupting the Smartphone Industry: An Interview with OnePlus CEO Pete Lau,* (July 2015).

"The invite-only model helped us manage our inventory better and after two years, we thought we had a fair understanding of the market. It also helped sell the phone."[350]

--Vikas Agarwal (General manager, OnePlus India)

Building off this hype and the exclusivity surrounding the OnePlus brand, the company has previously engaged in a number of campaigns in which lucky winners are given the chance to win early-bird invites, and in some cases purchase OnePlus products at greatly discounted prices. Given the novelty in obtaining invites in the first place, such campaigns provide a perfect opportunity to build extra hype around the release of new smartphone models, and to help the company remain exciting and relevant amongst consumers.

However, a number of campaigns were strongly criticised for their insensitivity to wider societal concerns, such as: the environment; health and safety, and gender rights. As a result, the high impact that OnePlus hoped to ignite through campaign competitions, was somewhat over-shadowed by public criticisms. In a few instances this eventually called for OnePlus to either alter the terms of its campaigns, or terminate them all together.

9.4 Sales Campaigns

One such scenario was witnessed in April 2014, upon the release of OnePlus' first branded product: the OnePlus One. The company, which was only a couple of months old, publicly announced that in line with its "Smash the Past" Campaign, it would be giving away OnePlus One phones for just USD $1. The prizes were up for grabs to 100 lucky cus-tomers who would be randomly selected from a list of email addresses

---

[350] TechinAsia, Merlin Francis, *OnePlus Radically Revamps India Strategy, gets More Aggressive,* (October 2016).

submitted by participants. The 100 participants with the chosen email addresses would then be required to send in video evidence of destroying their existing phones to finalise their victory.

Exhibit 9.4

Source: OnePlus

Via Android Community, Robert Nelson, OnePlus "Smash the Past" Campaign now Accepting Appli-cants, (2014).

Yet the terms of the competition remained unclear upon its initial announcement. Full details of the competition rules had not been fully disclosed, in the hope of building excitement around the campaign prior to its launch. Accordingly, it was observed that some OnePlus fans attempted to prematurely get ahead of the contest, misinterpreting the campaign as one in which the first 100 customers to have sent in video evidence, would automatically win the $1 give away. This resulted in a frenzy of people who had smashed their phones and sent in videos to OnePlus, misunderstanding the rules of the campaign [see Exhibit 4 for OnePlus' attempt to rectify this error]. As a result, the unsuspecting participants were left without a working phone and with no greater chances at winning the competition.[351]

---

[351] Android Authority, Andrew Grush, *Ahead of the OnePlus 'Smash the Past' Contest, People are Already Murdering Innocent Smartphones,* (April 2014).

Some have since argued that the campaign was ill-advised from its very conception, resulting in nothing more than the arbitrary waste of 100 phones. As such it was criticised for promoting a wasteful mentality and contributing to environmental problems. From a practical perspective, such unnecessary waste led some participants to question why they should be expected to smash a perfectly decent product, which at the very least could be recycled, sold on or donated for a just cause. Such reservations, along with health and safety concerns voiced about the toxicity of breaking mobile phone components, led to mixed public reception.

As a result, OnePlus was eventually led to alter its conditions, prompting that the 100 winners would now have the additional choice of donating their old phones to the non-profit charity, Medic Mobile.[352] The charity was selected for its cause, specialising in recycling old phones to fund healthcare projects in developing countries, providing health care workers with the technology needed to improve their outreach.

"The lesson learned is that sometimes it's OK to be a little polarizing. You're never able to satisfy everyone."

--Carl Pei, (OnePlus CEO)[353]

Whilst the amendment to the campaign rules was welcomed and even praised by OnePlus fans as evidence that the company listens to customer feedback, such a marketing strategy gives rise to key oversights. A key goal within marketing is to promote a company and its products in a way that reflects positively on the business. Most importantly, is the need to depict the company in line with its own business culture, values and mottos. However in the case at hand, OnePlus' ac-

---

[352] OnePlus Official Website, see <<https://forums.oneplus.net/threads/the-smash-is-over-donate-your-flagship.7481/>> [accessed on 21st September 2017].
[353] Supra note 7, Advertising Age.

tions in condoning wasteful behaviour, was at odds with it's own afore-mentioned objectives: *"Respect comes from doing right things the right way and building something that matters."*

What's more, the company overlooked the importance of diversification, as a tool for engaging new audiences and a wider array of consumers with varying interests. Indeed, diversification is especially useful for a new company just starting out, so that it may begin from a more generalised standpoint. In turn it may better identify it's own niche, in analysing market reactions to determine which target consumer group best suits its products. On the contrary, the net result of OnePlus' campaigns was to alienate subgroups of their target market. This same attitude resulted months later in a particularly controversial OnePlus campaign; one that was not simply "polarizing" but alienating and offensive to consumer subgroups.[354]

Misgivings by the company to appropriately vet and consider the foreseeable implications of its marketing tactics, gave rise to the "Ladies First" campaign in August 2014. The campaign was aimed directly towards female consumers, in the hopes of increasing female involvement within the tech world more generally. Accordingly, the company offered 50 women the chance to win "invites" in exchange for posting a photo of themselves with the OnePlus logo either printed on a piece of paper or written somewhere on their body. In turn, OnePlus' online community forum members would be given the chance to "like" the entry photos. The top 50 most liked entries, would subsequently win the chance at purchasing the company's OnePlus One phone alongside a branded T-Shirt [Exhibit 9.5].

---

[354] Forbes, Mike Elgan, *How Bad PR Can Kill a Great Product,* (August 2014).

Exhibit 9.5

Source: OnePlus Via BGR Group, Brad Reed, OnePlus's Latest Marketing Stunt is a Disaster in the Making, (2014).

Within a matter of hours, the campaign was shut down having faced wide spread criticism for its sexist and inappropriate approach towards promoting its products and brand. In fact, some female participants utilised the campaign platform to circulate images depicting their own outrage at the contest's demeaning nature, utilising hand gestures to portray their disapproval of the company's actions.[355]

In defending the face of OnePlus, the company announced that the campaign had been initiated without the consent of higher management, embodying a "misguided effort by a few isolated employees."[356]

---

[355] Supra note 15, Forbes; The Verge, Jacob Kastrenakes, *OnePlus Asks Women to Participate in Degrading Contest to get a Smartphone,* (August 2014).

[356] Supra note 15, Forbes.

"During that time a lot of staff [were] not in the office, people were on vacation or traveling for business, and we didn't have time to approve it. As soon as we saw it we removed it."

--Carl Pei (CEO OnePlus)[357]

This demonstrates problems relating to internal management, lacking the checks and balances to safeguard against such risks. Large scale promotional materials and marketing strategies should always require the final "go-ahead" from senior members prior to publication; given the impact that they may have on the company's reputation as a whole. In fact in any organ of the corporate structure, levels of responsibility and accountability need to be appropriately distributed, with mechanisms in place for monitoring individuals at a horizontal and vertical dimension. This is so as to ensure that individual decisions and actions do not easily influence, or become reflective of the company as a whole.

Indeed, it is not enough to excuse the campaign's misgivings by attributing such actions to "isolated employees." Rather mechanisms ought to have been in place to restrict the ability for lower members of staff to establish such strategies without a higher authority. Given this oversight, the company still faced backlash as the overall representative for the conduct of its employees. The net result not only gave rise to widespread public criticism, but given the impact of such campaigns in reflecting upon the company's own value systems, affiliated the OnePlus brand with sexist undertones.

Nevertheless, it is conceded that OnePlus had been very quick to identify the problem and remove it accordingly. In light of any offense caused by the initiative, the company further offered gifts of compensation to all participants that had submitted their photos to the company forum. After all, it is noted here that misguided advertising attempts are

---

[357] Supra note 7, Advertising Age.

experienced even by the largest of companies (see the previous chapter on Responsible Advertising and Effective Communication).

To avoid such controversies, companies ought to ensure that marketing strategies are well managed, strategically implemented and assessed from a 3600 perspective in attempting to foresee any controversial reactions it may give rise to. Utilising such a lens, the environmental and health and safety risks inherent in "Smash the Past," along with the social risks in the "Ladies First" campaign, may have been acknowledged and mitigated before their launch.

The use of a more diversified approach rather than polarizing, is noted in light of OnePlus' later collaboration with India's Ola Cabs (a transportation company specialising in providing shared services, similar to Uber). Under the OnePlus-Ola campaign, customers would have the chance to purchase OnePlus products, invite-free, within a short stipulated timeframe (less than a day per host city). Products purchased in time would be delivered to the customer's door within 15minutes of purchase via Ola Cabs.[358] The campaign was so successful that following its release in December 2015 for the promotion of the OnePlus X[359], it was relaunched the following year in December 2016 to promote the OnePlus 3T.[360]

Such success is attributable to its well thought out, pragmatic design; accounting for the needs of a wider audience without utilising any form of controversy to create its hype. To begin with, OnePlus ensured strategic selection of a well trusted and popular local company to enter into

---

[358] Business Insider, *OnePlus Partners Ola to Sell Devices Through Taxi App,* (December 2015).

[359] See OnePlus Marketing Blog <<https://blog.oneplus.net/india/2015/12/05/oneplus_ola/>> [accessed on 22nd September 2017].

[360] See OnePlus Marketing Blog <<https://blog.olacabs.com/preview-the-oneplus-3t-at-your-doorstep/>> [accessed on 22nd September 2017].

the campaign, enabling it to attract a wider audience given the particularly large 80% market share that Ola Cabs already dominated in India back in 2015.[361] As a result, even those consumers who did not belong to the OnePlus community, would have the chance to purchase it's products straight off the frequently used Ola App. In this way, the company allowed for greater diversification, emphasised by the campaign's sale of products without necessitating an invite.

Along the same vein, OnePlus' decision to roll the campaign out to 7 major cities across India, enabled its products to be easily accessible to a large variety of new and existing consumers. At the same time, it strengthened its word-of-mouth advertising approach and even developed new business relationships. After all, the collaboration benefitted Ola Cabs too; demonstrating the speed and efficiency of their transportation services, as well as encouraging new customers to download their app.

In fact, the 2016 campaign went a step further. In order to guarantee that customers would not lose out from participating, OnePlus ensured that those whose orders were not received in time would be given compensation in the form of a 10,000mAH power bank[362]. Accordingly, the campaign not only provided a win-win for Ola Cabs and OnePlus, but for customers taking part too.

Such a mechanism evidences that the decision making process was better structured, with the company recognising the importance of investing time into developing safeguards for situations where the campaign failed in its intentions. This coupled with acknowledging the differing interests and needs of its consumer market ensured success; having neither singled out a sub-group of consumers, nor requested any controversial conduct on behalf of participants. Rather, the campaign

---

[361] Forbes, Ellen Huet, *World War Uber: Why the Ride-Hailing Giant Can't Conquer the Planet (Yet),* (September 2015);

[362] Supra note 21, OnePlus Marketing Blog.

built upon the company's existing values and business strategies; focusing on exclusivity by virtue of the time deadline imposed for orders, and creating a campaign "that works hand in hand with users."

9.5 Positive Customer Feedback

However as previously noted, when using a strictly word-of mouth advertising approach, creating a hype to ensure that a company's brand and products become well known is not the only factor worth considering. Rather, it is equally important that general customer feedback remains positive; a factor paramount to establishing OnePlus as the better, respected brand it strives to be.

In order to promote such a positive image, it is necessary for companies to secure a loyal consumer base; solidifying its position and competitive edge long term. This requires a high level of service and attention to detail, to provide customers with the kind of retail experience that the brand later wishes to be affiliated with.

Yet, the company's past reputation with respect to false promises, misrepresentation and inefficient customer complaint services, have hindered the ability for its brand to truly achieve such a reputation. In response, a number of OnePlus customers demonstrated their disappointment in 2017, by supporting a page posted on the crowd speaking platform: Thunderclap. The platform enables individuals to spread awareness on a certain topic, leading OnePlus community member David Monteiro to create and circulate a negative post about the company: *"Get to know how #OnePlus treats its earlier customers and breaks its promises."* The page gained 2,724 supporters in just under one month, and surmised that OnePlus' mistakes could be attributed to the fact that it *"cares more about marketing than it does about its customers."*[363]

The matter in question that had triggered the response was down to the company's promises that all OnePlus 2 phones would be updated to the Android 7 "Nougat" system. However, after 2 years of making such commitments, the company publicly announced that this would no longer be the case.[364] The most apparent problem in this situation lay with the company's failure to live up to its word. Indeed, on multiple former occasions, similar promises were made and broken with specific regards to the OnePlus 2 phone.

Take for instance commitments made at the phone's initial launch, which voiced that it would be easier and quicker for customers to obtain the new smartphone. The assurances made, arose in light of the negative feedback that customers had given during the launch of the OnePlus One phone regarding delays and problems acquiring "invites." In the hope of receiving a more positive response with the OnePlus 2, it was thus promised that such delays would no longer be a problem. However, notwithstanding these assurances, logistical mismanagement still resulted in lengthy delays, with phones shipped out nearly a month after the company's targeted date. In acknowledgement of its broken promise, OnePlus announced[365]:

"We messed up the launch of the OnePlus 2...This delay has brought huge opportunity cost...We don't plan on making further promises for

---

[363] ThunderClap, David Monteiro, *Promises Matter, OnePlus,* (April 2017). <<https://www.thunderclap.it/projects/55301-promises-matter-oneplus?locale=en>> [accessed on 22nd September 2017].

[364] Android Authority, Kris Carlon, *OnePlus Finally Confirms no Nougat Update for the OnePlus2,* (June 2017).

[365] See OnePlus Community Forum Thread <<https://forums.oneplus.net/threads/sorry-for-the-delay-guys.362497/>> , [accessed on 22nd September 2017].

future launches, and will instead focus on showing the world how we've improved through our actions.

--Carl Pei (CEO OnePlus)

Yet contrary to the sincere apology, the company still failed to safeguard itself against breaking other promises that had been made for the OnePlus 2. Commitments for ongoing customer support and upgrades of the phone every 1-2 months for the 2 years after its launch, had been adhered to only for the first year; up until the release of the company's newer OnePlus 3 model. The result was to imply a certain fickleness to the company: only willing to invest its attention and resources into its newest product. This, coupled with the aforementioned failure to upgrade the One Plus 2 to the Android 7 "Nougat" operating system, demonstrated that despite the company's reassurances, it still took the making and breaking of promises rather light-heartedly.

The company's omission, intentional or not, highlights a weakness in its long term customer support and services; a factor crucial to building an affinity and loyal consumer base with the OnePlus brand. In turn, earlier customers were left feeling underappreciated for the input that they had had in catapulting the company's reputation from an unknown start-up to a fairly prominent smartphone supplier today.

In fact, the Thunderclap viral campaign following the companies "false promises," comments on the company's continuous failure to tackle problems head on. Notwithstanding its admission of error concerning the shipment of OnePlus 2 phones; other failed commitments were rarely commented on by OnePlus members, leaving customers unaware of whether promises made would be fulfilled by the company or not. Given OnePlus' dependency on social interactions for growth, in light of the consumer-centric focus it adopted, communication ought to be regularly maintained between the company and end users. Yet as evidenced by David Monteiro, consumers were faced with nothing but a lack of transparency and communication gap when things went wrong.

Indeed, OnePlus has often come up against challenges relating to its customer support, with many consumers having complained that said services are inefficient at handling their problems. Customer feedback claiming long delays between submitting a problem and receiving a reply from the support team, only exacerbates distrust and frustration with the company; preventing it from living up to the better, more respectable phone brand underlying its philosophy. In acknowledgement of these problems, it is conceded that the company has since upgraded its customer support teams in 2017, expanding its number of employees and providing multilingual support to better aid a wider range of consumers. In addition it has even opened up repair centres in the US and Europe, so that negative customer feedback and problems relating to OnePlus devices may be remedied much faster.[366]

Still, dishonest and misleading actions have continued to inhibit the transparency and trust of the OnePlus brand. Evidence that the company had been cheating on its Benchmark scores in 2017 prior to the release of its OnePlus 5 device, reiterate concerns that the company *"cares more about marketing than it does about its customers."* The company had previously been accused for the same behaviour with regards to the OnePlus 3T model; using performance boosters to improve the ability of mobile phone units handed out to the media in determining the smartphone's function and reliability.[367]

Unsurprisingly the company has received widespread criticism for its repeated blunder. Following the OnePlus 3T controversies of manipulating benchmark scores, OnePlus ought to have embedded monitor-

---

[366] The Verge, Vlad Savov, *OnePlus Touts Improvements to Customer Care in Anticipation of OnePlus 5,* (June 2017).
[367] The Verge, Vlad Savov, *OnePlus Touts Improvements to Customer Care in Anticipation of OnePlus 5,* (June 2017).

ing systems and policies to prevent the same scandal from arising again. After all, building trust does not require that no mistakes are ever made by a company, as logistical errors and marketing blunders are an intrinsic risk of every management decision. However what is required, is that companies demonstrate the ability to grow and develop in light of past mistakes, remedying faults to assure consumers that the same mistakes won't happen twice. Only in this manner, can customers feel confident that they can still depend on a company's brand long term, even where things have previously gone wrong.

Indeed, the real problem with the false promises surrounding the OnePlus 2 launch and after care services, is the fact that the company has failed on several occasions to honour its word; repeating the same behaviour that consumer feedback has openly identified to be a problem. After receiving consistent feedback identifying the same contentions, it is the responsibility of a company to investigate, monitor, assess and remedy the matter of contention. Only where this occurs, can it be said that the company possesses a well-integrated customer service system for handling complaints. In the case of OnePlus however, the biggest contentions centre on this very customer complaint system and its inability to provide remedy; it's no wonder then, that OnePlus customers had to turn to alternative platforms such as Thunderclap, to have their feedback heard.

9.6 Conclusion

"OnePlus's future growth strategy depends on its ability to build brand trust and affinity, so the company is keeping a closer check on its marketing output."[368]

Whilst OnePlus is still a relatively new company, and ought to be credited for the phenomenal growth it has achieved within a short time

---

[368] Supra note 7, Marketing Week.

span, lessons can be learnt from its failed marketing campaigns alongside the company's false promises and lack of transparency. Such shortcomings are exacerbated in the case of the company, given its dependency on consumers for circulating word-of-mouth driven advertisement.

Interestingly, the company has since made a dramatic move away from its word-of-mouth approach, taking on more conventional routes for doing business. In 2017, OnePlus contracted a celebrity endorsement from the Bollywood Superstar, Amitabh Bachchan. Whether this is as a result of its failure to properly secure long term loyalty from consumer advertising, or simply because the company has *"to think integrated and cross-platform to be most effective"*[369] is debatable. Either way, bringing some conventionalism to the company's controversial past may be warranted for defining itself as a respectable brand.

9.7 Questions for Thought

1. Is all publicity, good publicity?

2. Companies are likely to evolve and change over time. How can a company ensure it maintains the loyalty of its earlier consumers notwithstanding its own evolution?

3. How far should consumer after-sales care extend? One year after purchase, two years...? Does this differ depending on the type of goods sold?

4. Is a company always responsible if it's sales campaigns/marketing promotions are misinterpreted by a handful of the public? To what extent is it reasonable to hold them accountable?

---

[369] Economic Times, Amit Bapna, *Is OnePlus Revamping Its Brand Strategy? Bringing in a Celebrity Endorsement Paves the Path to Success,* (March 2017), quoting Girish Menon (KPMG India, Media & Entertainment Director).

5. Should companies always take a neutral stance when commenting on social issues, or is it ok to be a little bit polarising and somewhat controversial at times? If so, when?

9.8 Appendix

OnePlus: Unique Marketing Model

Exhibit 9.6 OnePlus Online Forums

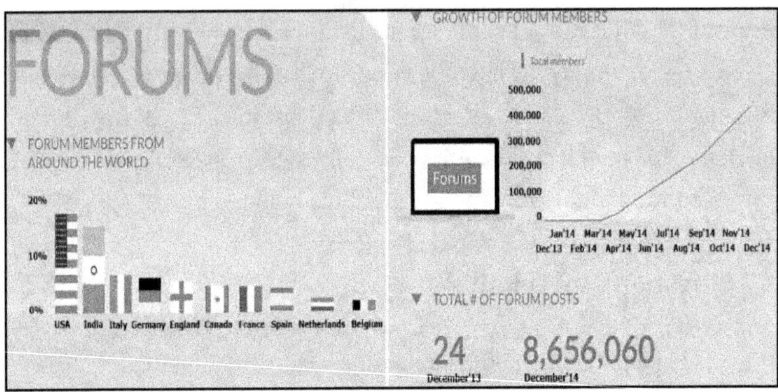

Source: OnePlus Annual Report, 2014

<<https://oneplus.net/au/annual-report-2014>>

OnePlus' marketing model establishes an online communi-ty through OnePlus Forums. These forums are central to the company's word of mouth advertising strategy, providing a direct platform for communication with consumers, as op-posed to reliance on traditional advertising methods for infor-mation exchange.

Exhibit 9.7 OnePlus Brand Growth and Data Traffic

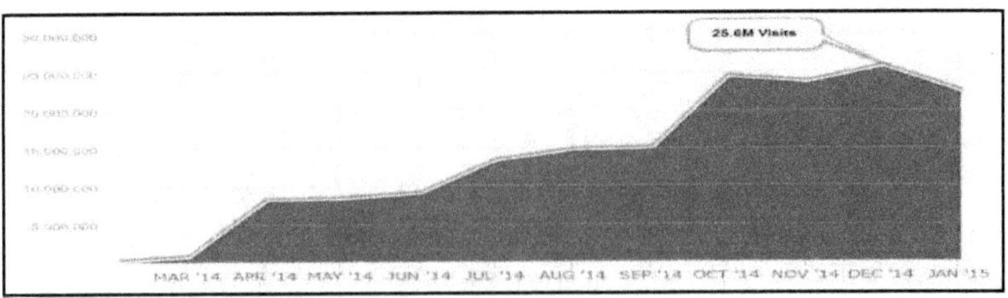

Source: SimilarWeb

Via: The Next Web, Ariel Rosenstein, How the OnePlus' Marketing Strategy made it the most Desirable Phone in the World, (2015)

Despite the company having only been established in December 2013, the OnePlus word-of-mouth advertising and "invite-only" model saw a dramatic surge in brand growth within it's first year.

Exhibit 9.8 OnePlus Invite System Explanation Given by Co-Founder, Carl Pei

Buying a popular smartphone can be a frustrating experience, both for consumers and manufacturers alike. This is something we're trying to solve.

For consumers, a product they have anticipated for a long time might be sold out immediately before they even have a chance to place an order. Some offer pre-orders, which often means a long time between paying for your order and actually having it shipped. The worst experience for consumers is probably when a company decides to sell in batches where you have to set a reminder to patiently wait for a batch, log onto the website to disappointedly find out that it got sold out. When you eventually get a chance to buy one, it's actually a pre-order that you'll need to wait a long time to receive again.

Why do manufacturers do this? It's very hard to predict the future, and hardware is expensive. Producing larger batches means tying in more capital and increasing risk. Making too many devices that end up not being sold can bankrupt a business easily. In addition, there's always a production ramp up period where production yield increases by time. This is another reason to why it's hard to have a lot of stock from the very beginning. When the choice is between selling to a few users first, or stocking up and delaying launch, it's not a difficult decision to choose the former.

[Updated May 9] Another reason to the invite system is because we're still learning. Launching a product worldwide is ambitious for a 5 month old startup. We are sure that there will be hiccups along the way and that the purchasing experience will not be perfect from the very start. With invites, we can control and ramp up availability, giving a chance for our logistics and customer service teams to catch up if anything unexpected happens.

Good Products Shared Among Friends

To solve these problems, we have created a much more user friendly way of buying the device through the OnePlus Invite System. With an invite, you can be 100% sure that you'll actually be able to buy it, and it ships within a few days. In contrast to staying up in the middle of the night trying to buy one along with 20,000 other people. So in the true spirit of the OnePlus name, a good product gets spread by word of mouth, shared among friends for that extra personalized touch.

> So how do you get an invite? Invites will also be made available through friends, contests, and on this forum (you have not been forgotten). We value thoughtful contributions from active fans. Once you've bought a OnePlus One, you'll also become eligible to invite your friends in the future.
>
> In the beginning, they'll be available in limited quantities, but as time progresses they'll become easier and easier to come by.

Source: OnePlus Official Forum

OnePlus: Market Dominance

Exhibit 9.9 OnePlus Growth_India

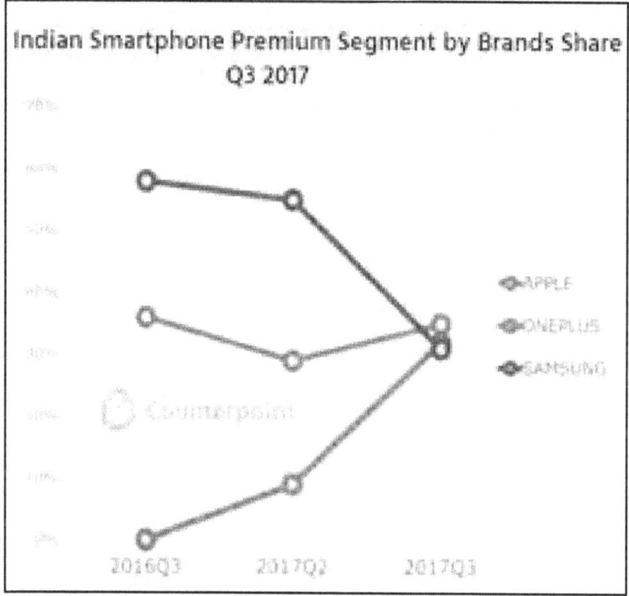

Source: Counterpoint, Karn Chauhan, OnePlus 5 Was the Best Selling Premium Smartphone Model in India in Q3 2017, (2017).

Exhibit 9.10 OnePlus Market Share_India

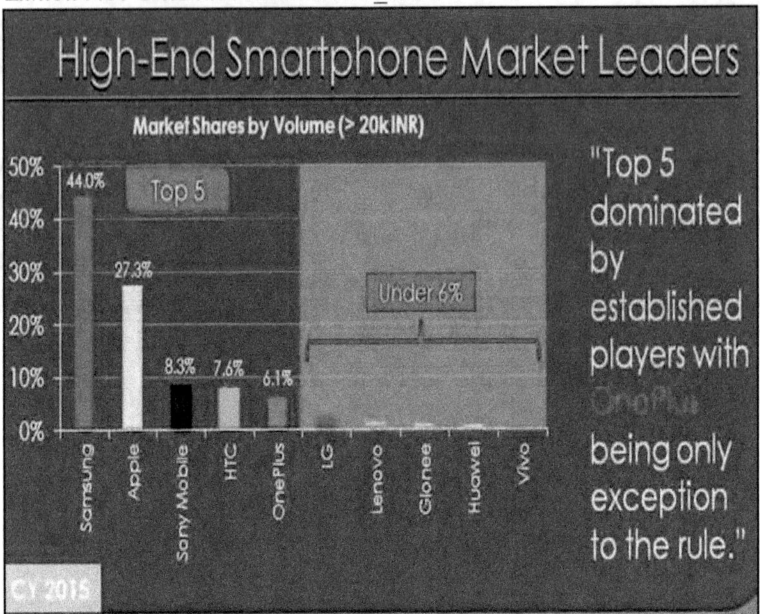

Source: Cyber-Media Research

Via Indian Express, Premium smartphone segment grows, OnePlus emerges as big winner: CMR, (2016)

Note: OnePlus' market share and dominance is particularly large and growing within the Indian emerging market. However, within the global market and even the domestic one, the company is still yet to be named as one of the key competitors in the smartphone industry (see Exhibit 9.11 and 9.12 below).

Exhibit 9.11 Domestic Smartphone Market (China)

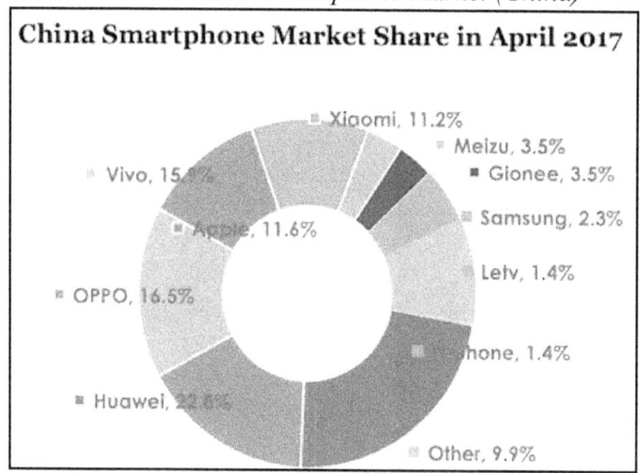

Source: Gesellschaft für Konsumforschung (GfK) (May 2017)

Via China Internet Watch, Top 10 smartphone brands in China in April 2017.

Exhibit 9.12 Global Smartphone Mar-ket

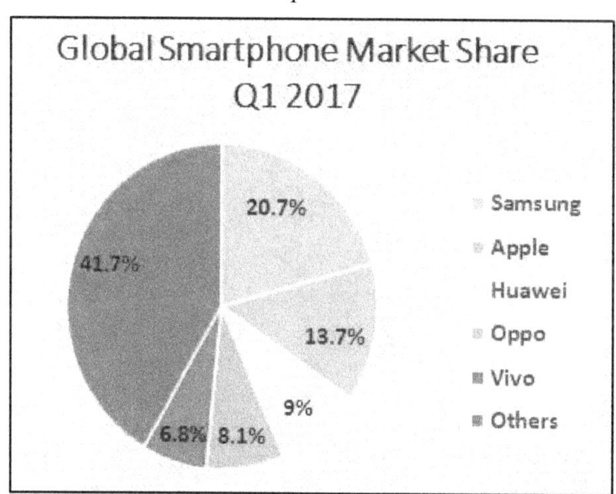

Source: Gartner

Via Android Headlines, Kristijan Lucic, Gartner: Worldwide Smartphone Sales Grew 9% YoY in Q1 2017, (2017).

10

NEW AGE BUSINESS

Cases for Thought

The Virtual World

The case studies examined thus far portray lessons learnt from past failings in Chinese ODI, particularly with regards to: the extractive industries; infrastructure building; mergers and acquisitions; the export of manufacture, and consumer retailers. Collectively, such examples reiterate general needs within ODI for: long term strategy, diligent preparation, localisation of projects, adequate environmental and social impact assessments, responsible advertising, and efficient customer complaints mechanisms. Such factors are crucial to securing business success, whilst respecting the needs and interests of relevant stakeholder groups.

However, an interesting question arises as to how such factors might apply in light of the new age virtual world. Indeed, today's industry sectors are all beginning to embrace the surprisingly fast growth of the internet, recognising its capability in allowing a business to better target itself towards potential consumers through the use of internet-related products and services. At the same time, utilising other online technologies such as apps, system software and social media messaging platforms, have increased efficiency at every stage of business. Such products and services have arisen in a wide range of different contexts, revolutionising an entirely new form of "Silicon Valley" innovation-driven company; whereby traditional business models and supply chain structures are somewhat subverted in place of novel concepts for corporate management and revenue creation.

Of the influx in software programmes, tech companies have capitalised on the ability for their products to better enhance and streamline existing industries. Some have achieved this by providing new and alternative ways of compiling data and market research; identifying trends in market behaviours and developing a means by which third party businesses may better streamline their P.R. and Marketing departments alongside ever-changing consumer needs.

Others have utilised technology for the purposes of establishing more direct platforms by which to bypass certain stages of the more traditional linear-based supply chains. As such tech companies may become able to sell services or information accrued by proxy of their online platforms at a B2B level (business-to-business); or alternatively embody the role of facilitating interchange between businesses (B2B) and consumers (B2C), adopting a mutual role between both groups. Such services enable companies to promote the cost-cutting benefits and increased efficiency that their technologies can provide to the traditional consumer sales process.

Analysis of the way in which these alternative business models may give rise to their own unique challenges, highlights the manner in which responsible business concepts such as: sustainability, strategic planning and due diligence, may need to be approached from a slightly different perspective when dealing with apps and online platforms. In demonstrating as much, the case of China's Meitu App shall first be explored, highlighting the obstacles that entertainment and social appware companies face when developing sustainable business strategies and executing diligent risk management as is advocated for more traditional business sectors.

Following on, the case of Ctrip, China's leading online travel agency, shall demonstrate the challenges that may be faced by exchange platforms, which aim to better connect industry providers with end users. Herein, the obstacles relating to safeguarding consumer safety and consumer rights alongside operating an open marketplace online, shall demonstrate the difficulties in navigating responsibility along a more triangular based business model.

11

THE CASE OF MEITU INC.

Monetising downloadable free appware

11.1 Case Background

The increase in today's market sectors for innovation, integrated with the power of the internet, has led to the emergence of tech based companies operating in a different capacity; moving away from the need to entrench themselves within existing industries and supply chains. Online platforms and free apps which depend on social functions to generate growth, have introduced completely novel industry sectors; expanding upon traditional concepts of entertainment and communication exchange, to establish online virtual networks of social activity.

Such industries have revolutionised both B2B and B2C based business models, sequencing them in reverse [Exhibit 11.1]. Accordingly, where traditional supply chains focus on B2B exchange, with the ultimate aim of facilitating end users (B2C); downloadable free appware focuses on B2C exchange, with the ultimate aim of facilitating third-party businesses in their advertising, market research and development (B2B). In this way, the profits made by free-appware relies most heavily on the sale of B2B based services, generated by proxy of B2C user engagement.

Crucially, appware companies achieve this by introducing an entirely new dimension of: C2B (consumer-to-business). This crucial stage enables tech companies to garner information from consumers, which is then passed on to other businesses for profit, such as: survey results; consumer preferences; market trends etc. Indeed, it is on this basis that majority of apps available today operate as free downloadable software for the average consumer; with the C2B stage in turn, acting as the commercialisation element of the business strategy in allowing the company to monetise from its large user base.

Exhibit 11.1

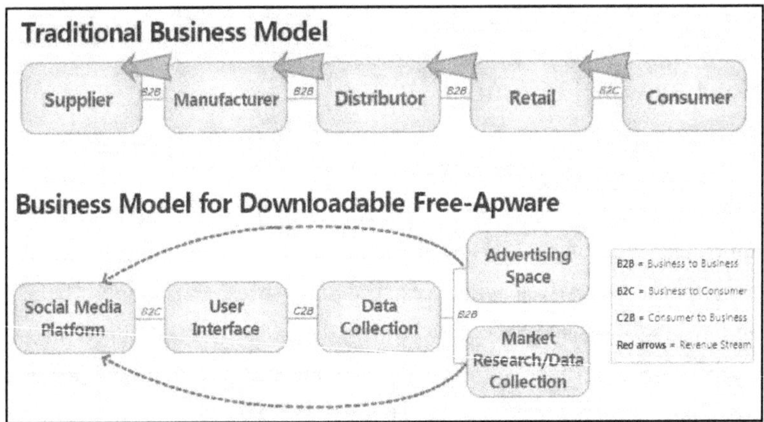

Source: Created by the Author

However, this alternative business strategy for revenue creation, means that the traditional tools for risk identification and assessment may no longer be so fitting. As opposed to tried-and-tested industry sectors such as mining or construction, app-based companies are currently faced with a greater number of uncertainties, making the task of quantifying risks much harder. This is by proxy of the dual nature of the internet and social trends, which are not only continuously progressing and developing, but which are prone to changing at alarming rates. Such dynamism makes it much harder for appware companies to strategically orchestrate themselves, as market trends become difficult to predict in the relevant industry sector, be it: gaming; travel and leisure; photography; fashion etc.

The result renders internet-based companies, particularly ones whose software is free, as bearing an intrinsic risk that what is of interest online today, may be quickly replaced with something entirely different tomorrow. A classic example is that of MySpace, an online social networking site that provided users with the chance to upload photos, videos, music and even blogs. Whilst the company was once the largest social media site in the world (from 2005 to 2008), it has since fallen in popularity and profitability emphasising:

"The fragility of social media, where fickle consumers and changing tastes can make sensations out of services like Tribe and Friendster, which quickly fade from public imagination."

-- Chunka Mui (Forbes)[370]

This fast paced intrinsically uncertain nature of software companies, coupled with the primary need for such companies to secure a large user base prior to establishing a reputation that is capable of monetising on; has meant that the entire business model for free appware is inherently different. Like all companies, there is a need from the outset to initially invest with higher chances of risk. However, unlike most companies which can steadily capitalise on their products and services whilst growing, appware companies whose apps are available for free download, can only truly capitalise on their product once they have grown a large enough reputation that is capable of earning revenue through B2B-based advertising and data collection. Subsequently, as demonstrated by Exhibit 1 (above), the flow of revenue streams for these companies emerges further down the line, interrupting the classic approach whereby revenue streams are achieved at each progressive stage of business.

---

[370] Forbes, Chunka Mui, *Why Facebook Beat MySpace, and Why MySpace's Revised Strategy will Probably Fail,* (January 2011).

11.2 B.A.T.: Software on the Rise

Yet the huge potential that the internet industry embodies has meant that despite higher risks, highly unpredictable market trends and delayed profitability, it is still a highly attractive industry that has been rapidly growing in both size and investment. It is no wonder then that within China, the technological boom as in all other areas of the world, has not gone unnoticed.

As such, whilst Chinese ODI may have focused most heavily within industry sectors of natural resource management and infrastructure building, China is also home to some of the largest internet based companies in the world. B.A.T, an acronym for China's three more profitable and renowned companies: Baidu, Alibaba and Tencent, are notable for the substantial sums of capital that they are able to generate through their own internet-based platforms and services. In terms of ODI, all three companies have been eagerly expanding globally in the hopes of dominating foreign markets in much the same way that they have managed to capitalise on China's own growing consumer appetite.

And they are not alone. As the Go Global push encouraged many traditional industry sectors to go abroad, it has also had an impact on Chinese internet and technology based companies. Although it has been argued that the main strategies for global expansion adopted by the B.A.T trio have focused on mergers and acquisitions[371], there are still a fair number of mid to small start-up companies, who have proved the ability for all types of Chinese apps and software products to organically expand overseas in countries such as: South East Asia, India, Latin America, USA, Germany and Canada [Exhibit 11.2].

---

[371] Economic Times, Amit Bapna, *Is OnePlus Revamping Its Brand Strategy? Bringing in a Celebrity Endorsement Paves the Path to Success,* (March 2017), quoting Girish Menon (KPMG India, Media & Entertainment Director).

Exhibit 11.2 How China's App Perfmance around the World

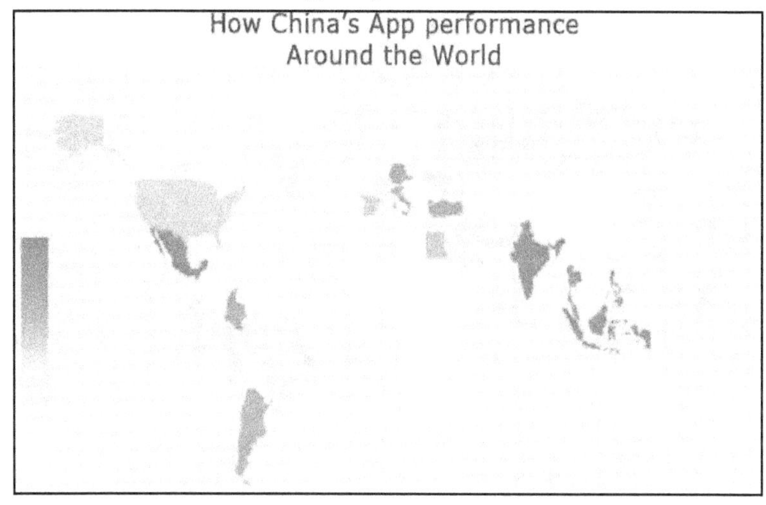

Source: Cheetah Lab <<http://data.cmcm.com/report/detail/152>>

Such appware companies have been as diverse as they have been plentiful, operating in a multitude of industry sectors from news to fitness, shopping to entertainment, and the aforementioned social media and communication sectors [Exhibit 11.3].

"China is now an indispensable part of the global developer community..."[372] "...Some of our most successful developers today are Chinese ones who export apps and games to the rest of the world."[373]

--Ben Galbraith (Google, Head of Product and Developer Relations)

---

[372] China Daily, Liu Zheng, *Application Developers Come of Age,* (January 2017).

[373] The Telegraph, Liu Zheng, *Google Executive Sees Potential for Developers' Economy,* (August 2016).

Exhibit 11.3 Chinese Apps that Made It into the Top 3,000 List in the Overseas Market Source: Cheetah Lab <<http://data.cmcm.com/report/detail/152>>

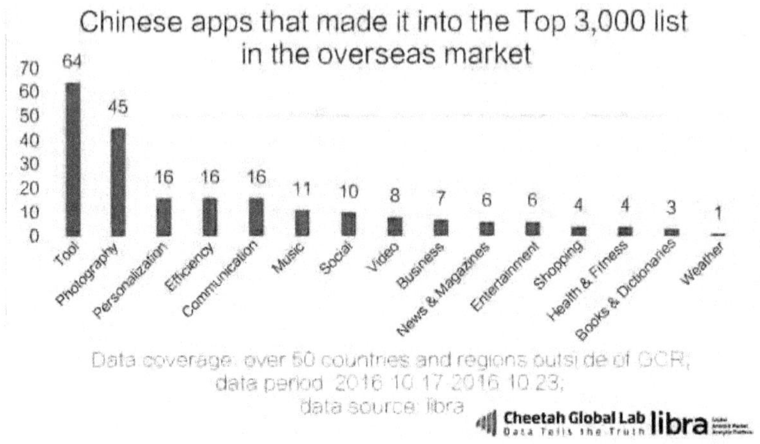

11.3 Meitu Madness

Amongst these companies lies one that acts as a testimony to the impressive development of Chinese made software applications: Meitu Inc. The company, as of 2017, has witnessed an unexpected surge in overseas markets, revitalising popularity for its photo image editing software.

First established in October 2008, Meitu began as a PC based photo-editing developer. Since then it has grown in both size and reputation into a leading developer of beauty-related mobile phone apps, available for free download on both Apple and Android devices. Following the company's first selfie app developed in 2013, it has made for itself an impressive repetoire of 13 software applications available on both iOS and Google Play, alongside leading Chinese app stores such as: Xiaomi, Tencent's Myapp, and Huawei.

The company's more famous products currently include:

1. Airbursh, Beauty Plus, Selfie City: photo editing software which enables users to retouch photos in much the same way as Photoshop, but with simplified user interface.

2. Meipai: live-streaming software (a particular fruitful industry currently within China).

3. Meitu: the company's most globally famous app which transforms photos into hand-drawn cartoon style images, personalised to create quirkier selfies.

The latter app, Meitu, has gained popularity both within China and overseas; with a network of over 1.1 billion users worldwide as of October 2016, and monthly active users reaching 520 million by January 2017.[374] Amongst consumers, overseas profiles account for 500 million originating from a whole host of different countries, spanning: Latin America; South Korea; India; South East Asia and the U.S.

To aid in it's global expansion, efforts have been invested into making Meitu apps available in over two dozen languages,[375] and localisation offices have been formed in: New Delhi (India); Sao Paulo (Brazil); Palo Alto (California); Singapore and Tokyo (Japan). Yet notwithstanding such efforts, the sudden claim to fame of the Meitu app in Western countries such as the U.S. and Europe, happened rather unexpectedly, and is yet to be fully understood.

In fact it has been theorised that the hype surrounding Meitu's beauty driven photo editting software had occurred more or less by fluke as opposed to well considered strategic investment. Statistics indicate that the apps popularity was somehow influenced by American politics; although it is noted that the company's 2017 update allowing images to

---

[374] Meitu Official Website, Company Profile: <<http://corp.meitu.com/en/about/overview/>> [accessed on 26th July 2017]; <<http://corp.meitu.com/en/news/news/49.html>> accessed: 2017/07/26>>.

[375] Technode, Mike Cormack, *Meitu, China's Leading Photo App Developer, Has reached 800m Accounts Worldwide,* (February 2015).

be recreated under six thematic styles, was the particular aspect to go viral.[376] Data analysis shows that on the same day of President Trump's inaguaration (January 20th), the Meitu App soared from its 1000th or so listing on the United States Apple store to 11th position. As a result, the bizarre turn of events aided Meitu's expansion in North America, surprising the Managing Director of Meitu Inc.'s International Business Department, Mr Fu Kan:

"我们甚至没用任何付费推广。"

(Translation: We did not even have to use any promotion.)[377]

The random turn of events reiterates the aforementioned difficulties inherent in predicting market trends for tech based industries, which are not only especially dynamic, but sensitive to social phenomenons.

Nevertheless, prior to the recent 2017 hype surrounding the company, the Meitu app was still doing phenomenally well within China and greater parts of Asia. It's impressive growth in usage had led to it's repeated ranking between June 2014 to October 2016, as one of the top eight non-game related iOS apps; placing it on par with appware from companies such as Facebook, Apple and Google.[378]

11.4 Making Profits?

Yet issues have been noted with regards to the company's long term sustainability. Concerns are voiced that despite Meitu Inc.'s large user engagement and growing reputation, the company has yet to turn a net profit, having steadily accrued accumulated losses [Exhibit 11.4]. In-

---

[376] International Business Times, *What is Meitu? Chinese selfie app goes viral as famous faces get anime 'hand-drawn' makeovers,* (January 2017).

[377] Meitu Official Press Release, 26th January 2017 <<https://corp.meitu.com/news/press/33.html>> [accessed on 28th July 2017] Chinese version of site.

[378] Supra note 5, Meitu Official Website.

deed, since its very conception of popular selfie related apps, Meitu Inc. has been investing more into its products than it has been getting out.

Exhibit 11.4 Revenue and Net Loss of Company from 2013 to 2016 H1

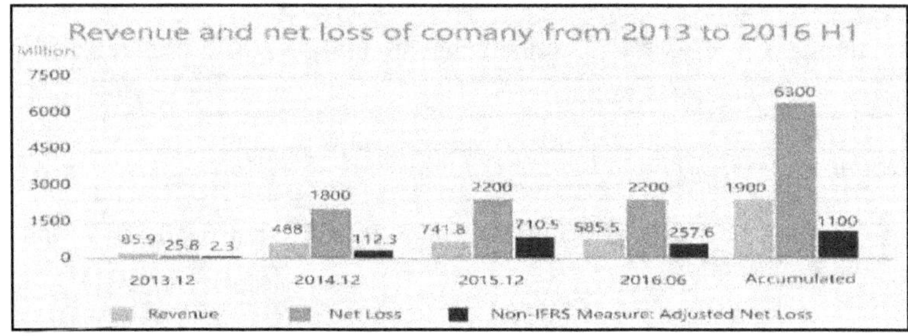

Source: Meitu Inc. Prospectus
Via China Tech Insights, What is this Selfie App Meitu from China that just Blew Up in the U.S.? (2017).

Consequently, whilst Meitu Inc.'s software may be rising in terms of popularity and consumer usage, the company has still been unable to find a way to properly and sustainably monetize from it's free-to-subscribe applications. This in turn is noted to undermine the overarching interests of its shareholders.

Thusfar in keeping itself afloat, 95% of Meitu's earnings have stemmed from its sideline business selling hardware luxury mobile phones; despite its primary business operations focusing on the development of software. Interestingly, this renders MeituKiss (the company's niche phone series dedicated to taking selfies), as arguably one of its more valuable assets, given the company's dependency on the revenue streams that the phone brand generates.

The problem here however, is that whilst MeituKiss may be capable of turning a small profit (with 750,000 units sold in 2016)[379]; it is not capable in the long run, of competing with other big name brands in the

---

[379] Reuters, Sijia Jiang, *Chinese Selfie App Firm Meitu Reduces Loss, aims for Expansion Abroad,* (March 2017).

mobile phone hardware industry. As previously mentioned, within China alone, Huawei, Oppo, Vivo and Xiaomi already present grave competition, having jointly dominated just under 60% of the Chinese market [Exhibit 11.5].[380] As such Meitukiss' only chances of success, rest on remaining within its niche, evidencing limitations in the phone brand's future prospects for growth.

Exhibit 11.5 Smartphone Vendors Market Shares, 2016 Q3

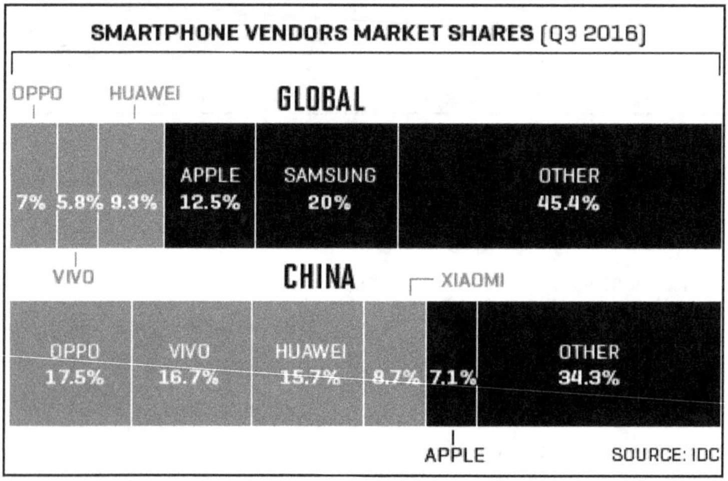

Sources: International Data Corporation.
Via Fortune, Scott Cendrowski, How China's Smartphone "Big Four" are fighting for Global Customers, (2017)

For Meitu Inc. this effectively signifies the need to gravitate away from its current reliance on hardware sales, and devise a strategy upon which to capitalise on the company's main business product: mobile phone software. Herein it is conceded that the company's revenue streams from software related products in the form of online adverts, fee-based add-ons and ecommerce, have been gradually improving; with

---

[380] Fortune, Scott Cendrowski, *How China's Smartphone 'Big Four' Are Fighting for Global Customers,* (January 2017).

December 2016 presenting a 481% increase in software-generated revenue as compared with the first half monthly average of 2016.[381] Nevertheless, in order for the company to truly make a difference to its net profits and continue increasing its overall share price, it may be time to introduce new business strategies that will enable the company to commercialise on its products much faster.

Some have since argued that this is already long overdue. Criticisms have been voiced that the company's failure to turn a profit, compromising the overall interests of its shareholders, is down to it's failure to diligently outline a realistic long term business strategy capable of securing growth.

"Meitu's big problem has always been that it came up with this killer app -- and the usage is unbelievable. It's crazy. But they never had a clear business model underneath it."[382]

--Jeffrey Towson (Peking University)

Professor of Investment

Such contentions reiterate the problems noted in the market entry case studies explored in preceeding chapters; whereby the experiences of Chinese companies with white elephants, failed mergers and acquisitions and poor localisation, can all be attributed to a lack of due diligence, long term focus, and strategic planning from the outset of ventures.

However, as previously explored (Exhibit 11.1), the business model of companies selling free-appware is inherently different to other industries. The pivotal difference here lies in the stage at which commercialisation occurs. This is because, by virtue of the fact that the revenue

---

[381] Tech in Asia, Ziwei Li, *Can Meitu Cash in on its Popularity to Make a Profit?*, (February 2017)

[382] Gadgets 360, Agence France-Presse, *Meitu, China's Selfie-App Leader, Seeks to 'Beautify the World'*, (February 2017).

streams for free-apware tend to arise much later on, by proxy of the B2C-C2B-B2B business structure; the inability for Meitu to yet yield a profit, does not immediately suggest that the company is lacking in business strategy. Rather, given the models typically used in light of the industry sector to which Meitu belongs, for some it is arguably even normal that no net profit has yet accured.

The company's Chairman and investor has since reiterated this fact, emphasising the need for internet based companies to first establish for themselves a positive and widely known reputation, before they can hope to capitalise on their product:

"For most internet companies, it is a long process to grope a business model. Previously we were focusing on acquiring users and cared much about user experience, but now we will start our commercialization."[383]

--Cai Wensheng

The statement suggests that Meitu's divergence from traditional practices, whereby a solid business model should be established prior to entering a new venture; was neither an accident nor an oversight. Indeed, upon going public with its listing on the Hong Kong stock exchange, the company remained confident in its business approach, with ambitions that despite its lack of profits it would be capable of securing for itself an IPO worth USD 500 million and a company valuation between USD 5-6 billion. In response to such ambitions, analysts and investors voiced heavy skepticism that these prospective valuations would be attainable by the company:

"Given its lack of a profitable and sustainable business model, Meitu's target valuation is a pricey one."[384]

---

[383] Supra note 12, Tech in Asia.
[384] Forbes, Yue Wang, *China's Meitu Eyes A Too-Pricey IPO,* (August 2016).

Nonetheless, the reality proved Meitu's suspicions to have been rather well-founded. In December 2016, the company's IPO raised a total of USD 629 million, over 25% more than it's anticipated USD 500 million target. This rendered Meitu Inc.'s IPO as the largest Hong Kong public offering since Alibaba's listing back in 2007. At the same time, despite securing a 10% lower company valuation than expected (at USD 4.6 billion),[385] the company's share price has continued to grow since, matching its previous ambitions with a current valuation of approximately USD 6 billion (a mere 7 months after having gone public).[386]

What this notably represents is a paradigm shift in conventional investment strategies, whereby a company's future potential is considered more highly than its past credentials. I.e. It is no longer about whether you have a history of profit-making to show:

"It's about whether you have the potential users to generate future profits."[387]

--Wang Xiaofeng (Forrester analyst)

This forward thinking approach operates in stark contrast to the Venezuelan case of the Tinaco-Anaco railway. In the aforementioned example, it was the oversight of the Chinese company to look backwards into the Venezuelan government's credit history, which underpinned much of its failings. However, in the case at hand, it appears that by proxy of the alternative business model employed:

"For tech companies, the future is more important than the past."[388]

--William Chou (Deloitte)

---

[385] Forbes, Yue Wang, *China's Meitu Eyes A Too-Pricey IPO,* (August 2016).

[386] Correct to the date: 2017/07/27.

[387] Financial Times, Yuan Yang and Gloria Cheung, *Selfie App Meitu Set to be valued at $5.2bn after IPO,* (December 2016).

[388] Supra note 13, Gadgets 360.

11.5 Monetising: The Meitu Method

Indeed, the problem facing Meitu is not uncommon amongst many other appware enterprises whose primary services and products are free for the wider public, e.g.: the likes of Facebook, Twitter, Snap (Snapchat) and LinkedIn. All these companies despite their grand size and reputation, have all experienced similar issues conceptualising sustainable business models for monetization.

"Converting Facebook data into money is harder than it sounds..."[389]

--Antonio Garcia-Martínez

(Former Facebook Executive)

In resolving this issue, a popular model heavily utilised by apps and free online platforms relies on the sale of advertising space and corporate sponsorships for revenue generation. This approach aims to capitalise on the substantial boom of online advertisements, whereby 41% of ad spending amongst large companies has already transitioned to digital media formats.[390] Within this digital capacity, simple codes and algorithms can be devised to track patterns in search behaviour and in a member's usage of apps, enabling third-party enterprises to better target themselves towards desired consumer markets.

Simultaneously, monetization methods may further adopt an additional layer relating to the sale of information obtained from users about their social habits, interests and wider behaviours. This not only strengthens the effectiveness of targetted advertising, but provides appware companies with valuable assets: market research, data and statis-

---

[389] The Guardian, Antonio Garcia-Martinez, *I'm an ex-Facebook exec: don't believe what they tell you about ads,* (May 2017).
[390] Harvard Business Review, *Do Search Ads Really Work?,* (March-April 2017 Issue).

tics. These assets (private information on public behaviour), may then be sold to third-party companies in the furtherance of their own research and development, enabling them to better understand social, political and market trends for integration into business strategies.

However, such a model for revenue creation raises doubts as to its long-term sustainability. Skepticism first arises with regards to the sale of online advertising space, as it is noted that the effectiveness of online advertising on millennials is yet to be properly understood or even substantiated. This, along with fears that online advertising will only last so long before the general public are once again put off (repeating the same cycle that had occurred with other more traditional forms of media),[391] have led analysts to ponder whether dependency on advertising for appware monetization is really sustainable.

What's more, reiterating the aforementioned concerns surrounding Superfish in the Lenovo scandal, this method of monetisation gives rise to public safety concerns, threats to privacy and online security, and ethical issues. Questions arise as to the onus on tech companies to act responsibly, in light of the way in which withholding private user information enlarges their sphere of influence over wider stakeholder groups.

Indeed, quickly following Meitu's unexpected boom in the US alongside European countries, concerns were noted about the privacy and personal security related to the app's download and function; evidencing the resistance of consumers (particularly within western countries), against the collection of online information. The app has since been defended by software experts to be no more of an immediate threat to personal security or privacy as most other apps on the market,[392] however it is apparent that obtaining revenue through the sale of user

---

[391] Aurora, Tariq Ziad Khan, *The brave new world of social media IPOs,* (April 2017).

[392] The Verge, Russell Brandom, *Meitu has a tracking problem, not a spying problem,* (January 2017).

information will be a much harder strategy to employ in today's more and more scrupulous market. After all, even appware belonging to well established companies such as Apple and Facebook, have struggled with public tensions concerning user privacy.[393]

In light of these concerns for the long term sustainability of advertisement and data-collection as methods for monetising appware; Meitu Inc. is noteworthy in its novel attempts of commercialisation. Rather than focus on the sale of private data, the company has chosen to focus its attention on developing a fashion based online "eco-system," where revenue is generated through its role as an e-commerce platform. In line with its new aim, the company declared the launch of two new ventures in 2017: *Pushion,* a fashion-focused social e-commerce platform [Exhibit 11.6]; and *Meitu Personalised,* a platform upon which Meitu Inc. can sell it's own merchandise, personalised by users with their own Meitu-made photographs. It was announced that through the two ventures, the company: *"marks a pivotal step towards monetization and platformization for Meitu."*[394]

Herein, the former of the two ventures is worth particular analysis, as it exemplifies the way in which the new age of the internet can establish more co-dependent relationships between different stakeholder groups. In turn, traditional concepts of corporate responsibility and sustainability may be redefined.

---

[393] Business Insider, Lisa Eadicicco, *One of the Biggest Features we're expecting to see in the new Apple TV is really troubling for privacy, experts say,* (September 2015). Forbes, Chunka Mai, *Facebook's Privacy Issues Are Deeper Than We Knew,* (August 2011) ;   Forbes, Thomas Fox-Brewster, *Facebook is Playing Games With your Privacy And There's Nothing You Can Do About It,* (June 2016); Business Insider, Avery Hartmans, *What you need to know about the privacy of the new smart camera Amazon wants to put in your bedroom,* (April 2017).

[394] Supra note 5, Meitu Official Website.

Exhibit 11.6

Source: Courtesy of Meitu (Corporate News)

The Pushion venture hopes to secure profits for Meitu Inc. by establishing an e-commerce platform with exclusive fashion launches, whilst establishing a more interactive and social element to e-commerce. Simply speaking, the platform shall operate by enabling popular users, termed "trendsetters", to sponsor particular clothing items or full outfits that are available on Pushion. This is done by displaying favourited items in a *Trendsetter's* virtual shop, which their followers may then peruse. Should a person (follower) choose to purchase an item of clothing that the trendsetter has sponsored, the trendsetter shall have the opportunity of earning commission from the relevant retailer. This approach to e-commerce not only provides users with a more interactive role within Meitu, but establishes a much closer and more integrated online community. In this way, Pushion establishes a method of monetizing downloadable free-appware in a long-term sustainable manner.

The novelty herein, lies in the way in which the platform shall be able to unite the different interests of stakeholder groups: providing a virtual space in which businesses, consumers and even outsourced agents (i.e.: trendsetters) may co-exist. Cleverly, the platform panders to the needs of retailers to engage in targetted advertising and data collection, however does so in a manner that is less intrusive to the general public. This is because with the existence of Trendsetter sponsorships, consumers themselves become involved in the very advertising that retailers are looking for; providing a mutually beneficial relationship whereby fashion retailers are able to directly target desired audiences, whilst consumers are able to earn some extra money for themselves.

From a data collection point of view, Pushion is also useful to third-party companies as it provides retailers with a platform upon which they may deduce future trends by proxy of it's social element. Notably however, this ability for data collection and market research occurs without Meitu Inc. having to encroach upon user privacy through the sale of personal information.

Subsequently, through creating more interconnected relationships between companies and consumers, Meitu Inc. may better facilitate the integration of business and society needs and interests; creating an online market environment, which is conducive to all involved. At present, the future of the new venture may not be certain, however it will certainly be interesting to see whether this approach is successful in establishing channels for direct communication between end users and third-party companies, with Meitu Inc. acting as the bridge between the two. If all else fails, there is always the option voiced by Meitu Inc.'s CEO Wu Xinhong: "collaboration with smartphone giants by exporting our software technology."[395]

11.6 Conclusion

All in all, the example case of Meitu Inc. provides an interesting insight into the unique challenges faced by downloadable free-apware companies; who by virtue of the dynamism of the internet and social

---

[395] Supra note 10, Reuters. Although note that this too may be a short-lived approach, given consumer attitudes towards preinstalled software (as outlined in the *Lenovo and Superfish* case).

trends, employ an alternative business model for revenue creation and risk identification. In turn, whilst the key phrases of corporate responsibility and sustainability are still very much applicable to the internet industry, i.e.:"long-termism", "due diligence", "strategic planning" and "localisation"; the manner of their application may differ as compared with more traditional industry sectors.

This is particularly true with regards to the timing and method of their monetisation. Herein, the Pushion model represents a commendable approach. However, for it to be successful, it must be capable of overcoming the inherent risks posed by online platforms. After all, such platforms, in which businesses, consumers and outsourced agents may coexist, give rise to an online virtual marketplace, which is increasingly harder to standardise and monitor. The following case of Ctrip evidences such problems, acting as a warning for Pushion to ensure that it has implemented adequate mechanisms for regulating the activity of those operating on its fashion based e-commerce platform.

11.7 Questions for Thought

1. Why is it that for software related companies "it's about whether you have the potential users to generate future profits," yet when investing in traditional industry sectors, it's about what is on the existing balance-sheet that counts?

2. Software and social media platforms have managed to accrue substantially high IPO valuations. Are these justified, or is it part and parcel of the hype surrounding these new industry sectors?

3. Meitu has only just strategized a method for monetising on its large user base. Do you think its timing is opportune? Maybe it's too late, or even too early to do so?

4. What considerations ought to be made by Meitu prior to releasing its new Pushion platform?

11.8 Appendix

"Trendsetter": Influencer Marketing

Exhibit 11.7 Social Media Based Marketing_Benefits to businesses

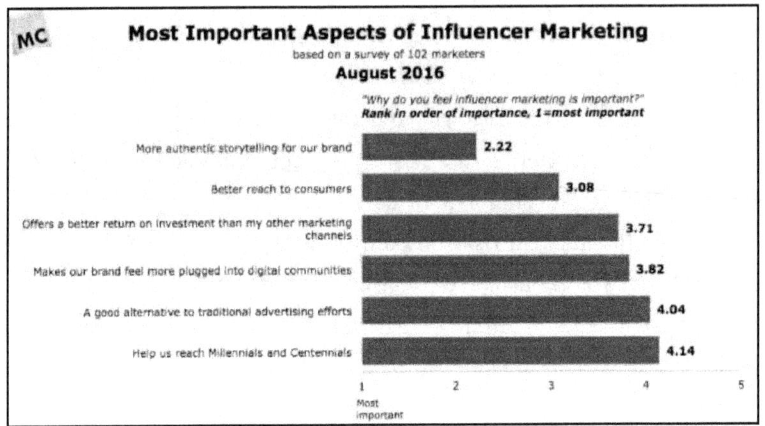

Source: TapInfluence, Altimeter Group, Brian Solis, The Influencer Marketing Manifesto, (2016) Via Marketing Charts.

Exhibit 11.8 Social Media Based Marketing_Benefits to Influencers

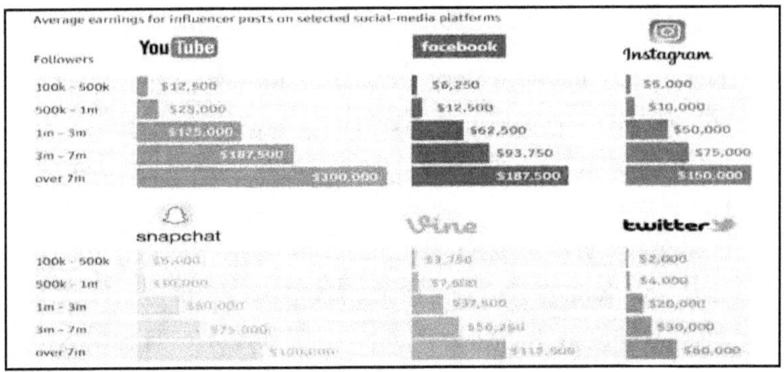

Source: Capitv8 Via The Economist, Celebrities' Endorsement Earnings on Social Me-dia, (2016)

The above exhibits demonstrate the benefits to be had for businesses and consumers utilising online social media platforms for sponsored market-

ing ("influencer marketing"). Meitu's new "Trendsetter" model capital-ises on this model whilst incorporating "affiliate marketing" in the form of commission-based sales. In this way users to the platform may earn money by influencing trends, whilst fashion brands adver-tised on Push-ion increase their outreach in a more cost-effective man-ner than tradi-tional advertising.

Meitu: Moneting Potential

Exhibit 11.9 Meitu Userbase_Volume

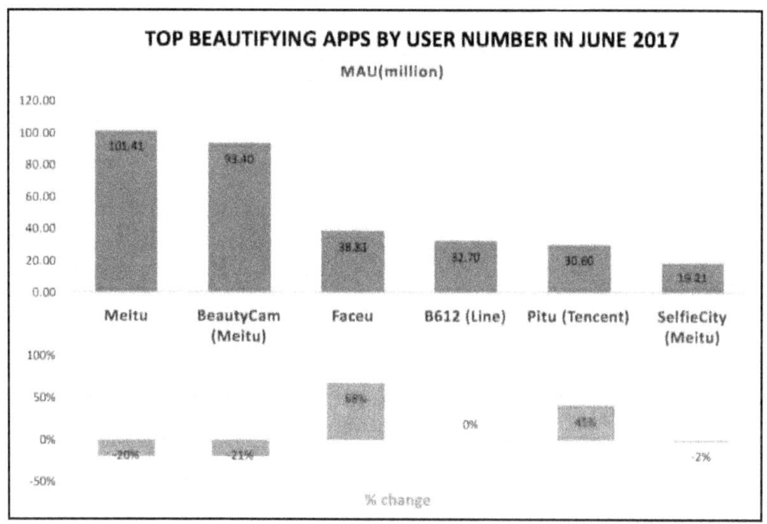

Source: QuesstMobile

Via Technode, Rita Liao, Will China's Biggest Beautifier Meitu Ever be Profitable?, (2017) <<http://www.iresearchchina.com/content/ details7_30567.html>>

Exhibit 11.10 B2B Based Platforms_Potential for Small-Medium Sized Enterprises

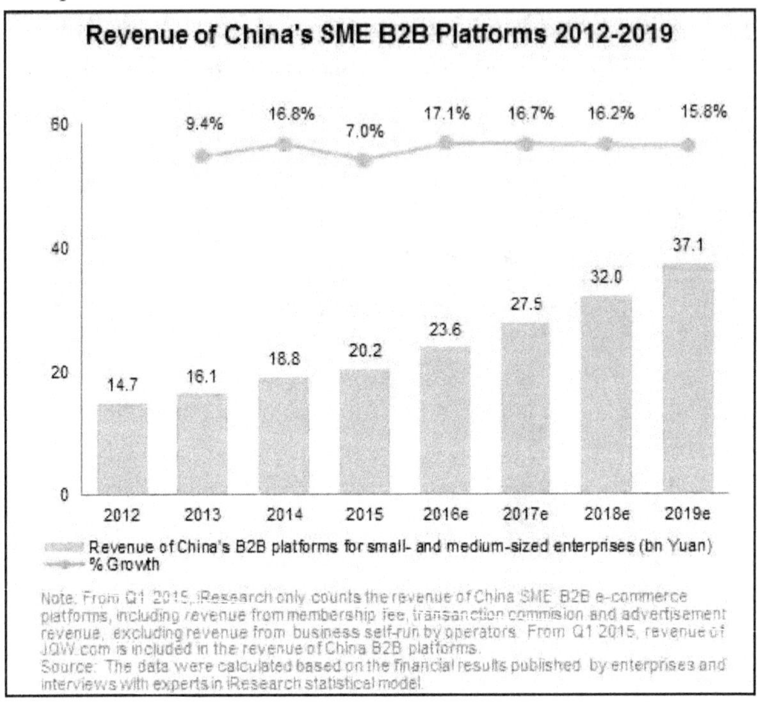

Source: iResearch Global Group (December 2016)

<<http://www.iresearchchina.com/content/details7_30567.html>>

The monetisation potential for generating revenue via B2B is substantially large within the Chinese market and steadily increasing.

Tech Companies: IPOs vs Profitability

Exhibit 11.11 IPO valuation vs Profitability_Tech Companies

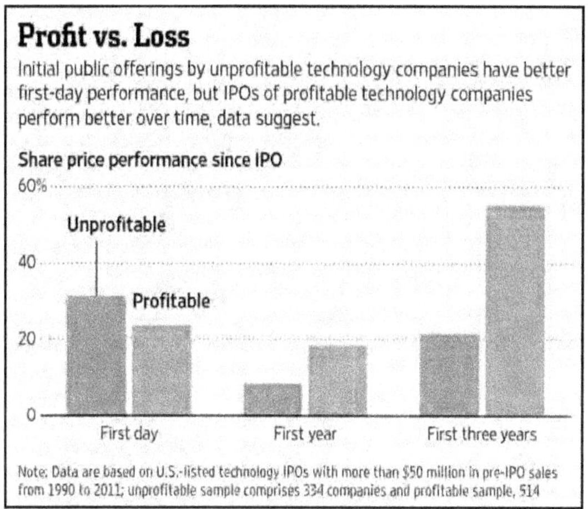

Source: Jay Ritter, University of Florida

Via The Wall Street Journal, Telis Demos, In Latest IPOs - Profits Aren't the Point, (2013)

Exhibit 11.12 Volume of Tech IPOs vs Profitability

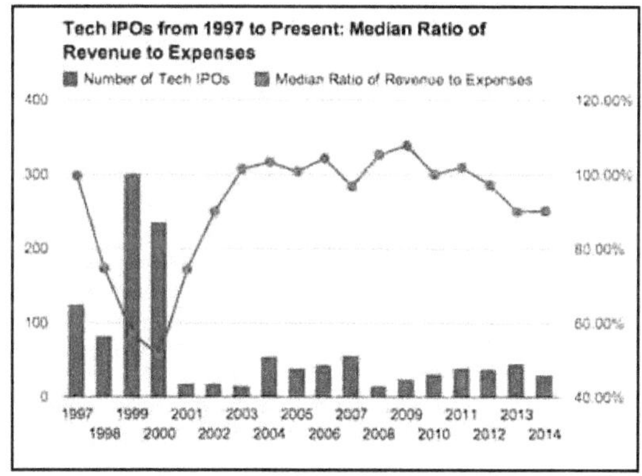

Source: Mattermark Research, Crunchbase, AngelList

Via Mattermark, Danielle Morrill, A Data-Driven Exploration of Tech IPOs from 1997 to Present, (2014).

12

THE CASE OF CTRIP.COM

Regulating e-commerce and comparison websites

12.1 Case Background

The role of e-commerce and exchange platforms, which focus on connecting businesses and consumers in a more direct manner, once again operate in a fundamentally different way to both traditional business models and the aforementioned free-appware. This is in respect of the role of such platforms, which act as databases of information tasked with helping to find the perfect match between industry providers and end-users. In other words, a type of online *"yellow pages."*

Such platforms operate by establishing an online marketplace, whereby the goods and services of industry providers can be directly compared and contrasted by internet users.

The effect of this has been to completely revolutionise market trends, as evidenced by e-commerce platforms such as Amazon, Taobao and Jingdong; which have had a heavy impact upon the need for real-life stores, altering the very dynamics of consumptive behaviour. In turn these virtual outlets become middlemen between traditional B2C models (business-to-consumer), whilst further reshaping traditional supply chain management from supply-driven models to demand-driven solutions. Simultaneously, new streams of revenue may be created at a C2C level (consumer-to-consumer), facilitating the sale of goods between users on the platform.

In this way, exchange platforms are able to connect and facilitate a whole range of different transaction types. They benefit those who are looking to sell their own goods and services (be it businesses or individuals) by acting as advertising space; whilst also helping consumers to navigate their own way around the cornucopia of products available in today's increasingly competitive markets

Exhibit 12.1

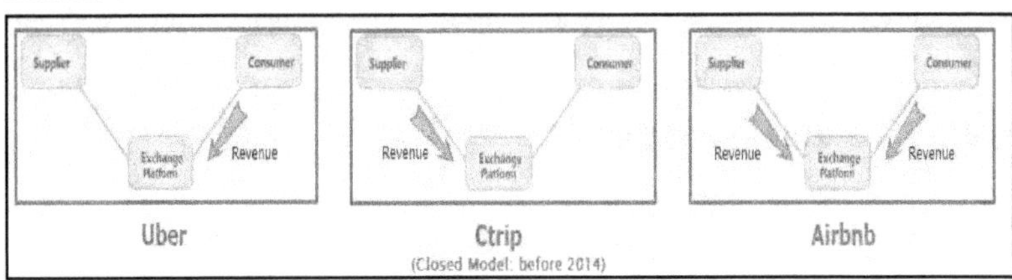

Source: Created by the Author

The business models for such platforms alter considerably in that they take on a more triangular structure as opposed to linear [Exhibit 12.1]. Accordingly, the platform can be utilised to generate revenue from consumers and/or industry providers alike. In some cases the exchange platform shall charge a small fee for membership or usage of their service, allowing the tech company to earn a direct income from users, e.g.: Uber. In other cases it may be free for consumers to use the platform, however revenue is generated by charging a commission on all sales made by registered industry providers, e.g.: Ctrip (pre-2014). Equally, the platform may choose to generate revenue from both ends, through the industry suppliers and consumers alike, e.g.: Airbnb.

This structure of exchange platforms differs from traditional manufacturing supply chains, as well as the free entertainment and social appware models previously analysed [Exhibit 12.2]. This is because, unlike the aforementioned business models, a tech company who has developed an exchange platform, acts as an agent for both ends of the supply chain. As such, unlike with social media apps which must first build a large user base (B2C) before establishing B2B connections; a company acting as an exchange provider wishes to build its B2B and B2C relationships simultaneously. This is fundamental, as its intrinsic role is to establish a flourishing marketplace in which suppliers and end users may be connected.

Exhibit 12.2

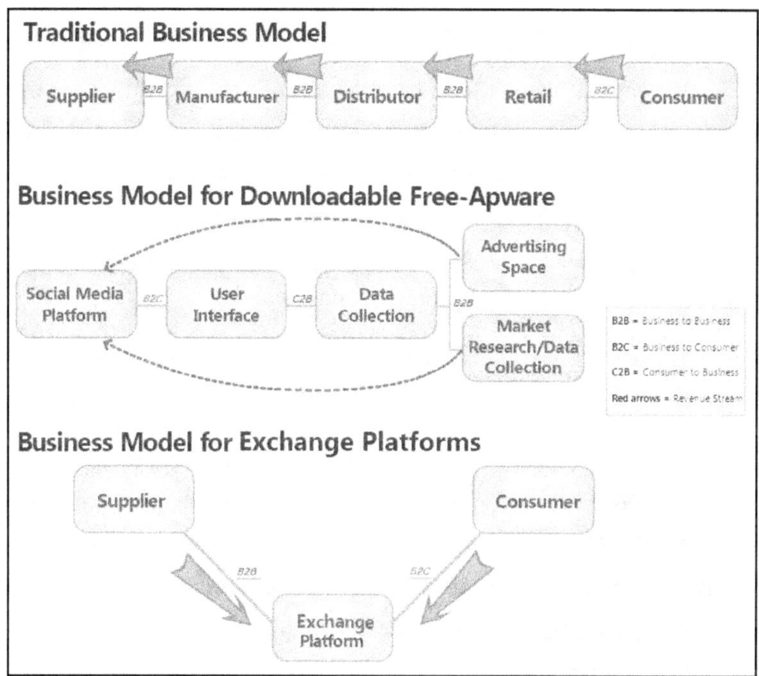

Source: Created by the Author

What's more, exchange platforms do not suffer from the same risk management problems as social appware companies; as monetisation of the platform occurs from the outset (in the same vein as traditional business models). Accordingly, unlike appware, which has to wait until it has built a large enough user base before B2B monetisation, exchange platforms can utilise traditional concepts for dealing with risk identification and business strategy. It is for this reason that Pushion is a strategically smart investment decision by Meitu: allowing the company to start earning revenue from the very outset of the venture's release.

However, exchange platforms contain added risks for maintaining due diligence across the supply chain. As a marketplace for connecting third party businesses with consumers, the role of the platform as an agent for both parties, extends unto it a responsibility to verify the authenticity of both sides. For instance, if a third party business loses money on a sale generated through the platform, even if just as a result of the customer's actions, the platform provider shares some liability. Equally, where a consumer purchases goods or services through the platform, only to discover that they were misrepresented, malicious or false; once again the platform provider may share liability.

Of course mechanisms to mitigate such problems are plentiful, and may even be as simple as providing reasonable indemnity clauses where possible. However in all cases, the platform provider's reputation shall be at stake. After all, the very job of the platform is to manage and oversee the virtual market that it has created. Having to balance the external activities of the marketplace alongside the company's own responsibilities for monitoring internal operations, increases the risk that fraudulent, negligent or improper conduct goes unnoticed. A prime example of this is demonstrated by the 2016 controversies surrounding the Chinese travel provider: Ctrip.com. Here problems arose concerning fraudulent and inappropriate sales conduct by agents utilising the platform to facilitate customer transactions.

12.2 Ctrip Business Model

Ctrip is recognised to date as China's largest online travel agency, providing services including: domestic and international air travel, train ticket reservation, package tours, accommodation bookings and corporate travel services. Founded in 1999, the company has steadily grown in both size and prestige with listings on NASDAQ since 2003, a current market valuation of approximately USD 30 billion, and a marketplace spanning 200 countries across six continents, confirming its status as an internationally renowned corporation.[396]

The online platform facilitates exchange between third party businesses and consumers (operating as a "middleman" exchange), as well as offering some travel services of its own at a B2C level. In doing so, Ctrip maintains its online marketplace as free to use for consumers, with its main revenue generated from service providers in the form of commission for all transactions made on the company's platform.

Indeed, for a long time the company adopted a close platform model, by which only Ctrip employees were capable of handling transactions between consumers and third party travel providers. In this way, the company could ensure easier and more direct management over its online marketplace, safeguarding that transactions remained in line with the company's own policies and value system.

However by 2014, with Ctrip's rival competitor Qunar gaining steam in the Chinese market with its alternative open platform for purchasing travel services; the company altered its business model to open up the marketplace [Exhibit 12.3].[397] In turn, third party agents became able to sell tickets to consumers utilising Ctrip's platform. In essence, what this meant was that Ctrip no longer acted as a direct middleman between service providers and end users, but rather by outsourcing third parties, transitioned into a platform connecting: businesses, consumers and agents alike.

---

[396] Correct to the date: 2017/09/08.

[397] Forbes, Trefis Team, *Ctrip Fourth Quarter 2014 Earnings Preview: Strategic Investments in Focus,* (March 2015); Seeking Alpha, Doug Young, *Ctrip Joins Open Platform Crowd, Oversight Needed,* (December 2014).

Exhibit 12.3

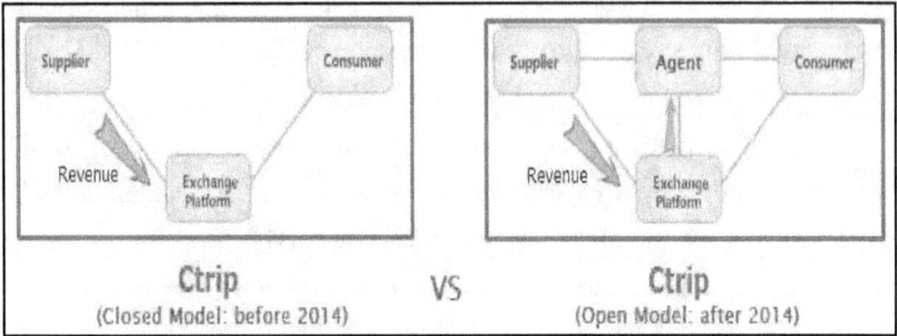

Source: Created by the Author

Consequently, through its new open model Ctrip became able to elevate its competitive edge, expanding upon the range of consumer choices available on its platform. As a result, the website welcomed a new branch to its online network, with over 5,000 independent travel agents now able to provide a greater range in services at more competitive prices[398]; establishing a better all-rounded marketplace.

Yet, notwithstanding the positive implications of operating an online open platform, negative repercussions in the form of less effective monitoring and regulation, led to the company's reputation taking a hit just over a year later in early 2016.

12.3 Flight Ticket Scams

Controversies arose when improper conduct by third party agents on Ctrip's online platform were uncovered. In January 2016, the experience of a Mr Fu Jingnan who had purchased a round trip flight from Beijing to Tokyo's Haneda Airport, were circulated around Chinese social media, drawing attention to misdemeanours from travel agents on the platform.

---

[398] China Radio International, Li Jianhua, *Ctrip Involved in Row Over Fake Flight Tickets,* (January 2016).

Mr Fu had purchased his tickets through the convenience of Ctrip only to discover on his return journey back from Tokyo to Beijing on the 7th January 2016, that his Japan Airlines flight ticket was invalid on the grounds that it had been purchased using another customer's air mileage points. Accordingly, given that the flight was listed under the name of a Japanese customer with no relation or connection to Mr Fu, the tickets had been cancelled notwithstanding the payment made; leaving Mr Fu with no way of discovering this fact until the time came for him to check into his flight.

Unable to use his pre-paid ticket, Mr Fu contacted Ctrip to help him remedy the situation, at which point he was referred to the original third party agent who had handled his transaction.[399] After a few minutes an alternative flight was provided for, however once again the ticket was rejected on the same grounds; it had been purchased using somebody else's customer mileage points in order to be sold at a discounted price.

As a result, Mr Fu was pulled aside by the Tokyo Haneda Airport security and asked about the details surrounding his purchase of the ticket. Requested to "cooperate with the investigation,"[400] he was re-peatedly asked if he had personally bought the tickets, and whether or not he bore any relationship with the Japanese customer whose mileage points had been used for their purchase.

"这个事情是我最尴尬的地方，因为日本人非常在意信誉这个问题， 他其实很难理解为什么中国最大的旅行服务提供商会卖三张假机票给我。"

"This was my most embarrassing experience. The Japanese were very concerned about the credibility of the issue, and found it very diffi-

---

[399] Shanghai Daily, Yang Jian, *Passenger 'detained' in Tokyo after buying ticket on Ctrip.com that turned out to be illegal"* (January 2016).
[400] Supra note 4, Shanghai Daily.

cult to comprehend that China's largest travel service provider could have sold me three fake tickets."[401]

"I felt humiliated after being investigated for three hours at the Japanese airport and was almost detained...I want Ctrip to apologize and remove the negative records created by the airport and airlines."[402]

--Mr Fu Jingnan

The issue highlighted Ctrip's failure to ensure adequate oversight of its marketplace and agents, resulting in improper sales techniques and undermining the overall integrity of the platform provider. Indeed, the sale of flight tickets using mileage points is highly regulated by airline policies, in which majority of airline providers (including Japan Airlines [Exhibit 12.4]) expressly state that such points may not be swapped in any way, and can only be used for tickets purchased by the account holder or his/her family.[403]

Accordingly, the actions of the ticketing agent in selling Mr Fu tickets purchased with third party mileage constituted a breach of airline policy; motivated by an attempt to sell the flight at a more competitive, discount price. As a result, the action amounted to a deceitful and fraudulent sale of an invalid ticket given that: a). payment had already been charged to Mr Fu's bank account, and b). The sale utilised the property of another without prior consent.

---

[401] CCTV13 News1+1, Live Broadcast, (January 11th 2016) <<https://www.youtube.com/watch?v=hhr15SDJEks>> [accessed on 04/09/2017].

[402] The Nanfang, Charles Liu, *Beware of Ctrip: Company Accused of Fraud After Customers Stranded Abroad,* (Updated May 2016).

[403] Supra note 7, The Nanfang.

Exhibit 12.4 Japan Airlines policy: Who is eligible to claim airline awards redeemed via mileage

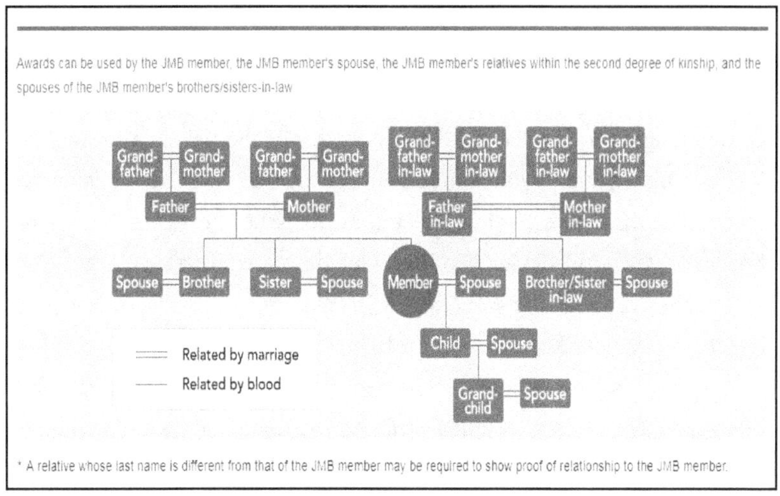

Source: Japan Airlines Official Website

In response to the matter, Ctrip publicly apologised to Mr Fu and was eventually able to fly him back to Beijing on a new ticket. The company announced that any other customers, who encounter similar problems regarding tickets purchased off the platform, would be entitled to triple compensation and a full refund.[404] Notably, the company agreed that it was in need of better mechanisms for monitoring the actions of its agents.

Indeed, just two days after Mr Fu experienced problems with his flight ticket, another case came to light of a Mr Li Miao who had purchased two return flights for himself and his partner from Beijing to Sapporo (Japan). Mr Li, a Ctrip Diamond Club customer for more than 11 years, found himself and his girlfriend unable to check in for their outgoing Air China flight on the 9th January 2016, on the grounds that the tickets they had purchased from Ctrip were invalid. The couple were

---

[404] Supra note 4, Shanghai Daily.

told by staff that their flight details could not be found anywhere on the Air China system, leaving Mr Li to conclude: *"That means they did not actually sell the tickets."*[405] As such they were left with no other choice but to purchase two entirely new flights for their trip to Japan.

In the case of Mr Li, Ctrip announced that the problem arose as the ticketing agent had failed to ensure issuance of the tickets after the sale was completed and payment made. In this regard, it has been challenged that rather than pure negligence, failure to issue the tickets may have been motivated by backhanded sales techniques, whereby:

"Some agents scout for cheaper tickets, especially for last minute deals, and then make an actual booking."[406]

Nonetheless, regardless of whether or not there had been any malicious intent, the case coupled with Mr Fu Jingnan's aforementioned experiences, resulted in great injury to Ctrip's reputation. Mr Fu's posts on Weibo commenting on the matter, coupled with Mr Li's posts on wechat, gave rise to notions of the company as a "scam" as both cases went viral. Indeed, Mr Li Miao's reputation as an online travel writer saw his Wechat post in particular, reposted and re-read over 100,000 times within just two days.[407] In addition, many mainland Chinese newspapers and media groups reviewed the cases shortly after, giving rise to an unveiling of a series of similar situations and experiences that customers had faced when purchasing travel services off the Ctrip platform.[408] The two scandals highlightedthe problems inherent in the company's monitoring and regulation of transactions on its platform.

---

[405] Supra note 4, Shanghai Daily.

[406] Caixin, Liu Xiaojing and Lu Xiaoxi, *Online Travel Agents Hit by Turbulence As Airlines Tighten Scrutiny"* (May 2016).

[407] See: <<https://www.huxiu.com/article/136946.html>> for the article Mr Li Miao posted on his Wechat account on January 12th 2016.

[408] See: <<http://news.163.com/16/0121/18/BDSFT4AU00011229.html>> on a customer who had ordered two train tickets for the same train with overlapping times, only to discover that one of the train tickets had been purchased using

In fact just a week earlier, tensions had already built up against Qunar (China's second largest online travel intermediary). Nine leading Chinese airlines terminated their business dealings with the online platform provider due to the frequency of problems encountered by customers [Exhibit 12.5]. Problems included: customers facing unexpected additional fees, problems with refunds, and arbitrary changes to conditions of ticket use. Such problems were once again attributed to the failings of online platforms to appropriately regulate and standardise the conduct of third party agents:

"[Third party agents] employ unethical practice to make extra money while offering low-priced airline tickets to price-sensitive consumers."[409]

In light of such controversies, an investigation into the sale of flight tickets by online travel intermediaries (including both Ctrip and Qunar), was conducted by the China Consumer Association. The association, whose primary task concerns consumer rights issues within China, found that out of every 10,000 tickets sold on Ctrip, an average of 2 encountered problems. Notably, their investigations showed that all the blame could not simply be pinned on third party agents, as similar problems had even been found in cases where the tickets had been administered directly through Ctrip employees.[410]

What this demonstrates is the challenge faced by all online platforms to ensure effective internal management of the virtual marketplaces they

---

another person's I.D. The booking agent had done so in order to circumvent the train rules which disallow the buying of multiple tickets in this way. Having decided which travel time suited the passenger best, the passenger arrived at the train station to refund one of the two tickets. At this time they were asked to provide a *"released from prison certificate"*, revealing that the additional train ticket had been purchased under the I.D. of a person in prison.

[409] Global Times, Zhang Ye, *Major Airlines Abandon Online Travel Agency, Citing Customer Complaints,* (January 2016).

[410] Supra note 11, Caixin.

create. It would be easy to recommend that Pushion avoid such problems by ensuring that their e-commerce platforms maintain a closed network, and thereby prohibits the use of third party agents in facilitating purchases. However as the China Consumer Association's investigation highlights, problems encountered are not always attributable solely to third parties. Rather it seems that irrespective of whether an online platform is open or closed, it is likely to face regulatory challenges by virtue of the fact that it is operating in the more lucid, virtual domain. Accordingly, it will always be much harder to implement effective mechanisms for overseeing and standardising online conduct. Not to mention that maintaining a closed network for Pushion would irreparably undermine the underlying social identity of the platform, as the use of Trendsetters automatically opens up the platform to third party agents.

Exhibit 12.5

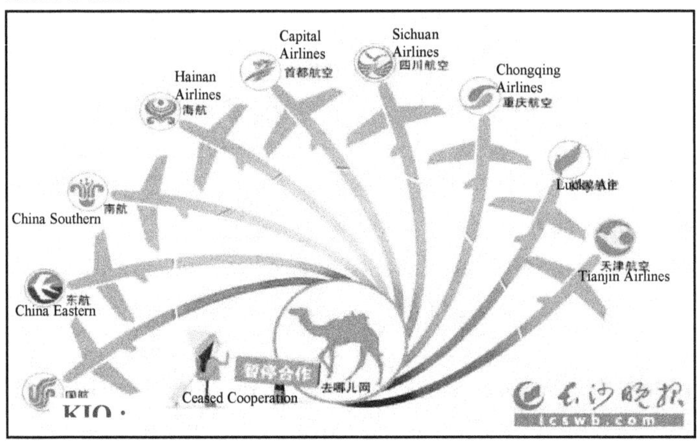

Source: Courtesy of Changsha Evening News Net, 去哪儿网被直销砸了小蛮腰, (2016) << http://www.sohu.com/a/53909483_359083>>

Nevertheless, it is conceded that where a platform takes the form of an open model one, such challenges are exacerbated, as the risk of improper conduct becomes higher due to the indirect management structure employed. In this regard, it is important for companies to remember that even where problems encountered are attributable by and large to third parties, this does not exonerate the platform completely. After all, its sole purpose is to provide a marketplace which can be trusted, facilitating engagement between service providers and end users in a manner that maintains the integrity of traditional purchasing mediums.

"携程是以机票代理商的身份面对用户"

"For end users, Ctrip is the face - it represents all agents [on its platform]."[411]

Where an exchange platform is unable to create such a reliable marketplace, it becomes more cost effective for businesses and consumers to use traditional purchasing means, rendering the services of companies like Ctrip obsolete. Such a reaction was even noted in light of controversies surrounding both Ctrip and Qunar, with customers stating that they would rather purchase flight tickets directly from the airline provider in future. The same applied for airlines, with a shifting focus on selling tickets directly to passengers. In fact, already a year earlier in 2015, the China State Assets Supervision and Administration Commission had initiated movement away from using online travel platforms. It was mandated that Air China, China Eastern Airlines and China Southern Airlines (the top three Chinese State-owned airlines), were to increase the number of their direct sales up to 50% by 2018.[412]

12.4 Tighter Regulations

The need to maintain a trustworthy and reliable marketplace is essential, and fundamentally requires that e-commerce and exchange plat-

---

[411] Caixin, 覃敏 (Tan Min), *携程"假飞机票"风波后的灰色产业链* (January 2016).

[412] China Daily, Paul Welitzkin, *Ctrip CEO says Acquisition Starting to Pay Off,* (March 2017); Supra note 11, Caixin (Liu Xiaojing and Lu Xiaoxi).

forms ensure adequate regulation along the entire transaction process. This necessitates:

1. full disclosure of key information regarding transactions that have been placed on the platform,

2. departments or mechanisms for monitoring the conduct of those involved in facilitating business exchange, and

3. appropriate customer response in cases where problems might have arisen.

12.5 Public Disclosure

In Ctrip's case, the problem at hand emerged with regards to all three elements. Firstly, it is noted that there existed a lack of transparency concerning the company's relationship with third party agents. From a user interface perspective, it is not apparent that the agent selling a customer their ticket is not actually a Ctrip own employee.

Even where it is known, the company failed to publicly disclose the nature of business dealings it held with outsourced agents; particularly with regards to the extent to which information could be accessed between the two. Had such information been publicly announced, Ctrip's liability and the level of responsibility that it held over the fraudulent and/or negligent actions of third parties, would have been much clearer and less controversial from the outset.

In any case, the company would have still had to face reputational loss in light of inherent consumer rights issues; as the role of exchange platforms in representing all parties on its virtual marketplace, renders it accountable. Still, improved transparency would have likely mitigated negative repercussions, as it would have given rise to enhanced consumer awareness of how Ctrip works and the risks therein; conducive to a more sympathetic public response.

12.6 Monitoring Mechanisms

"没有人知道携程对代理商的违规行为是否是睁一只眼闭一只眼，可以知道的是携程本身有能力做这件事情，但它现在监管不力."

"No one knows whether or not Ctrip turned a blind eye towards the irregularities of its agent's actions. However what is known, is that Ctrip had the ability to discover what was going on. The problem lies with poor supervision."[413]

--Ctrip Ticketing Agent

The second and biggest issue that arose in the case of Ctrip, lay with a failure to properly vet transactions made by ticketing agents. It was admitted by Ctrip that whilst manual checks were conducted regularly, they were only made on a randomised spot-check basis. Accordingly, only a small percentage of total transactions are monitored, and deemed representative for all.

The problem here lies in the vast number of third party agents used by Ctrip; with previous figures indicating that at least 5,000 independent agents operate on the platform.[414] As such, there is bound to exist variations in the expertise and regulatory frameworks of agents, with some employed by larger-scale agencies and others operating in a smaller capacity. With this in mind, whilst random sampling may be a useful and cost-effective method for monitoring activity, to be truly reliable, it would need to ensure that it had sufficiently taken such variables into account.

In addition, alongside Ctrip's manual checks, the company ought to have integrated further online mechanisms and systems for flagging up potential discrepancies. For instance, in cases where a flight passenger's name fails to correspond with other crucial information, such as the

---

[413] Supra note 16, Caixin.

[414] Supra note 3, China Radio International.

name of the mileage point's holder whose discount had been applied to the ticket. Such a simple mechanism for tracking transactions, would allow problems to be detected much faster by flagging up red flags. These could then in turn be investigated through the manual systems that are already in place.

"从技术层面，携程是可以监管这个事情的。"上述代理商人士称，携程可以通过机票信息的校验，了解供应商提供的机票来历。

"From a technical perspective, Ctrip can regulate this." Third party agents said that Ctrip should be able to check the ticket information to understand the origin of the sale made.[415]

In recognition of their shortcomings, shortly after the 2016 incidents, Ctrip dramatically improved the safeguards in place for regulating the conduct of ticketing agents online. The company committed to checking 100% of transactions, ensuring that they would all be manually monitored and audited on a case-by-case basis.[416] At the same time they implemented a next day policy with regards to the payment of third party agency fees.[417]

Such changes are welcome, particularly in and amongst the changing landscape of the Chinese tourism industry in which airline providers have been gravitating away from the use of online travel intermediaries.[418] Nonetheless, the changes only operate to monitor the behaviour of agents further down the line. As such, a better tactic is the one employed by Alitrip (Alibaba's rival online travel intermediary). The company monitors agents from the very beginning of the supply chain, pre-

---

[415] Supra note 16, Caixin.

[416] Supra note 16, Caixin.

[417] China Travel News, *Ctrip Halt Agents Listings of Domestic Flights Scheduled After September 1,* (July 2016).

[418] China Travel News, *Alitrip, Ctrip Remove Agents' Listings of International Flights,* (June 2016).

venting air ticketing agents from simply self-listing their services on the Alitrip platform. Rather, Alitrip ensures that only those agents with professional experience and a high enough calibre may be trusted with platform listings. Accordingly it is safeguarded that each third party agent has been appropriately vetted, using random spot-checks to confirm their authenticity.[419] In this way all third parties are taken into account, systemised and regulated from the outset.

12.7 Customer Response

Finally the third area which Ctrip underestimated, exacerbating the situation of Mr Fu Jingnan in particular, was that of: customer response. Indeed, it is notable that in any company, even one with impeccable monitoring standards, problems may always arise.

In this regard, it is noted that responsible business practice is concerned with the way in which a business reacts and considers the needs of its stakeholders. As such, the existence of errors in themselves are not immediately 'irresponsible'; as in practically all scenarios and business industries there exists a reasonable margin of error. Rather it is essential that where problems do arise, they are handled in an efficient and effective way, whereby the interests and concerns of the relevant stakeholder have been properly understood and appropriate remedies employed.

In the case of Ctrip and Mr Fu Jingnan, it was seen that the company failed to do precisely this. Upon receiving Mr Fu's call concerning his invalid flight ticket back to Beijing, Ctrip's response had been to refer him back to the original agent dealing with his transaction. Whilst this may be rationalised on the grounds that the third party agent ought to have been more familiar with his case, had Ctrip dedicated some extra time to discovering the root of the problem behind his invalid ticket, it

---

[419] Supra note 14, Global Times.

would have become quickly apparent that the issue lay with the original ticketing agent in the first place.

What this once again iterates is the need for online exchange platforms to have access to information on all transactions on their marketplace, by virtue of their sole purpose in operating as a communication exchange. With such mechanisms in place, it ought to have been fairly easy and quick for Ctrip's customer complaint helpline to detect Mr Fu's underlying problem and resolve it themselves. This would have spared Mr Fu the embarrassment of discovering that the new ticket issued to him in resolution of his initial problem, was once again invalid on the same grounds; a factor which greatly contributed to Tokyo Haneda Security's hesitation in believing Mr Fu's story.

It is thus recommended that for all companies (even open platform based ones), the company's customer response team ought to be in house. In turn all customer complaints and customer problems ought to also be dealt with directly by the company's own employees. Only in this way, can the company ensure that a customer's problems are dealt with in a genuine manner, able to vouch for the credibility and accountability of its own staff. This in turn would directly reflect on the values and reputation of the business itself.

Such a recommendation stems from the very purpose of a customer complaints service, which is intended to establish a means of reliable two-way communication between consumers and businesses. As such, this specific branch of the corporate structure is paramount in maintaining the credibility of a company, whilst upholding its positive corporate image.

With this in mind, the problems inherent with Ctrip's actions in referring a customer complaint on to a third party agent are notable. In acknowledgement of this fact, Ctrip has agreed to upgrade its customer protection plan, establishing that in future, if a passenger is unable to fly due to some error on behalf of the company or an agent; Ctrip would bear the burden of communicating with the airline provider to fully explain the situation.[420] Hopefully such changes will spare Ctrip customers from having to relive the embarrassing experiences of Mr Fu, who was left having to single-handedly defend his honest intentions in purchasing the flight tickets.

12.8 Back to the Real World

In fact the complexities in managing an online marketplace, particularly one that is open and therefore involves an additional stakeholder (third party agents), may have led to Ctrip's most recent decision to "go offline."

Towards the end of 2016, adding to the list of partnerships Ctrip had already formed with rival travel intermediaries (including the aforementioned Qunar)[421], the company entered into a partnership with Traveling Bestone; an offline Chinese travel agency [Exhibit 12.6]. Under the strategic investment agreement, Ctrip gained access to over 5,500 retail outlets located in 22 provinces across China. The retail outlets, operated under a franchise system, are located in second and third tier cities and aim to establish an alternative means for customers to purchase the products already available online [Exhibit 12.7].[422]

Such a move does not necessarily signify gravitation away from the company's online business. Rather it is more likely an investment decision focused towards expanding Ctrip's current reach and market share. Nevertheless, it does demonstrate that despite the perks that the virtual

---

[420] Supra note 16, Caixin.

[421] China Daily, Wang Wen, *Ctrip and Qunar Join Hands to Create Biggest Travel Agency,* (October 2015).

[422] China Tech News, *Ctrip's Online Travel Goes Offline With 5,500 Stores Across China,* (March 2017); Forbes, *Ctrip's Strategic Investments Complementing its Efforts to Gain Market Share",* (May 2017); Beijing Times (京华时报), *携程战略投资旅游百事通,* (October 2016).

world and the internet have to offer, for some companies like Ctrip, long term business strategy and business growth is seen to depend more strongly on the collaboration of both online and offline services; not simply on the development of new technologies.

Exhibit 12.6

Source: Courtesy of China Travel News

Reads: "Ctrip + Bestone, A new start, A new Journey"

Exhibit 12.7 Ctrip Offline Store

Source: Courtesy of Cixi News Network (慈溪新闻网)

Herein, an offline retail franchise may help the company better regulate its operations; as the creation of physical outlets provides greater accountability for monitoring the actions of Ctrip representatives and third party agents. Yet on the other hand, it could be argued that the introduction of such stores may further complicate the already highly interwoven business model that Ctrip employs; creating a bigger and more diverse offline-online marketplace which is even harder to control. Either way, the company seems to have set its sights on expanding its offline business in the near future.

"We plan to have 6,500 stores in operation by the end of this year [2017]."

--Jane Jie Sun (CEO Ctrip)

12.9 Conclusion

The case of Ctrip highlights the problems that exist for exchange platforms that have created vast online marketplaces. These problems primarily focus on the regulation and monitoring of the varying actors on the platform. In turn, issues relating to consumer protection and consumer rights may arise, as well as general difficulties in management and accountability; as the virtual domain creates more complicated business structures with greater rifts and separations between the varying business organs.

Indeed, the situation becomes ever more complex in the context of open platform models, in which third party agents are outsourced to facilitate transactions. This is by virtue of the additional stage that they introduce to the business model, creating a more complex web of relationships. Herein, third party agents may not always take the form of those tasked with listing offers, but may also be involved in other areas facilitating business e.g. advertisement (the model Pushion hopes to employ).

Nonetheless, whilst the Ctrip case highlights problems of regulation and accountability with specific regards to open-model online travel intermediaries, the same remains true for any exchange/e-commerce platform. The 2011 controversies surrounding e-commerce giant Alibaba demonstrate as much; with Alibaba having run into similar problems of fraudulent conduct regarding its own employees and the violation of general consumer rights.[423] Such problems are thereby universal challenges that may arise when navigating online industries, especially with the alternative business strategies and models that they employ.

12.10 Questions for Thought

1. Do you think that the benefits associated with an open platform model outweigh the additional risks that come with a decentralised marketplace?

2. "Problems relating to the regulation of employee conduct is not simply a problem for e-commerce and exchange platforms, but for any business operating online." Do you agree?

3. Ctrip's recent decision to purchase over 5,500 brick-and-mortar retail outlets is somewhat reminiscent of OnePlus' recent decision to utilise traditional advertising in the form of a celebrity endorsement by Amitabh Bachchan. These decisions appear to be motivated by a desire to become better integrated and cross-platform. Is this the future for business, i.e.: online-offline hybrids?

4. How far should an e-commerce platform's responsibility extend to ensuring that the goods/services sold on the platform are

---

[423] See: The Economist, *An Online Fraud Scandal In China: Alibaba and the 2,236 Thieves,* (February 2011); Forbes, Gady Epstein, *Alibaba's Jack Ma Fights to Win Back Trust,* (March 2011).
The case involves Alibaba's "Golden Status" scheme, in which the company attempted to establish greater trust in its platform by granting special status to those online traders deemed both legitimate and trustworthy. However, the scandal uncovered fraudulent behaviour on behalf of 100 Alibaba staff members who intentionally and/or negligently allowed fraudsters to list themselves with "Golden Status", charging consumers for fake goods that never actually existed.

reliable and genuine? How might this compare to the responsibility of Baidu and other search engines to verify the authenticity of sponsored advertisements? Further still, how might this compare to the responsibility of traditional businesses in ensuring quality control along the supply chain?

12.11 Appendix

China Online Travel Industry: Trends

Exhibit 12.8 Chinese Online Travel Market

Source: iResearch Global Group
<< http://www.iresearchchina.com/content/details7_33852.html>>
[accessed on 15th October 2017].

Exhibit 12.9 Ctrip Market Share Q1 2016 and Ctrip Market Share Q1 2017

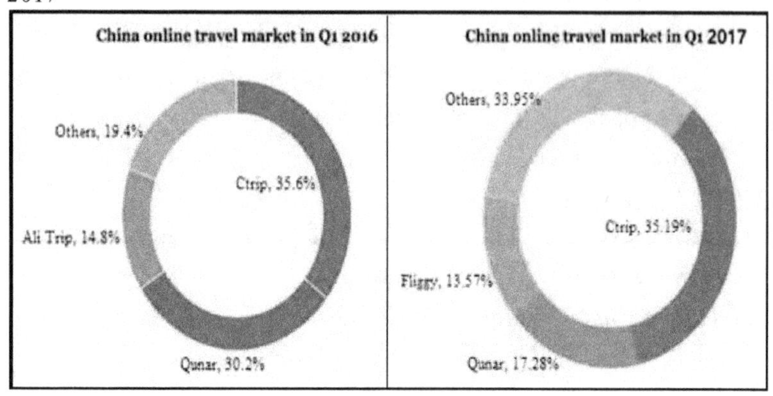

Source: Analysys (June 2016)

Via China Internet Watch, China Online Travel Market Overview Q3 2016, (2016), and Analysys [accessed on 18th October 2017].
<<http://www.analysyschina.com/view/viewDetail-229.html>>

专项整治陆续展开 专家：以法制化思维治理方能奏效

从去哪儿网下架机票产品，只是航企开展销售代理专项整治工作的其中一步。2 月，中国国际航空公司率先在国内航线，全面推出将机票价格打印在登机牌上。只要购买了航班号为 CA 开头且是国航实际承运的国内航线机票，在国航境内官网或国航无线客户端办理自助值机时，登机牌上的票价（含税）栏内将显示实际支付的全航程机票金额，该金额包括机票票价、燃油附加费和机场建设费。近日，部分南方航空航班登机牌也被打印上了机票的价格。两大航空公司的目的均是避免代理商"卖高价票"给消费者，这也是航空公司规范机票市场的进一步措施。

有业内人士表示，近一两年，票代行业买卖积分、不合理退改签等"猫腻"愈发严重，操作手段也越发恶劣，严重损害乘客权益。从客观效果上看，登机牌明码标价是件好事，旅客可以方便地和购票时所支付的金额对比，知道票代有没有把低价机票以高价出售。

在航企展开行动的同时，连续遭遇几大航空公司"断供"的去哪儿网为加速与航企的"和好"，也在近日发布的《去哪儿关于整顿净化机票代理销售市场的公告》里称，已经发动全面自查行动，并与航空公司一起对不规范经营的代理商予以处理，目前已经处罚了 91 家有不合规经营行为的代理商，下线了 21 家严重违规的代理商并要求其整改，清退了 2 家严重违规服务恶劣的代理商永不合作。

Source: People's Network, Ye Xin, 航企下架去哪儿机票引关注 整治违规机票代理成关键, (2016).

Via China National Tourism Administration Official Website
<<http://www.cnta.gov.cn/xxfb/hydt/201603/t20160321_764427.shtml>>

Exhibit 12.11 Action Taken by Chinese Airlines against "Black Market"

> **Attention: Airline Carriers Shelving Qunar Plane Tickets:**
> **Regulation of illegal air ticketing agents has become key**
> **(2016)**
>
> *People's Network, Beijing, 21ˢᵗ March (Reporter Ye Xin)*
>
> From the beginning of the year when Ctrip's "redemption of air tickets" and "invalid e-ticket numbers" triggered a crisis of confidence, to recent events in which several airline carriers shelved their tickets on Qunar's website, it has become clear that illegal ticketing agents (hereinafter "ticketing agents") are the real "culprits" behind the problem. How to rectify the ticket agent marketplace is now the real crux between OTA [Online Travel Agents] and the airline companies; necessary for regulating the market in the interests of passengers.
>
> *Ticket agents, a mixed bag – The rights of Passengers are at stake*
>
> It is reported that the current domestic ticket agent market is a mixed bag. Mixed in with legal ticketing agents, there also exists a number of "black market agents", i.e.: those who failed to obtain the necessary qualifications issued by China Air Transportation Association [CATA] permitting them to sell tickets. In recent years these "black market agents" have begun to sell their tickets on large scale OTA platforms, and through doing so may even earn unreasonably high refund fees by binding insurance products of their own.

Online Ticketing Agents_Unofficial Translation of Extract 1

For all these reasons, we, the undersigned civil society organisations, declare that THE ENVIRONNEMENTAL PERMIT GRANTED TO JIUXING MINES S.A.R.L. FOR GOLD MINING IN SOMAHAMANINA IS NOT ACCEPTABLE.

We fully support and reinforce the opposition of our compatriots living in the affected area and neighbouring communities to this gold mining project, and hereby declare our determination to work with them and all stakeholders in order to find a sustainable solution which respects human rights.

Signed in Antananarivo on 23 June 2016

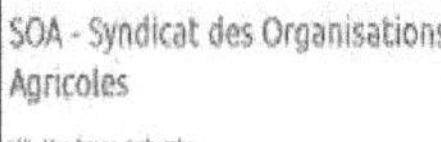

国家互联网信息办公室　　　　施行日期: 2016 年 8 月 1 日

互联网信息搜索服务管理规定

第六条.　　互联网信息搜索服务提供者应当落实主体责任，建立健全信息审核、公共信息实时巡查、应急处置及个人信息保护等信息安全管理制度，具有安全可控的防范措施，为有关部门依法履行职责提供必要的技术支持。

第七条.　　互联网信息搜索服务提供者不得以链接、摘要、快照、联想词、相关搜索、相关推荐等形式提供含有法律法规禁止的信息内容。

第八条.　　互联网信息搜索服务提供者提供服务过程中发现搜索结果明显含有法律法规禁止内容的信息、网站及应用，应当停止提供相关搜索结果，保存有关记录，并及时向国家或者地方互联网信息办公室报告。

第九条.　　互联网信息搜索服务提供者及其从业人员，不得通过断开相关链接或者提供含有虚假信息的搜索结果等手段，牟取不正当利益。

第十条.　　互联网信息搜索服务提供者应当提供客观、公正、权威的搜索结果，不得损害国家利益、公共利益，以及公民、法人和其他组织的合法权益。

Source: Translation by the Author

Exhibit 12.12 New Regulations for Airline Providers_Need to Increase Direct Sales Ratio to 50% by 2018

As of Now 9 Airlines Have Announced the Suspension of their Cooperation with Qunar.com

Economic Daily, 7th January 2016 (Reporter, Huang Rong)

…"Before 2014, the direct sales for flight tickets of several major airlines accounted for about 10% of all total sales, so [airlines] had no choice but to 'turn a blind eye' to the behavior of small to medium-sized ticket agents," said Ctrip Advisory CEO Wei Changren to reporters. With the rise of Ctrip, Qunar.com and other online travel intermediaries, [the situation of] small and medium-sized agents [has improved greatly], as they are able to get on the fast train for selling tickets online. However, the long-standing problem of their non-compliance has not yet disappeared. On the contrary, it has only gotten bigger….

… [However] in the first half of last year, regulators put forward the new "double-fifty" target to "three major airlines." [This held that] in the next three years, China's big three airline providers will need to increase the proportion of their direct sales so that it reaches up to 50%. At the same time, 2014 [regulations hold that] agency fees need to be dropped by 50%. Industry insiders informed reporters, although this appears straight forward, the rigid requirements for airlines to increase the proportion of their direct sales is a "going a bit too far." However, in reality the goal of the two measures is to ultimately decrease the price of air tickets.

It has always been that ticketing agents would normally charge airlines high agency costs. A spokesperson for one state-owned airline provider disclosed to reporters that in 2014 its agency fees

Source Economic Daily, Huang Rong, 截至目前已有9家航空公司宣布暂停与去哪儿网合作, (2016). Via XinhuaNet

<<http://news.xinhuanet.com/fortune/2016-01/07/c_128604503.htm>>

Exhibit 12.13 New Regulations for Airline Providers_Need to Increase Direct Sales Ratio to 50% by 2018_Unofficial Translation of Extract 3

第十一条．互联网信息搜索服务提供者提供付费搜索信息服务，应当依法查验客户有关资质，明确付费搜索信息页面比例上限，醒目区分自然搜索结果与付费搜索信息，对付费搜索信息逐条加注显著标识。互联网信息搜索服务提供者提供商业广告信息服务，应当遵守相关法律法规。

第十二条．互联网信息搜索服务提供者应当建立健全公众投诉、举报和用户权益保护制度，在显著位置公布投诉、举报方式，主动接受公众监督，及时处理公众投诉、举报，依法承担对用户权益造成损害的赔偿责任。

In actuality, as early as 2007, domestic airlines had already started to explore ways in which to reduce business costs by increasing their direct sales ratio. For example, China Southern Airlines took the lead in announcing that agency commission for ticket sales would be reduced from 1% to 0%. However, it has to be admitted that the overall effect of this has been minimal, Wei Changren told reporters. According to an investigation by CTCNN [*劲旅*] towards the end of 2015, Air China, China Southern Airlines, China Eastern Airlines and Hainan Airlines (the big four major airlines) had an average direct sales ratio of between 20% to 30%.

"Airlines still hold a bigger voice. As a resource provider, corresponding policies introduced by the airline will still have a very big impact upon the market. There are many ways to regulate the market," said Wei Changren. "In the past, the airlines did not have an incentive to change, it saved them trouble not to. Now there is a hardline requirement and the airlines have made adjustments."

Source: Translation by the Author.

Education Ethics Series

Ikechukwu J. Ani / Obiora F. Ike (Eds.), *Higher Education in Crisis: Sustaining Quality Assurance and Innovation in Research through Applied Ethics*, 2019, 214pp. ISBN: 978-2-88931-323-5

Obiora F. Ike, Justus Mbae, Chidiebere Onyia (Eds.), *Mainstreaming Ethics in Higher Education, Vol. 1*,2019, 779pp. ISBN: 978-2-88931-300-6

Deivit Montealegre / María Eugenia Barroso (Eds*.), Ethics in Higher Education, a Transversal Dimension: Challenges for Latin America. Ética en educación superior, una dimensión transversal: Desafíos para América Latina*: 2020, 148pp. ISBN: 978-2-88931-359-4

Education Praxis Series*

Tobe Nnamani / Christoph Stückelberger, Resolving Ethical Dilemmas in Professional and Private Life. 50 Cases from Africa for Teaching and Training, 2019, 235pp. ISBN: 978-2-88931-315-0

Copublications & Other

Patrice Meyer-Bisch, Stefania Gandolfi, Greta Balliu (éds.), *L'interdépendance des droits de l'homme au principe de toute gouvernance démocratique. Commentaire de Souveraineté et coopération*, 2019, 324pp. ISBN : 978-2-88931-310-5

Obiora F. Ike, *Applied Ethics to Issues of Development, Culture, Religion and Education*, 2020, 280pp. ISBN: 978-2-88931-335-8

Obiora F. Ike, *Moral and Ethical Leadership, Human Rights and Conflict Resolution – African and Global Contexts*, 2020, 191pp. ISBN: 978-2-88931-333-4

Kenneth R. Ross, *Mission Rediscovered: Transforming Disciples*, 2020, 139pp. ISBN: 978-2-88931-370-9

Praxis Series

Oscar Brenifier, *Day After Day 365 Aphorisms*, 2019, 395pp. ISBN: 978-2-88931-272-6

Christoph Stückelberger, *365 Way-Markers*, 2019, 416pp. ISBN: 978-2-88931-282-5 (available in English and German).

Benoît Girardin / Evelyne Fiechter-Widemann (Eds*.), Blue Ethics: Ethical Perspectives on Sustainable, Fair Water Resources Use and Management*, 2019, 265pp. ISBN: 978-2-88931-308-2 (available in English and French)